Conducting Qualitative Research of Learning in Online Spaces

For my parents, who instilled in me a love for inquiry.
Hannah

For my children, who help me to see the world through ever-changing perspectives.
Sandra

For my son, as always.
Jen

For my parents, my earliest teachers in the art of observation and questioning.
Alecia

Conducting Qualitative Research of Learning in Online Spaces

Hannah R. Gerber

Sam Houston State University

Sandra Schamroth Abrams

St. John's University

Jen Scott Curwood

University of Sydney

Alecia Marie Magnifico

University of New Hampshire

Los Angeles | London | New Delhi
Singapore | Washington DC | Melbourne

FOR INFORMATION:

SAGE Publications, Inc.
2455 Teller Road
Thousand Oaks, California 91320
E-mail: order@sagepub.com

SAGE Publications Ltd.
1 Oliver's Yard
55 City Road
London, EC1Y 1SP
United Kingdom

SAGE Publications India Pvt. Ltd.
B 1/I 1 Mohan Cooperative Industrial Area
Mathura Road, New Delhi 110 044
India

SAGE Publications Asia-Pacific Pte. Ltd.
3 Church Street
#10-04 Samsung Hub
Singapore 049483

Acquisitions Editor: Helen Salmon
Editorial Assistant: Anna Villarruel
Production Editor: Olivia Weber-Stenis
Copy Editor: Ellen Howard
Typesetter: C&M Digitals (P) Ltd.
Proofreader: Sally Jaskold
Indexer: Diggs Publication Services
Cover Designer: Candice Harman
Marketing Manager: Nicole Elliott

Printed in the United States of America

Library of Congress Cataloging-in-Publication Data

Names: Gerber, Hannah R., author. | Abrams, Sandra Schamroth, author. | Curwood, Jen Scott, author. | Magnifico, Alecia, author.

Title: Conducting qualitative research of learning in online spaces / Hannah R. Gerber, Sandra Schamroth Abrams, Jen Scott Curwood, and Alecia Magnifico.

Description: Thousand Oaks, California : Sage Publications, Inc., 2016. | Includes bibliographical references and index.

Identifiers: LCCN 2015038929 | ISBN 9781483333847 (pbk. : alk. paper)

Subjects: LCSH: Web-based instruction—Research—Methodology.

Classification: LCC LB1044.87 .G47 2016 | DDC 371.33/44678—dc23 LC record available at http://lccn.loc.gov/2015038929

This book is printed on acid-free paper.

16 17 18 19 20 10 9 8 7 6 5 4 3 2 1

Brief Contents

Detailed Contents

List of Figures, Tables, and Spotlight Boxes

Figures

Tables

Spotlight Boxes

Foreword

Conducting Qualitative Research in the Moment

According to Denzin and Lincoln (2011), qualitative research has undergone the following nine moments that span from the beginning of the twentieth century to the present:

(1) *traditional (1900–1950)*, wherein many researchers who rejected logical positivism gravitated towards qualitative research;

(2) *modernist or golden age (1950–1970)*, wherein attempts were made to legitimize qualitative research (e.g., via grounded theory) by making its methods as rigorous as quantitative research; many textbook authors attempted to formalize qualitative research; and new interpretive theories emerged (e.g., ethnomethodology, critical theory, critical race theory, feminism, phenomenology in various forms [e.g., descriptive phenomenology, interpretive hermeneutic phenomenology]);

(3) *blurred genres (1970–1986)*, wherein qualitative researchers possessed a full arsenal of philosophical stances and methods; early forms of computer-assisted qualitative data analysis software programs became generally available to assist the analysis of textual data; new worldviews became popularized (e.g., poststructuralism); several qualitative research journals were launched; and naturalistic, postpositivist, and constructionist paradigms gained prominence;

(4) *crisis of representation (1986–1990)*, wherein qualitative research and writing became more reflexive, culminating in research questions being posed regarding issues of gender, race, class, sexuality, and other issues that previously had been considered to represent taboo research topics; quality criteria used by quantitative researchers, such as reliability, validity, and objectivity, were problematized; the triple crises of representation (i.e., qualitative researchers being unable to capture lived experiences directly), legitimation (i.e., problematizing the traditional [foundational] criteria for

evaluating and interpreting qualitative research), and praxis (i.e., involving asking whether it is possible to effect change in the world if society exclusively was represented by text) were highlighted;

(5) *postmodern period of experimental ethnographic writing (1990–1995)*, which marked a struggle for qualitative researchers to make sense of the triple crises; the emergence of new methodologies for conducting ethnography (e.g., auto-ethnography); the problematizing and ensuing drastic reduction in emphasis of the passive observer; and the promotion of action, participatory, and transformative-oriented research;

(6) *post-experimental inquiry (1990–1995)*, which involved researchers whose works were driven by a quest to move towards a free and equitable democratic society; and new forms of qualitative writings being published that reflected multidisciplinary, interdisciplinary, and transdisciplinary research;

(7) *methodologically contested present (2000–2004)*, which represented a period of conflict and tension, especially between qualitative and quantitative researchers, and the emergence of a growing body of literature on paradigms and methods;

(8) *unnamed (2005–present)*, which represented a period of confronting the methodological ramifications of the promotion of evidence-based research; and

(9) *fractured future (2005–present)*, wherein methodologists would divide themselves (i.e., "gold standard" of scientific research [i.e., randomized control designs] vs. various forms of qualitative research), and the value and significance of qualitative research might become marginalized (see also Ravenek & Rudman, 2013).

Just as the field of qualitative research is situated in a cultural and historical context, so too is the Internet. Indeed, the evolution of the Internet can be mapped onto the aforementioned nine qualitative moments. Specifically, the World Wide Web was invented in March 1989 by Sir Tim John Berners-Lee, a British computer scientist. Thus, Web 1.0, representing the first generation of the World Wide Web, and which was characterized by hierarchically arranged separate and static websites with information predominantly controlled by a small group of content providers (i.e., *read-only web*), came to the fore during the end of the fourth moment and the beginning of the fifth moment.

Further, the sixth moment marked the date when the phrase *Web 2.0* was first coined on April 1, 1999, by Darci DiNucci (1999, p. 32); the seventh moment marked the date when Web 1.0 officially was switched to Web 2.0 (i.e., November 20, 2001) and marked the period during which social media websites were developed and used, including the launching of MySpace (January 1, 2003) and Facebook (February 4, 2004), as well as the hosting of the first Web 2.0 conference on October 1, 2004, by O'Reilly Media Live, which popularized the term *Web 2.0*; and the eighth and ninth moments marked the creation of resources such as Wiki Spaces (January 1, 2005) and YouTube (August 20, 2005).

Since the introduction of Web 2.0, the number of users of Web 2.0 platforms has increased exponentially—leading my coauthors and me to call for a *10th moment* in qualitative research, which we labeled as "the period of *Methodological Innovation*, in which qualitative researchers go beyond the traditional ways of collecting primary and reflexive data" (Onwuegbuzie, Leech, & Collins, 2010, p. 697). In so doing, we argued that qualitative researchers would "transcend this methodological contestation and methodological divide by taking advantage of the innovative approaches to reflexivity . . . and the latest technology and computer-mediated communication" (p. 697).

The use of Web 2.0 platforms has permeated many communities and nations— for example, with more than two billion people using the Internet worldwide. According to the Pew Research Center (2015), in the United States, the proportion of adults who use the Internet increased from 14 percent by the end of the sixth moment (i.e., *post-experimental inquiry*) to 66 percent by the end of the seventh moment (i.e., *methodologically contested present*) to 87 percent within the eighth (i.e., *unnamed*) and ninth (i.e., *fractured future*) moments—specifically, as of January 2014. Of these Internet users, the proportion of adults who use social networking sites (i.e., social media) increased from 8 percent by the end of the seventh moment to 74 percent in January 2014. Further, by April 2015, 68 percent of U.S. adults owned a smartphone, 45 percent owned a tablet computer, 19 percent owned an ebook reader, 40 percent owned a game console, and 14 percent owned a portable gaming device (Pew Research Center, 2015).

Globally, Internet use has grown by 566 percent from the beginning of the seventh moment in 2000 to deep into the eighth and ninth moments in 2012. And even though every region has reported proportionally fewer Internet users than does the United States, Internet usage worldwide still is significant—with 34 percent, on average, of the world's population using the Internet: comprising 68 percent in Oceania/Australia, 63 percent in Europe (63 percent), 43 percent in Latin America/Caribbean, 40 percent in the Middle East, 28 percent in Asia, and 16 percent in Africa (Pew Internet & American Life Project, 2013). In the parlance of quantitative researchers (cf. Peters & Van Voorhis, 1940) and some qualitative researchers (cf. Onwuegbuzie, 2003), all of these proportions represent large effect sizes in the context of their sociocultural and geopolitical milieu. In fact, as someone who has been extremely fortunate to have travelled to numerous countries and states that represent six continents, I have witnessed first-hand the widespread and diverse use of Web 2.0 platforms—from Bedouin Arabs in Israel and Palestine (Bremaud, 2013) to members of the Masai Tribe in Kenya (Dimbleby, 2010)—to provide just a couple examples.

However, the use of Web 2.0 tools by researchers has not kept pace with the use by people in their daily lives. For example, in an article that I published as co–guest editor of a special issue in the *International Journal of Qualitative Methods*, Snelson (in press) used a systematic literature review process to examine trends in qualitative and mixed methods social media research literature published from 2007 through 2013 by searching the three major databases: Academic Search Premier, Web of Science, and Google Scholar. Of the thousands of articles published during this time period, Snelson (in press) identified only 174 peer-reviewed qualitative research journal articles wherein social media played a central role. Although this represents an increase in the qualitative media research literature in recent years, this low proportion of published articles involving the study of online environments relative to the study of offline environments does not reflect the popularity of Web 2.0 platforms as a means of communication. Thus, it is not surprising that Greenhow, Robelia, and Hughes (2009) declared, "A stronger research focus on students' everyday use of Web 2.0 technologies and their learning with Web 2.0 both in and outside of classrooms is needed" (p. 246). Interestingly, Windschitl's (1998) call, made between the sixth and seventh moments, for researchers to utilize qualitative research methods in order to explore, to discover, and to describe complex changes that occur in the context of Web-based teaching and learning, as well as to understand technological, ethical, educational, professional, and/or social practices pertaining to technology use not only across people's life span, but also across a whole day (e.g., home, institutions of learning, work place, social spaces) is still very much applicable today in the ninth moment, justifying the need for the tenth moment, as stated previously.

Despite the importance of studying online spaces (e.g., Facebook, Twitter, blogs, wikis, forums, and listservs), the major research methodology textbooks focus primarily—if not exclusively—on methodologies pertaining to the study of offline spaces, with not even a chapter allocated to methodologies that are applicable to the study of online spaces. Unfortunately, the methodological tools presented in standard research methodology books for studying offline spaces are insufficient, per se, for examining many Web 2.0–related research questions. Further, of the few textbooks devoted specifically to online research methodologies, most of them were published during the early years of the eighth and ninth moments, and although they contain some useful information, they need updating, such as Fielding and Lee's (2008) excellent edited book—which represents the year that the earliest forms of file hosting services (e.g., Dropbox) and Internet-based social bookmarking services (e.g., academia.edu) came to the fore. Further, very few graduate school programs provide students with the option to take formal courses on online research methods.

This lack of (current) published works in the area of online research methods coupled with the lack of formal and systematic instruction on conducting online research likely explain the relative lack of attention to the study of online spaces. And such lack of attention has dire consequences for the advancement of research methodologies in general. As an example, as noted by Leach, Kalinowski, Onwuegbuzie, and Leamons (in press), with very few exceptions (e.g., medical research), researchers representing many fields and disciplines still rely on printed consent forms to document participants' informed consent, instead of using online, or electronic, informed consent systems that "have the potential to help with logistical problems and possibly increase the consent rates among research studies because they are often more convenient to administer, to complete, and to submit" (p. xx).

Therefore, when I was asked to write the foreword for this book, I became very excited because it meant that I would get the opportunity to read a book that was much needed before it was released to the general public. And after reading it the first time, I was immediately able to declare unequivocally that this book delivered extremely effectively what the title promised! Now, I am a big fan of the most popular professional sport played in the United States, namely, the National Football League (NFL), being extremely fortunate to have attended Super Bowl XLVII between the San Francisco 49ers (my favorite team) and the Baltimore Ravens in New Orleans in 2013 (Yes, research methodologists do have a life!). Interestingly, a few weeks before I wrote this foreword, during halftime of a football game that occurred on a Monday night, while waiting for the teams to begin the second half, I decided to spend a few moments to read causally the Introduction chapter of this book. However, after reading this chapter, I found myself not being able to put the book down. Subsequently, I ignored completely the whole second half of the football game (which turned out to be an excellent game from the highlights that I watched later) and, instead, ended up reading the book from cover to cover. Those who know me would be surprised that I would give up a whole half of an NFL game to read *any* book—let alone a research methodology textbook—in its entirety and giving 100-percent attention to the task, at a time when I did not have to read it. As someone who has taught research methodology courses for more than two decades (Yes, this demonstrates how old I am!), I love reading about research methodology; however, I love football even more. And so my unconscious decision to read this book instead of watching the football game is a testament to how captivating the book is.

Throughout the book, the authors effectively explain, describe, analyze, apply, evaluate, synthesize, modify, support, refute, and extend many issues relevant to the emerging dialogue on online research in general and online qualitative research in particular. The importance of the information that they provide in their book cannot be understated, bearing in mind the aforementioned significant increase in the use of Web 2.0 tools worldwide and the corresponding lack of recent publications on online research methodologies.

Each of the eight chapters begins with guiding questions that motivate readers to think critically from the onset. Similarly, the questions at the end of each chapter help readers to reflect back on the information provided in that chapter as well as help them to situate the discussion within their own research. I particularly like what the authors call *spotlight boxes*, which reside at strategic places within each chapter and showcase an array of research studies by summarizing the methodologies, methods, frameworks, tools, concepts, findings, and/or meaning making that were described by the researchers.

A perusal of their reference list makes it quickly obvious that these authors respectfully stand on the shoulder of methodological, theoretical, and conceptual giants—building on their classic works. Further, each chapter is beautifully written using an appropriate combination of old, emerging, and new terminology related to both methods and online spaces. And, despite the fact that this book involves the work of four authors, it is presented in a seamless way wherein each chapter connects to both the chapters before and those that follow.

In a book wherein every chapter makes an important contribution to the dialogue on conducting research in online spaces, the chapter on ethical research is particularly noteworthy. Among the array of excellent information provided in this chapter, the authors provide thoughtful recommendations for obtaining approval from ethics review boards. It is clear that driving their discussion throughout this chapter is the importance of researchers maximizing non-maleficence (i.e., not causing harm to others); beneficence (i.e., working for the benefit of others); (social) justice (i.e., making decisions based on universal principles and rules, in an impartial and warranted manner in an attempt to guarantee fair and equitable treatment of all people), and fidelity (i.e., demonstrating loyalty, faithfulness, and commitment), as well as professional competence (i.e., recognizing limitations and undertaking tasks within the researcher's set of skills and knowledge of the topic explored and the results reported); integrity (i.e., being fair, honest, and respectful of others' data and representing their data appropriately); scholarly responsibility (i.e., adhering to best practices through documentation [i.e., leaving an audit trail] and reflecting on the methodological choices made); social responsibility (i.e., applying awareness of the social dimensions of the underling topic); and respecting rights, dignity, and diversity (i.e., striving to eliminate bias for misrepresenting others' data and not discriminating participants based on their exceptionalities) (cf. Onwuegbuzie & Frels, 2016)—the sum of which provide a pathway for researchers to be *meta-ethical*, which implies adherence to *virtue ethics* (i.e., referring to the *character* of the researcher as the impetus for ethical behavior, as opposed to focusing on rules) and *pragmatic ethics* (i.e., using the standards set by communities under the assumption that communities are progressing morally in line with the progression of scientific knowledge).

I close by commending the authors for writing such a visionary methodological primer that is both reader-friendly and far-reaching. Indubitably, these authors move forward the conversation on conducting qualitative research of learning in online spaces in an appropriate direction and pace. In so doing, they will help researchers "to pursue understanding of those opportunities and challenge existing barriers that prevent us (scholars, teachers, administrators, students, and families) from taking a step toward discovery" (Greenhow et al., 2009, p. 256). Simply put, this unique book provides a much-needed guide to help researchers consider their methods, tools, roles, affect, positionality, and, above all, humanness in the qualitative research process pertaining to the study of learning in online spaces. This seminal book begins to fill a void such that it will make a significant contribution to both the research methodology and online literatures. The biggest endorsement that I can give the book is that I intend to use it in my own research methodology courses because it provides a framework for helping researchers conduct research *in the moment*—specifically, the *Methodological Innovation* moment.

Anthony J. Onwuegbuzie
Sam Houston State University

References

Bremaud, J. (2013, May 9). Bedouins sitting around the fire listening to mobile phones [video file]. Retrieved from https://www.youtube.com/watch?v=RmhIKeiUd8A

Denzin, N. K., & Lincoln, Y. S. (2011). Introduction: The discipline and practice of qualitative research. In N. K. Denzin & Y. S. Lincoln (Eds.), *Sage handbook of qualitative research* (4th ed., pp. 1-25). Thousand Oaks, CA: Sage.

DiNucci, D. (1999). Fragmented future. *Print, 53*(4), 32, 221–222.

Fielding, N. G., & Lee, R. M. (2008). *The Sage handbook of online research methods*. Thousand Oaks, CA: Sage.

Greenhow, C. M., Robelia, E., & Hughes, J. (2009). Web 2.0 and classroom research: What path should we take now? *Educational Researcher, 38*, 246–259. doi:10.3102/0013189X09336671

Leach, L. F., Kalinowski, K. E., Onwuegbuzie, A. J., & Leamons, C. G. (in press). Investigating the efficacy of a basic online informed consent system in educational research. *International Journal of Multiple Research Approaches*.

Onwuegbuzie, A. J. (2003). Effect sizes in qualitative research: A prolegomenon. *Quality & Quantity: International Journal of Methodology*, 37, 393-409. doi:10.1023/A:1027379223537

Onwuegbuzie, A. J., & Frels, R. K. (2016). *Seven steps to a comprehensive literature review: A multimodal and cultural approach*. London, England: Sage.

Onwuegbuzie, A. J., Leech, N. L., & Collins, K. M. T. (2010). Innovative data collection strategies in qualitative research. *The Qualitative Report*, 15, 696–726. Retrieved from http://www.nova.edu/ssss/QR/QR15-3/onwuegbuzie.pdf

Peters, C. C., & VanVoorhis, W. R. (1940). *Statistical procedures and their mathematical bases*. New York, NY: McGraw-Hill.

Pew Internet & American Life Project (2013). *Demographics of Internet users (April–May 2013)*. Retrieved from http://www.pewinternet.org/Trend-Data-%28Adults%29/Whos-Online.aspx

Pew Research Center. (2015). *Internet user demographics*. Retrieved from http://www.pewinternet.org/data-trend/internet-use/latest-stats/

Ravenek, M. J., & Rudman, D. L. (2013). Bridging conceptions of quality in moments of qualitative research. *International Journal of Qualitative Methods*, 12, 436–456. Retrieved from https://ejournals.library.ualberta.ca/index.php/IJQM/article/view/11192

Snelson, C. L. (in press). Qualitative and mixed methods social media research: A review of the literature. *International Journal of Qualitative Methods*.

Windschitl, M. (1998). The WWW and classroom research: What path should we take? *Educational Researcher*, 27(1), 28–33.

Preface

••

For over two decades, researchers have been grappling with online inquiry, including gaining access to spaces, communicating with participants, and obtaining informed consent. Before the advent of Web 2.0, online research primarily examined static, heavily text-based forms and spaces, such as email, chatrooms, and websites. Though studies of the primitive Internet often were focused on content analysis or involved offline methods to clarify online data, such as face-to-face individual interviews (Reid, 1994; Turkle, 1995), near the end of the twentieth century, online spaces began to gain recognition as vehicles for recruiting and communicating with participants (Gaiser, 1997). More recently, researchers have conducted a range of online studies of behavior and meaning making, from examinations of teamwork and leadership in massively multiplayer gaming to investigations of youth literacy and writing development through fanfiction (Chen, 2012; Lammers, 2012).

In this book, we acknowledge the evolving nature of online spaces and advocate for a pragmatic approach to data collection and analysis that will support a rich understanding of meaning making in these environments. As such, *Conducting Qualitative Research of Learning in Online Spaces* provides guidance for researchers who wish to design and conduct diverse studies of learning in online contexts.

As researchers advance investigations of learning in online spaces, contemporary studies often target dynamic spaces that are user-driven, social, and collaborative, which we refer to as **networked field sites.** To capture the interactions within these sites, researchers can draw on a variety of theoretical frameworks, methodological approaches, and data sources to better understand learning in online spaces. For instance, methods for collecting data in online environments often include observation, in-depth interviews, focus group interviews, surveys, and artifact analysis. Though the examination of learning in online spaces may have features similar to traditional face-to-face approaches, some researchers have suggested that "online qualitative research cannot be considered a reproduction of traditional techniques on the Internet but is a different set of tools, with its own peculiar advantages and limitations" (Graffigna & Bosio, 2006, p. 68). Participants' experiences are informed by both the online and offline world, so it is important for researchers to consider how to attend to data that are drawn from both online and offline spaces.

In many ways, these points are related to Matthew Williams's (2007) questions about the role of the researcher in online spaces. He has challenged the field to consider these questions:

> To what extent is the researcher able to write in a convincing way about the people studied when anonymity inherent in Internet interactions casts doubts upon the identities of

research participants? How does the participant observer manage his or her identity in settings mediated by text and graphics, and what impact might this have on data collection? How are researchers to conceptualize the boundaries of online settings and the experiences of those observed? (p. 8)

Williams's prompts suggest that we need to do more than just select the appropriate method for accessing and collecting data. As online researchers, we argue that:

- we need to understand relationships between researchers' mental models and participants' experiences (see Chapter One);

- we need to grasp how researchers can trace learners' meaning making across various networked field sites, thereby initiating ways to extend the boundaries of knowledge and traditions (see Chapter Two);

- we need to consider how our theories of learning influence the studies that we design and conduct (see Chapter Three);

- we need to place greater emphasis on the complicated aspects of researchers' reflexivity, bias, and positioning as research tools (see Chapter Four);

- we need to determine how multiple data sources can be assembled and analyzed to capture richer pictures of online meaning making (see Chapters Five and Six);

- we need to support and conduct ethical research in online environments (see Chapter Seven); and

- we need to continually rethink research methods in light of evolving spaces and practices (see Chapter Eight).

These concepts have led us to contemplate how researchers approach online learning and advocate for moving beyond tradition; in order to understand multidimensional and multi-sited learning, researchers need to be creative in their approaches to data collection and analysis. Such a pragmatic stance is not about a cavalier disregard for tradition; rather it is about responding to an evolving learning landscape that supports not only new and creative forms of meaning making, but also more expansive research designs. As such, we see the future of research in online learning as requiring multiple approaches. Extending ideas from the mixed methods tradition, John W. Creswell (2015) proposed that multimethod approaches allow researchers to collect and analyze multiple forms of qualitative data to better understand a given study. By supporting a multimethod approach, we contend that researchers will be able to describe how people make meaning in online environments.

The Structure of This Book

Conducting Qualitative Research of Learning in Online Spaces is a methodological primer that examines multifaceted approaches to researching learning in online environments. Our book considers the affordances and constraints of conducting research within networked field sites to better understand the nature of online learning.

Because we look to mixed and multimethod approaches to research within online environments, each chapter supports readers by engaging them in critically questioning and applying the conceptual and theoretical perspectives to their own work. Readers are encouraged to think through their own studies by considering the guiding questions that are provided at the beginning of each chapter, as well as the Connecting to Your Work questions for reflection at the end of each chapter.

Additionally, to help readers make sense of the concepts and methods we discuss throughout, we provide Spotlight Boxes within each chapter that feature a variety of studies and their methods, tools, concepts, and findings. Our hope is that these support structures will guide readers in their own qualitative research.

This book builds on discussions of learning and online spaces, conceptual frameworks and research design, multiple methods for collecting and analyzing data, as well as established and evolving ethical philosophies. Inherent across all of the following chapters is the need for researchers to be creative, agentive, and purposeful in selecting and/or combining methods to aptly study meaning making in protean spaces.

Chapter One explains the underlying premise of what constitutes research of learning in online spaces. Highlighting the importance of researcher agency and creativity, the chapter looks to remixing as a frame for conducting multimethod qualitative research. In so doing, it underscores mental models and logics of inquiry as key elements in the pragmatic design of multimethod qualitative studies.

Chapter Two provides an overview of online spaces, such as blogs, wikis, and forums, that can inform online qualitative research. This chapter focuses on inquiries of meaning making in networked field sites that are not temporally or spatially confined. This chapter suggests that, because of the diverse range of participants' purposes for engaging in these spaces, researchers need to exercise flexibility in the way that they approach research design.

Chapter Three surveys various conceptual frameworks used to study learning and draws particular attention to behavioral theories, cognitive theories, and social theories of learning. Details about the three frameworks are provided, including a brief review of research employing each framework. The chapter then articulates contemporary frameworks for conceptualizing learning in online spaces, such as affinity spaces, connected learning, and participatory cultures. Finally, it discusses how researchers might align learning theories with their topic or online spaces of interest.

Chapter Four examines researcher positioning within online spaces. More specifically, it considers how researchers might participate in their research sites and interact with participants, providing a continuum from non-interactional "lurking" and "creeping," to full participation in an environment. Examining forms of participation and interaction is central to understanding the role of the online researcher, as well as the nuances of participatory practices, online cultures, and virtual data collection.

Chapter Five addresses data collection in light of evolving online spaces. Honoring traditional qualitative methods as well as a pragmatic approach to data collection, this chapter examines various contemporary methods to study online meaning making. It also outlines key questions to ask when considering data sources and data collection techniques.

Chapter Six focuses on data analysis. It begins by discussing research questions and data analysis plans and then reviews potential methods that may be used alone or mixed in creative ways. The chapter focuses on thematic, grounded theory, discourse, and artifact analyses, and it also examines studies that use multimethod approaches to describe learning and participation in online spaces. Readers will consider the theoretical assumptions embedded in different forms of data analysis, as well as how to align their data analysis with their overarching interests and study designs.

Chapter Seven considers ethical aspects of conducting research in online spaces. This chapter traces the history of cases and policies that have contributed to the field of research ethics, and it discusses how these cases are related to the various policies that inform the conduct of ethical research in online spaces. This chapter provides recommendations for navigating ethics review boards and discusses what constitutes public information and private information, including the impact of security settings on ethical data collection. Additionally, it considers how to ensure the anonymity of one's research participants in online research contexts through layers of concealment depending on the sensitivity of the data collected.

The final chapter, Chapter Eight, moves scholars beyond their current research and engages them in considering the next steps to take or new technologies to explore in future inquiries. This chapter encourages readers to think through practical applications for how their research informs their understanding of learning, as well as ways to examine the implications of their research.

Acknowledgments

We would like to thank our respective institutions, Sam Houston State University, St. John's University, the University of Sydney, and the University of New Hampshire, for the support necessary to complete this comprehensive text.

We appreciate colleagues' and reviewers' important feedback, which has helped us to extend how we perceive and study learning in online spaces. Conversations with colleagues and fellow scholars have helped us to clarify, confirm, and challenge (re)conceptualized approaches to qualitative research. Likewise, we thank the SAGE reviewers who took the time to provide us extensive feedback throughout the review process: Darnell Bradley, Cardinal Stritch University; Martin Oliver, UCL Institute of Education; Damiana Gibbons Pyles, Appalachian State University; and Pamela Whitehouse, Midwestern State University.

We would like to thank Tony Onwuegbuzie for providing thought-provoking insight in his foreword to our text.

We also would like to thank Helen Salmon and the SAGE editorial staff for their dedication and commitment to this project. Thank you for your continued attention and earnest support.

Authors' Note

Over the course of time, scholars have refined understandings and theories related to learning and the research of learning in online and offline spaces. Given the natural progression of thought, coupled with the inevitable and often swift evolution of technology, there may be multiple editions of a given text. In our book, we have carefully selected editions that have enabled us to situate theories, and our focus on any one particular edition brings to light that publication's unique contribution. We do not intend to privilege any one scholar's perspectives; rather, we build on the strength of historically situated thinking to enrich the discussion of contemporary research and the overall examination of learning in online spaces.

About the Authors

Hannah R. Gerber is an associate professor in the Department of Language, Literacy and Special Populations at Sam Houston State University in Texas, where she teaches graduate courses in digital epistemologies and virtual ethnography. Gerber's research has focused on adolescents and their videogaming practices, examining confluences of learning across various literacies in multiple online and offline settings. She has conducted research in such diverse environments as homes, libraries, and schools, and within inner-city, rural, and international contexts in North America, the Middle East, and Southeast Asia. She has given lectures and keynote addresses on her research at conferences and universities around the world. Gerber's recent publications can be found in *English Journal*, *Educational Media International*, and *The ALAN Review*. She is coeditor of *Bridging Literacies with Videogames*.

Sandra Schamroth Abrams is an associate professor in the Department of Curriculum and Instruction at St. John's University in New York. Her research of digital literacies and videogaming focuses on agentive learning, layered meaning making, and pedagogical discovery located at the intersection of online and offline experiences. Her recent work appears in the *Journal of Adolescent & Adult Literacy*, the *Journal of Literacy Research*, and *Educational Media International*. She is the author of *Integrating Virtual and Traditional Learning in 6–12 Classrooms: A Layered Literacies Approach to Multimodal Meaning Making* and the coeditor of *Bridging Literacies with Videogames*.

Jen Scott Curwood is a senior lecturer in English education and media studies at the University of Sydney in Australia. Her research focuses on literacy, technology, and teacher professional development. She has recently investigated young adults' writing practices in online spaces and teachers' integration of digital tools in content area classrooms. Curwood's scholarship has appeared in the *Journal of Literacy Research*, *Journal of Adolescent & Adult Literacy*, *Teaching Education*, and *Learning, Media, and Technology*.

Alecia Marie Magnifico is an assistant professor of English at the University of New Hampshire, where she teaches courses on English teaching, digital literacies, and research methods. Magnifico's research interests focus on understanding, supporting, and encouraging adolescents' writing for different audiences. Much of her writing in this area describes and theorizes composition across formal and informal contexts. She also works with teachers to design curricula and assessments that engage digital tools and multiple literacies. She enjoys the challenge of developing research methods to represent what happens in these complex social learning spaces. Magnifico's recent work can be found in *Literacy*, the *Journal of Adolescent & Adult Literacy*, and *E-Learning and Digital Media*.

Guiding Questions for Chapter 1

- Historically, how have qualitative approaches been used to study learning in online spaces?

- How does the concept of remixing multiple approaches lend itself to the study of learning within online spaces?

- What are some ways in which researchers can remix multiple qualitative approaches in order to study learning in online spaces?

CHAPTER ONE

How Can Learning in Online Spaces Be Informed by Qualitative Research?

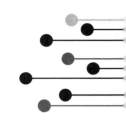

Introduction

Conducting research in online spaces can be challenging, but rewarding. Online environments often seem like brave new worlds filled with unknown and exciting areas for discovery. By exploring existing qualitative approaches to studying learning in formal and informal online spaces, researchers will be able to better understand the development of multimethod approaches.

Readers can expect to see how examples of online learning, from initial design to data collection to data analysis, are addressed in light of the porous boundaries that loosely separate online and offline worlds (Burnett, 2011; Burnett & Merchant, 2014). This chapter provides an overview of seminal constructs that impact qualitative inquiry—namely mental models, research traditions, and inquiry paradigms—and offers insight into methodological shifts as well as researcher agency and creativity.

Mediated Spaces and Online Learning

> For qualitative researchers wanting to understand the everyday, the Internet has therefore become almost unavoidable, but is also often troubling in the extent to which it seems to challenge our starting premises about who we study, where they are, and what they do there. (Hine, 2013, p. 2)

Advances in technology have led to new and shifting landscapes, often presenting researchers with multiple challenges in investigating evolving online spaces and practices. Consequently, researchers may grapple with questions about designing their study to best understand online meaning making (Black, 2008; Gee, 2007; Hine, 2000; Nardi, Ly, & Harris, 2007). This book highlights how scholars have examined learning in digital spaces, and it provides seminal examples and prompts to inform and inspire future research. This book pushes researchers to think through existing approaches and methodologies, and to consider alternative and multiple ways to approach the study of learning in online spaces.

The Internet and online learning are not new. In fact, online social spaces like Usenet and multiuser domains, also known as MUDs, were present in the 1970s. These eventually led to other variations, such as MOOs (a MUD that is object oriented) and MUVEs (multiuser virtual environments) that supported flexible environments and user creativity (Slator et al., 2007). Though research has attempted to define characteristics of online learners (Dabbagh, 2007), examining the features of online spaces will allow researchers to explore more deeply examples of meaning making.

In so doing, this book calls attention to the complicated nature of investigating learning in online spaces. Given that online environments continually and often dramatically change, this book avoids claims about what online learning spaces are. Instead, this book provides understandings of how researchers have collected, generated, and analyzed data, as well as (re)considered the affordances and limitations of their chosen approaches.

Making Pragmatic Choices About Methods

Questions of learning and education often cross traditional disciplinary boundaries and demand complex data collection and analyses. As such, it is possible and frequently useful for researchers in these areas to adopt, develop, and mix methodologies that draw from a variety of traditions. This tradition began with mixed methods scholars who initially sought to escape the "paradigm wars" of earlier generations. (An excellent history can be found in Tashakkori & Teddlie, 1998.)

Initially, it was most common to combine qualitative and quantitative measures. One definition of mixed methods describes it as "research in which the investigator collects and analyzes data, integrates the findings, and draws inferences using both qualitative and quantitative approaches or methods in a single study or program of inquiry" (Tashakkori & Creswell, 2007, p. 4). In current research, however, multiple combinations of methods, known as multimethod research, are possible and support the emergence of new descriptions and insights.

When beginning an investigation, researchers must hone their ideas for the study's focus. For example, rather than collecting all possible data in an online setting for learning, are particular kinds of interactions more interesting? Do online interactions suggest another relevant avenue to pursue? A number of different analyses or data sources might be investigated as ways to examine particular areas of the online spaces, or they could be used to tease out certain kinds of learning processes that become more evident as the researcher enters the space.

As educational research has evolved, the field has become more willing to accept mixed, open-ended, and naturalistic frameworks. In past years, many studies of learning environments were planned as deliberate experiments, and as such, frameworks for data collection and analysis were often seen as immutable contracts in which the researcher promised to study definite research questions in established, specific ways. This particular image of the analytical framework does not work as well in qualitative studies where interpretation and mapping are central activities to a study's development. For example, many ethnographers first engage in mapping field sites to inform their foci and early interpretations. Such activities are central to a study's development. Some mixed methods researchers have presented pragmatic frameworks that are particularly useful in new and evolving environments— that is, encouraging fellow researchers to choose philosophical stances, methods, and designs that speak most directly to their research questions (e.g., Johnson & Onwuegbuzie, 2004).

This kind of eclectic "alternative paradigm" (Greene, 2007, p. 82) design is both practical and somewhat controversial, in that some researchers (e.g., Lincoln & Guba, 2000, 2002) believe that initial paradigmatic assumptions are central to the way inquiry unfolds. In other words, if a researcher believes that social aspects of meaning making are central to learning, these ideas deeply influence the resulting settings chosen for study, data collected, and analyses undertaken. Despite this intertwined nature of philosophy and method, advocates for a pragmatic stance, including Burke Johnson and Anthony J. Onwuegbuzie (2004), claim that basing research in practical choices makes sense for many studies, and "taking a non-purist, or compatibilist or mixed position, allows researchers to mix and match design components that offer the best chance of answering their specific research questions" (p. 15).

Nevertheless, it is important to remember that foundational mixed methods work typically assumes that researchers will define a single research site and approaches to its study from the beginning of the inquiry and will include the collection of both quantitative and qualitative data sources (Creswell, 2015). Today, many online learning spaces are spread across several resources, websites, and social media. In the remainder of this book, we will theorize such environments as networked field sites to describe this multiplicity. In such environments, it may be difficult accurately to map a line of online inquiry at the inception of study, much less to devise hypotheses or clear directions for data collection. Online researchers often discover new artifacts, ideas, or ways of sharing meaning in the course of their inhabitation—information perhaps unconsidered in the initial study design or analysis plan. In such situations, practicalities may be even more central in completing a successful inquiry. Multiple methods and methodologies may become useful to a researcher's theorized understanding of a space, and a pragmatic frame allows for this kind of evolution to occur.

Jennifer C. Greene (2007) has noted that these ideas and decisions are complex ones. On one hand, researchers may make nominally pragmatic choices in response to a particular happening. On the other, researchers' actions are guided by their mental models of and assumptions about their inquiry, regardless of whether they explicitly state or interrogate these beliefs. Extending the ideas of Phillips (1996) and Smith (1997), Greene explained that mental models are borne from many aspects of a researcher's education, experience, and context, and they can profoundly affect how inquiry is carried out. Reflecting actively on these choices and evolving ideas strengthens the study overall, making it "more generative and defensible" (p. 59). Mental models, in other words, are tools for developing and staying true to a study's logic of inquiry. Periodically considering and interrogating expectations for how various data sources and analyses will contribute to meaning making in an ongoing way, researchers can consider such models as statements of philosophical and field-based commitments (Morgan, 2007). As Bloome (2012) has reminded the field, "The meaningfulness of any set of research methods and techniques must, after all, be derived from the principles in which they are embedded" (p. 8). While Bloome's discussion focused on classroom ethnography, the statement holds true across methodological traditions.

Choosing Among Qualitative Traditions

Qualitative research is an established form of inquiry that explores people's experiences in their natural settings (Creswell, 1998). These traditions can be used in concert, as a researcher sees the need emerge, as a means to appropriately attend to the research question and the examined online space. This is not suggesting that existing traditions be abandoned or misappropriated. Rather, harkening back to Christine Hine's (2013) discussion of researching online spaces, studying online meaning making can be challenging, and looking first to established traditions can help researchers appropriate the right methods for their studies. This book examines the core features of qualitative inquiry found in case study, ethnography, grounded theory, and phenomenology. However, this list of approaches is not exhaustive.

As Sharan B. Merriam (2009) aptly noted, other methodology scholars, such as Michael Quinn Patton (2002), John W. Creswell (2007), Norman K. Denzin and Yvonna S. Lincoln (2005), and Renata Tesch (1990), have called attention to a variety of approaches. Their classifications, which include a range of five to forty-five approaches, thereby underscore that there is "no consensus" in categorizing qualitative inquiry (Merriam, 2009, p. 21). We do not intend to offer or recategorize traditions. Instead, this book provides options—namely, options for researchers to take an agentive stance and extend existing approaches beyond the boundaries of their existing constructs. Following the discussion of the four aforementioned qualitative traditions, this book addresses research paradigms that inform research approaches.

Qualitative Approaches

Qualitative research predates the advent of the Internet, and established traditions have been used to study online spaces. Scholars have found four key approaches—case study, ethnography, grounded theory, and phenomenology—to be helpful in examining and understanding the processes, products, and interactions inherent in learning in online spaces.

Case Study

Researchers select a case study approach when they are interested in examining a phenomenon that is bounded. That is, data collection would be limited to examining a defined aspect, be it a particular person (e.g., a student), a group of people (e.g., a classroom, a school), or a program (e.g., a coding workshop). It can extend to include sites of study, activities, or processes (Johnson & Christensen, 2014). Robert K. Yin (2014) explained:

> The distinctive need for case study research arises out of the desire to understand complex social phenomena. In brief, case study allows investigators to focus on a "case" and retain a holistic and real world perspective—such as in studying individual life cycles, small group behavior, organizational and managerial processes, neighborhood change, school performance, international relations, and the maturation of industries. (p. 5)

Regardless of the focus of study, the case must fall within the bounded system that the researcher has defined.

According to Robert E. Stake (1995), there are three types of case studies. In **intrinsic case studies** the researcher attempts to understand a single case that is being studied, such as studying a particular student to better understand the strategies and methods that the particular student uses in learning processes. In **instrumental case studies**, researchers study cases to gain insight into issues that inform other situations and sites. For example, a researcher might study a student to better understand the impact of an innovative curriculum that has recently been implemented. The instrumental aspect is the area of interest, which is the impact of the curriculum, and the case of the student allows the researcher to dig into this question of importance. The **collective case study**, or multicase design (Yin, 2014), allows researchers to compare similarities and differences among cases in order to gain a more comprehensive understanding about a theory or issue. For example, the researcher may still have interest in understanding the impact of an innovative curriculum, but may choose to study several students and teachers simultaneously to address the question of the curriculum's impact.

Researchers have conducted case study research to understand learning in online spaces (e.g., Glazer & Hergenrader, 2014). Rish's (2014) instrumental case study of collaborative writing, digital cartography, and videogame design in a high school English classroom included classroom observations and student interviews. He analyzed the transmedia artifacts students created using programs such as AutoRealm, Terragan, and RPG Maker. Rish's use of case study allowed him to explore trial and error within online learning and the role of transmedia resources in collaborative world building.

Ethnography

Ethnography focuses on understanding cultures and communities. It emerged out of the field of anthropology in the early twentieth century and means "writing about people" (Johnson & Christensen, 2008, p. 44). Ethnography aims to better understand the perspectives, attitudes, shared values, norms, practices, and interactions of a given group of people through rich, thick description (Geertz, 1973). As such, ethnography requires researchers to become participant observers, immersing themselves in a specific community context in order to collect data such as artifacts, interviews, and extensive field notes. In online spaces, researchers have conducted investigations in situ (e.g., Black, 2008; Ito et al., 2010; Lee, 2014), adapting ethnographic methods to engage in online and connective ethnography.

Online ethnography, also referred to as virtual ethnography (Hine, 2000) and netnography (Kozinets, 2009), is concerned with the data collection methods used to understand interactions within online spaces. Online data collection methods build on traditional ethnographic principles, which include a bricolage (Lévi-Strauss, 1962) of methods and tools that are continually refashioned and reworked to address the needs of the researcher.

Participant observation in online environments, whether through interactions with participants in massively multiplayer gaming worlds (Nardi, 2010; Steinkuehler, 2007), or interactions with participants in fanfiction communities (Magnifico, Curwood, & Lammers, 2015; Martin, et al. 2013), has become a central component within online ethnographic research. However, this kind of research also creates the need for researchers to better understand how to define the boundaries of a learning space. As explained further in Chapter Two, a field site for an online study can be both moving and porous, and researchers need to remain aware of these changes and be flexible in their approaches. The field site is dictated by the interactions among the individuals, the resources and tools that they use, and the social context of the learning situations.

Because of the importance of both online and offline spaces in people's learning, many researchers have recognized that the online and offline worlds inform one another. Thus, researchers need to pay close attention to the intersections between worlds (Fields & Kafai, 2009; Leander, 2008; Leander & McKim, 2003). One way is through **connective ethnography**, which acknowledges the connection between online and offline practices and environments.

Kevin M. Leander (2008) explained that, stemming from Hine's (2000) concept of virtual ethnography, *connective ethnography* is "a stance or orientation to Internet-related research that considers connections and relations as normative social practices and Intent social spaces as complexly connected to other social spaces" (p. 37). Examples include, but are not limited to, the study of instant messaging practices among adolescents (Jacobs, 2004) or the ways in which immigrant youth develop their literacy skills through their computer-mediated communication (Lam, 2000).

Grounded Theory

Barney G. Glaser and Anselm L. Strauss (1967) introduced grounded theory to research actions, interactions, and social processes—areas where they felt that other qualitative approaches fell short. Though the two sociologists can be credited with the development of this approach, other researchers have worked to further develop grounded theory methods to enable scholars to have a more fluid and less restrictive approach (Charmaz, 2006; Corbin & Strauss, 2007; Johnson & Christensen, 2014). For example, Kathy Charmaz (2006) developed her constructivist grounded theory approach to expose the power dynamics between the researcher and the researched.

Grounded theory studies rely on visits to the field site—whether through interviews, observations, or chat logs—and data analysis begins when the researcher is still in the field. The researcher moves back and forth between collecting new data and comparing it to the emerging themes in the data, a process known as constant comparison. As the researcher begins to generate theory, he or she is involved in an initial coding stage, called open coding. In open coding, the researcher takes data and segments it into multiple categories. The second step is axial coding, where the researcher identifies a core concept and returns to the data to better understand how the concept is represented within the data. The final step, selective coding, is where the researcher takes the central concept and relates it back to other categories so that the central concept becomes more refined.

Grounded theory has been used to understand the experiences of students learning in online environments (Crittendon, 2006; Feeler, 2012; Gerber & Price, 2013; Yalof, 2014). For example, in order to understand in-service teachers' perceptions of games-based learning as a teaching practice, Gerber and Price (2013) conducted a grounded theory analysis of teachers' discussion boards to better understand teachers' views of games-based learning within literacy classrooms. Relying on discussion board logs, Gerber and Price studied thirteen teachers enrolled in a graduate class on videogames and literacy. Using constant comparison analysis (featuring open, axial, and selective coding), they analyzed over one hundred discussion boards to gain an understanding of teachers' views. The use of constant comparison allowed the researchers to continually reformulate their thoughts and theories, as grounded in the discussion board data, and it facilitated the emergence of themes related to collegial surveillance and the lack of available professional development opportunities.

Phenomenology

Phenomenology is rooted in the work of German philosopher Edmund Husserl and is focused on understanding the lived experience of participants in relation to a given phenomenon. For example, Leander and Boldt's (2013) account of two children playing with manga stories, related toys, and trading cards showed how literacy activities may not always be deliberately designed, but may be improvisational and responsive to current, changing emotions and play conditions. Similarly, Wargo (2015) documented how a participant used smartphone apps like Snapchat and Map My Walk, as well as the gestures that dictate their use (e.g., swiping, tapping), to create, re-create, compose, and share experiential narratives.

According to Creswell (2013) there are two types of phenomenology: hermeneutical phenomenology (van Manen, 1990) and transcendental phenomenology (Moustakas, 1994). Hermeneutical phenomenology is oriented toward understanding the lived experiences by researching the texts of life, which are referred to as the hermeneutics. According to the approach used by Max van Manen, researchers first identify a phenomenon, reflect on essential themes, and maintain a personal connection to these happenings. In their study of the online educators' experiences, De Gagne and Walters (2010) employed a hermeneutic phenomenological approach in order to gain insight into participants' narrative accounts. This allowed for a reflection on "how they interpret and express their experiences through interviews" (Polit & Beck, 2004, p. 358).

Given that "phenomenology is not only a description, but also an interpretive process in which the research makes an interpretation . . . of the meaning of the lived experiences" (Creswell, 2013, p. 80), Clark Moustakas's transcendental phenomenology seeks to keep researchers' interpretations separate from the data. In so doing, transcendental phenomenology begins with researchers "describing their own experiences with the phenomenon and bracketing out their views before proceeding with the experiences of others" (Creswell, 2013, p. 80), thereby acknowledging preconceptions prior to data collection and analysis.

Participatory Approaches

Though not an established tradition, and often combined with aforementioned approaches, **participatory research** is used by researchers who wish to privilege participant voices, reduce researcher bias, and engage in "translocal" understanding (Burnett, Davies, Merchant, & Rowsell, 2014). Rooted in a nonconforming perspective of research design (Johnson & Onwuegbuzie, 2004), **participatory learning** encourages participants to be part of the research, from its conceptualization to the dissemination of findings. Some researchers have suggested that participatory approaches are crucial for overturning power dynamics inherent in traditional research approaches (Bergold & Thomas, 2012; Morrell, 2006; Onwuegbuzie & Frels, 2013).

Researchers using participatory approaches often strive to empower underrepresented, underserved, marginalized, or oppressed individuals and groups. For instance, when Michelle Fine and colleagues (2005) engaged in an "ethnographic analysis of the political economy of schooling as lived by youth in and around the New York City metropolitan area" (p. 500), they purposely included youth researchers who "played a vital role in determining the research design, questions, methods, interpretations and products" of the study (p. 501). In so doing, they found that the youth-as-researchers developed critical stances related to racism and social justice. Fine and colleagues featured some of the youth researchers' reflections and discoveries, such as, "I used to see flat. No more . . . now I know things are much deeper than they appear. And it's my job to find out what's behind the so-called facts. I can't see flat anymore" (p. 523). This suggests that participatory research could inspire a critical awakening among youth-as-researchers.

Critical dialectical pluralism (CDP) is a research philosophy that embraces the ethos of participatory research. In particular, critical dialectical pluralism creates pathways for participants to be maximally involved as researchers throughout the process, especially with respect to the dissemination and utilization of the findings (Onwuegbuzie & Frels, 2013). Adopting a CDP stance, Gerber, Abrams, Onwuegbuzie, and Benge (2014) worked collaboratively with adolescent participants to understand their engagement with multiple online and offline gaming resources as used in a public school remedial reading class. Given that the research took place during the school day, the participatory approach underscored the disruption of power dynamics between the teacher and the student, as well as between the researcher and the participant. The CDP stance allowed the research team to collaboratively trace learning across these resources and spaces, while honoring the perspectives and voices of participants through the entire research process—from conceptualization through research dissemination.

Participatory approaches may suggest that power structures and hierarchies can be eliminated, but such a stance seems idyllic and inaccurate because the reality is that youth-driven research participation remains under adult auspices. Barry Checkoway and Lorraine Gutiérrez (2006) underscore this point in their introduction to their edited volume on youth participation. Not only did they acknowledge the benefits of participatory research, but also they addressed the possible limitations: "Although participation initiatives might be youth-led, adult-led, or intergenerational in their origins, we recognize that none of the ones described here is truly youth-led. However, we reiterate that the quality of participation is not contingent on this approach" (p. 6). These concerns should not undermine participatory research; rather, they remind researchers to be cognizant of inherent power structures, thoughtful of their own presuppositions, and careful in their approach to include participant voices and decisions.

Research Paradigms and Philosophical Stances in a Study's Design

Creswell (2012) relied on the metaphor of a loom to address the traits of qualitative research. Creswell stated that qualitative research is like

> an intricate fabric composed of minute threads, many colors, different textures, and various blends of material. This fabric is not explained easily or simply. Like the loom on which fabric is woven, general assumptions and interpretive frameworks hold qualitative research together. To describe these frameworks, qualitative researchers use terms—constructivist, interpretivist, feminist, postmodernist, and so forth. Within these assumptions and through these frameworks are approaches to qualitative inquiry, such as narrative research, phenomenology, grounded theory, ethnography, and case studies. (p. 42)

Creswell (2012) pointed out that philosophical assumptions, mental models, interpretive frameworks, and approaches to methods are woven tightly together. In other words, researchers' own understandings, beliefs, and biases are difficult to separate from the tools that they use and craft in order to engage in inquiry, even when the intention is to be as objective as possible.

Methodological approaches to conducting a study should not be chosen arbitrarily. The design of the research questions are determined by the defined research purpose, the research questions, and the worldview, or paradigm, that a researcher brings to a study. A study's design, and its corresponding research questions, will be strengthened by researchers' regular reflections on their own assumptions and mental models.

Various researchers (Creswell, 2013; Guba & Lincoln, 1994; Tashakkori & Teddlie, 1998) have identified major **research paradigms** that shape a study's design, including positivism, postpositivism, critical theories, constructivism, and pragmatism. While other paradigms and philosophical stances exist, these broad categories shown in Table 1.1 highlight major defining ideas that frame researchers' inquiry. In short, using the concept of a "paradigm" to refer to a set of shared beliefs among researchers can be traced to Thomas Kuhn's (1962) text, *The Structure of Scientific Revolutions.*

Morgan (2007) has noted that this term has been taken up by social sciences researchers in several ways that are not always easy to distinguish from each other: "Paradigm" can define something as broad as a researcher's worldview—an epistemic stance that reflects beliefs about knowledge, beliefs that are shared across members of a field—or something as narrow as a model for research. Morgan explained that "these four versions of the paradigm concept are not mutually exclusive. Nor is one of them right and the others wrong. Instead the question is which version is most appropriate for any given purpose" (p. 54). Despite the noted range in definition, the word *paradigm* is most often used to describe an epistemic belief about knowledge, as in Table 1.1.

A **positivist** paradigm—a stance that was common through World War II— suggests that it is possible to use scientific methods to identify true, verifiable, value-free statements about the world. However, a **postpositivist** paradigm places some critical limits on that truth, acknowledging that "truth" and "reality" are by nature imperfect constructions because observations and findings are never free of human theory and intervention.

Table 1.1   Research Paradigms

Research Paradigm	Traits
Positivism	An assumed reality exists that can be tested and verified through research methods.
Postpositivism	Belief that an assumed reality exists, but that researchers can come to know it only in part.
Critical Theories	Seek to understand various situations and multiple realities. The researcher must take into account social, political, cultural, economic, ethnic, and gender factors.
Constructivism	Knowledge is a human and social construction where realit(ies) are co-constructed. A participatory paradigm extends from constructivism and attends to participant-researchers who co-construct knowledge with investigators.
Pragmatism	Concerned with the practical and with what works.

A **constructivist** paradigm might note that facts and truths are constructed by scientists and social scientists within human contexts, and so are unlikely to be verifiable by all observers, while a **critical theorist** paradigm would seek to understand the value systems that affect how such findings might be perceived among different groups of people or historical periods. (For more detail on these definitions, see, e.g., Lincoln & Guba, 2000; Tashakkori & Teddlie, 1998.)

While approaches to research are rarely directly associated with methods, typically quantitative experimental methods have been associated with positivist and postpositivist paradigms, and qualitative and naturalistic methods with constructivist and critical paradigms. When viewed in this way, it begins to become clear why mixed methods research has been such a significant and controversial evolution in methodology: How is it possible to combine techniques that have different views about the nature of knowledge itself?

Several approaches to mixing paradigms and methods exist, but Greene (2007) favors a "dialectical" stance (pp. 59–60), wherein the multiple knowledge paradigms, methods, and mental models about what those methods help researchers learn or accomplish are brought deliberately into conversation with each other. In this way, researchers can gain insight into more complex findings and perspectives that may be possible only when these contradictory stances are interrogated together.

Still other researchers favor a pragmatic stance toward mixing methods, in which the focus is placed not on broad epistemic or ontological claims, but on how particular methods will help researchers to inquire more successfully into particular settings or research questions. This position is derived from the work of American theorists such as Charles Peirce, William James, and John Dewey, who sought to develop a philosophy of how actions, ideas, and methods reflect human experience and advance democratic ideals.

Taking up this position, Morgan (2007) questioned the usefulness of paradigmatic assumptions: "Although paradigms as epistemological stances do draw attention to the deeper assumptions that researchers make, they tell us little about more substantive decisions such as what to study and how to do so" (p. 52). In other words, thinking about such questions as the nature of truth and knowledge may pull researchers away from more immediate questions, such as their reflections on the design of their inquiry.

Additionally, Johnson and Onwuegbuzie (2004) explicitly championed **pragmatism** as a paradigm for mixed methods. They did so to help scholars find a middle position between a "purist" stance (where mixing methods or paradigms is not defensible) and an "a-paradigmatic" stance (where methods are chosen without regard to broader philosophical concerns). Instead, pragmatism helps research designers to choose philosophical stances, methods, and procedures that speak most directly to their research questions. As Greene (2007) explained, "To approach mixed methods inquiry pragmatically does not mean to ignore or set to one side philosophical assumptions and stances when making practical methods decisions. For that is the a-paradigmatic stance. Rather, a pragmatic paradigm signals attention to transactions and interactions; to the consequential, contextual, and dynamic nature of character of knowledge; to knowledge as action; to the intertwinement of values with inquiry, and so forth" (p. 85).

We call attention to the pragmatic research paradigm to emphasize the connection between research methods and context. In other words, researchers may need to select multiple methods to gain a rich understanding of learning at a particular time and place, particularly in online spaces where learning often happens across many times and places. Although we emphasize this approach, we do not intend to privilege it; rather, we believe that there are multiple valid perspectives in and across research of learning in online spaces, and that it is important for researchers not to feel confined or constrained by one paradigm.

Pragmatic Research and Remix: Considering Multimethod Approaches

Given that pragmatic research connects research design and contexts, researchers have opportunities to take creative and agentive approaches to data collection and analysis. In this section, we introduce the concept of **remix** as it has been understood in literacy research. Then, we apply the remix framework pragmatically to mixed approaches to suggest that researchers can find the most appropriate and effective methods for their study when they can customize their approach.

Drawing on Creswell's (2015) concept of multimethod research, this section introduces how researchers might draw on multiple forms of qualitative data from networked field sites. Creswell (2015) indicated that researchers should not conflate mixed methods research with multimethod research. As he explained in *A Concise Introduction to Mixed Methods Research*, "When multiple forms of qualitative data are collected, the term is *multimethod* research, not mixed methods research" (p. 3, emphasis in original). Using multiple aspects of various traditions and data sources can lead to methodologically rich inquiries of online learning.

Remix

The concept of remix existed long before the age of the Internet and new media. One can look back to the Star Trek fandom magazines for a brief glimpse into the spaces of remix in popular culture. Star Trek fanzines were magazines written by "Trekkie" fans and based on different episodes, characters, and ideas posed in the various televised episodes. Popular culture and media scholar Henry Jenkins (1992) examined the concept behind Star Trek fandom magazines through Michel de Certeau's (1984) concept of textual poaching. He found that reclaiming textual materials reflected fans' beliefs and thoughts versus authorial imposed concepts, thereby providing fans a sense of ownership. As Jenkins claimed, traditional academic writers have been quick to place fans in a marginalized community, disparaging multiple fandoms as infantile, rudimentary, and unsophisticated in their approaches to experiencing texts. However, Jenkins suggested that this type of fan-based textual poaching not only allows for new engagement in and creative remixing of media texts, but also provides a moral economy (a set of rights and ownership) to fans who might otherwise be further marginalized.

More recently, new literacies scholars Michele Knobel and Colin Lankshear (2008) explained that remix has deep roots within the music industry, noting how audio-editing techniques have allowed artists to take apart and reorganize original songs and transform them into other musical creations. Building on this discussion of restructured song creation, Knobel and Lankshear argued that there are many avenues for individuals to engage in remix, particularly in the age of online media creation. Some contemporary examples of remix include:

- **Fanfiction**—narrative or poetic text that enthusiasts create, using and extending characters, ideas, and information from a particular book, movie, videogame, or other fandom.

- **Machinima**—derived from the portmanteau of machine and cinema, it is the creation of films through manipulation of videogame graphics.

- **Mash-Ups**—remixed musical tracks created by blending two or more songs together to create a hybrid song. Mash-ups often combine instrumental music with the vocals from another song.

- **Memes**—first introduced by Dawkins (1976), who used the term to address genes and DNA mutations. The meaning of this word now also characterizes cultural transmissions, often graphics or short animations with textual captions that pass from one person to the next, with slight variations between each passing.

What is central to each of the explanations of remix is the concept of creators' agency, especially as it involves one building on and reworking established texts and concepts. With remix, customization is both acceptable and encouraged. When applied to discussions of research methods, remix offers flexibility, but it also requires the researcher to constantly negotiate and rationalize methodological and paradigmatic choices. Currently, mixed methodology supports the combination of qualitative and quantitative research methods, and we call attention to remix to highlight researchers' agentive and creative possibilities when designing and conducting a multimethod qualitative investigation. More specifically, we suggest that a remix-inspired **multimethod approach** can be used to examine meaning making across online and offline spaces.

As introduced earlier, connective ethnography is an example of researchers taking creative and agentive stances as they investigate learning in online spaces. Leander (2008) acknowledged that "connective ethnography is informed by developments in several other fields, where notions of the research 'site' are being disrupted and relations are being traced among sociocultural practices and agents" (p. 37). Deborah A. Fields and Yasmin Kafai (2009) conducted a connective ethnography to examine how inhabitants of the virtual world Whyville moved and participated across the site. Not only did the researchers use a combination of data collection methods—from video to back-end data tracking to field notes and interview—but also they relied on the "insider gaming practice" of teleporting to investigate knowledge sharing and movement within the site (p. 48).

In this way, Fields and Kafai (2009) investigated networked field sites, as the site of the study was neither relegated to a singular space nor temporally limited. We argue that such thoughtful and productive remixing of methods is similar to what Greene (2007) and other mixed methods researchers might call a "dialectical" or "complementary strengths" combination of methods. There, seemingly disparate approaches (e.g., back-end data mining and face-to-face field notes) were brought together to create new insights about how participants learned to inhabit Whyville online and offline. Such innovative study designs advance the field of educational research and challenge researchers to attend to how learners move across and through multiple spaces.

Networked field sites allow researchers to trace how individuals move through multiple online spaces (e.g., from a Facebook site, to a fanfiction site, to a blog space) in order to make meaning. Researchers may call on multiple approaches to understand meanings made across spaces, just as Fields and Kafai (2009) did when examining participatory practices in Whyville. In this way, we can see how an emphasis on agency and creativity can move the field forward because researchers can be encouraged to view the boundaries of methodological traditions as porous; that is, researchers can see how methodologies can be combined to customize a research approach that is appropriate for a particular context of inquiry.

Inspired by remix, researchers may bring together a number of methodological approaches in order to investigate and understand meaning making within and across online spaces. Customizing a research approach, however, needs to be done with care. It would be irresponsible to simply draw from different traditions without an appropriate lens and purpose. As such, researchers should reflect on the affordances and limitations of the multiple methods, and ask questions such as these:

- In what ways will the various methods work in concert to capture and discover meaning making that spans online and offline environments?

- How will the remixed approach support the investigation of diverse field sites?

- How will the approach enhance critical reflection of researcher positioning and bias?

Using the lens of remix, this book features examples of agentive and creative research approaches from design to data collection to data analysis. More specifically, we highlight how drawing on multimethod approaches and traditions can enable researchers

- to move across various online sites, following participants, events, or networking residues (see Chapter Two and Chapter Four);

- to traverse and analyze online and offline data (see Chapter Four);

- to collect and gather participants' cultural productions and systematically (whether chronologically, spatially, or another category) trace the evolution of those productions (see Chapters Five and Six);

- to gather available back-end data (keystrokes, log-in data, and other algorithm data) and combine those data with traditional qualitative data, such as interviews (see Chapter Six);

- to understand and implement ethical approaches to entry into networked field sites (see Chapter Seven); and

- to engage in cocreation and coproduction in designing research studies with participants, even across disparate studies (see Chapter Eight).

As researchers embrace multiple approaches to study meaning making in a variety of online spaces, it is important to examine the creative and agentic techniques promoted by the concept of remix that one might take in designing his or her study. As more scholars enter their various fields of study (e.g., nursing, education, cultural anthropology, social work) recognizing that online spaces are important, scholars may be concerned with, and interested in, the diverse ways people engage in learning in online spaces. This might influence how researchers design studies to better understand these practices and meaning-making experiences. Judiciously selecting multiple appropriate methods to get to the heart of a research question is one of the biggest promises in looking at online research through the lens of remix.

Conclusion

The study of learning in online spaces can be vastly enriched when researchers consider the plethora of ways that learning unfolds dynamically in and across networked field sites. Because contemporary frames for meaning making within online environments cannot be relegated to a one-size-fits-all model, methodological approaches also must be reconsidered. As indicated, researchers should examine the framing of mental models and logics of inquiry that help to further shape their analytic frames. From there, researchers can adopt a research paradigm that aligns with their study's design.

CONNECTING TO YOUR WORK

Referring back to the various studies provided in this chapter, several different methodological approaches were introduced. The following questions can help you think through a future study, while drawing on the concepts that were introduced in this chapter.

- In what ways do you think that your potential research questions might be adapted to draw on a remixing of multiple approaches? How would this allow you to see different elements of your research?

- What benefits might be gained by introducing remixing

multiple approaches to a study's design?

- How do the theories behind mental models and logic of inquiry lend themselves to developing your study in an online environment?

Guiding Questions for Chapter 2

- How can online spaces be conceptualized as field sites?
- What kinds of online spaces support collaborative learning, social networking, media and project sharing, microblogging, and exploring virtual worlds?
- What are networked field sites, and how do they shape online qualitative research?

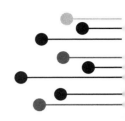

CHAPTER TWO

What Kinds of Online Spaces Exist?

Introduction

Research in online environments can focus on a single field site, such as a blog, wiki, or discussion board, or it can traverse multiple spaces and social media tools. For that reason, online researchers need to be flexible with both their methods and their approach to uncovering, participating in, and analyzing online spaces. Online spaces shape how, when, and why people learn, including through social networking, microblogging, photo and video sharing, and constructing and disseminating knowledge. Because of the ever-changing nature of technology, these spaces are rapidly emerging and evolving, and they include both formal and informal spaces for learning. To illustrate the present state of online qualitative research, in this chapter, we consider how researchers can conceptualize and map online spaces, and we share specific examples from contemporary studies.

Conceptualizing Online Spaces as Field Sites

Today's digital tools and online spaces challenge the traditional notion of field sites. Whereas previous research may have focused on a specific physical site in an effort to understand the interplay of individuals, practices, beliefs, and cultures, contemporary technology expands the boundaries of potential field sites. No longer geographically restricted, researchers can readily explore new contexts and interact with diverse artifacts. Scholars interested in collective action, for instance, can investigate how social media has played an integral role in revolutions in the Middle East (Herrera, 2012; Lynch, 2011). Not only can they access publicly available Twitter feeds and Facebook posts, but also they can connect with potential participants from any part of the world. In this way, qualitative research is increasingly digitally mediated, especially as researchers seek to understand how online spaces shape how people learn by engaging with semiotic resources, constructing meaning, and interacting with others. In order to examine how this occurs, it is first necessary to consider what defines and bounds contemporary field sites.

A field site can be conceptualized as a "network composed of fixed and moving points including spaces, people, and objects" (Burrell, 2009, p. 189). Consequently, a field site is inevitably complex and malleable. Rather than defining a field site by physical boundaries, the concept of a network offers a dynamic visual representation of the interaction between individuals, their tools, and their contexts. Notably, individuals often have substantial agency in interacting with each other, selecting their tools, and navigating their contexts. According to Christine Hine (2008), "The problem in defining appropriate field sites is that it is not always possible to identify in advance where the relevant social dynamics for understanding a particular technology are going on" (p. 4). Though it may be possible to identify a specific website for a learning community, rarely does the learning process exist in isolation.

Spotlight Box 2.1
Programming, Designing, and Learning With Scratch

Consider Scratch, a free programming language and online community where individuals can create their own animated stories, videogames, and other creative work (Resnick et al., 2009). Since its launch in 2007, Scratch has grown to nearly three million users worldwide, mostly youth ages 11 to 18. With ten million shared projects (Scratch Wiki, 2015), the Scratch community encourages interactive learning (see image below). Not only can users share their projects online, but also they are able to engage in social networking and collaborative learning through leaving

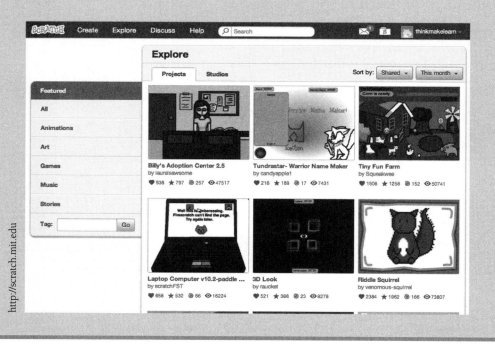

http://scratch.mit.edu

comments, favoriting projects, and friending other users.

Research suggests that in comparison to traditional programming, Scratch offers a more accessible, creative, and visual approach to creating environments and languages (Brennan, Monroy-Hernández, & Resnick, 2010). In addition, the design of the Scratch website supports collaborative learning since every project is fully public, and users can directly access and even edit the programming, graphics, and sound of the project. However, learning with Scratch is not restricted to Scratch.mit.edu.

The Scratch community involves a number of related online spaces and groups (Fields, Magnifico, Lammers, & Curwood, 2014). For instance, a user-created wiki is a collaboratively written source of information about the programming language, including scripts and tutorials, as well as the history, statistics, and other information about Scratch. According to Grimes and Fields (2012), many groups work together on projects, including games and interactive stories within the Scratch site. In addition, there are a number of live role-playing groups that use projects for inspiration for user-created characters and stories. Consequently, collaborative agency is instrumental to learning within the Scratch community. Collaborative agency emphasizes the active role that learners take when they participate within communities in order to build knowledge, design artifacts, and interact with others (Kafai, Fields, Roque, Burke, & Monroy Hernández, 2012).

Defining the Field Site

For qualitative researchers who seek to understand learning within the Scratch community, it is vital to first define their field site. For example, will they focus on the process of collaborative knowledge construction exclusively within the wiki? Will they analyze the comments on specific projects in order to gain insight into the interactive and public nature of programming within Scratch? Or, instead of focusing on particular features or spaces within the broader Scratch community, will researchers follow specific users across multiple sites as they write, design, and create with Scratch? Can they construct case studies of individual users, conduct interviews, and consider how they access projects and use the available programming tools to remix them, as in Figure 2.1? If we think of a field site as a network of fixed and moving points, researchers are then compelled to consider how the spaces, individuals, and objects shape the framing of the study and the ways in which learning can be conceptualized, traced, and analyzed within online environments.

The shift in the conceptualization of field sites is concomitant with the change in our understanding of culture. Previously, culture was thought to be a fixed

Figure 2.1 Example of a Scratch Project

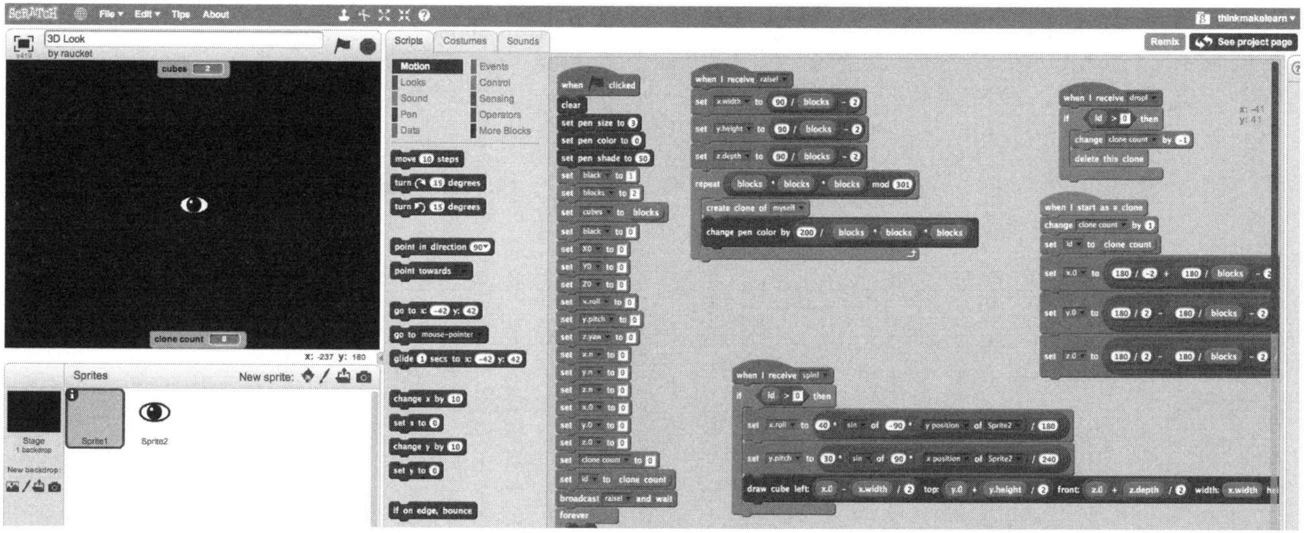

http://scratch.mit.edu

entity; today, scholars such as Arjun Appadurai (1996) and George Marcus (1998) argue that culture is marked by both intersection and flow. Digital culture is a prime example of this change. While all cultures change over time, "what makes the Internet so confounding for research is that the fundamental architecture also changes rapidly" (boyd, 2008a, p. 26). Because the tools and spaces are always in flux, so too are the related social practices. Online environments offer individuals around the world opportunities to engage in different social and cultural activities as part of the learning process; moreover, they afford qualitative researchers the opportunities to trace these activities across time and space. Research design, therefore, "should be a reflexive process which operates throughout every stage of a project" (Hammersley & Atkinson, 1995, p. 24). If digital culture involves networks, intersections, and interactions in online spaces, the ways in which researchers define and bound field sites must take this into account.

Multi-sited research can be designed around "chains, paths, threads, conjunctions, or juxtapositions of locations" (Marcus, 1998, p. 90). While Marcus suggested that researchers must establish some form of presence within the field site, his conceptualization of research transcends physical boundaries. For online researchers, it is possible to readily establish a virtual presence. This will then allow them to engage in the field site in different ways as well as to build meaningful relationships with participants across multiple countries and time zones (Lammers, Magnifico, & Curwood, 2014).

As Marcus (1998) noted, the researcher may follow the ways in which a person, an object, a symbol, or a metaphor moves within and across the space. Each approach may offer different insights into the processes and products involved in online learning. This movement is central to social practices and cultural processes; moreover, it may take place across great distance and serve to link disparate entities (Burrell, 2009). Mitchell (1996) described the Internet as "profoundly antispatial. . . . You cannot say where it is or describe its memorable shape and proportions. . . . But you can find things in it without knowing where they are" (p. 8). The task for qualitative researchers, then, is to ensure that their methodological approach effectively accounts for the pathways and the movements inherent to online spaces.

Understanding Networked Field Sites

Digital culture involves networks, intersections, and interactions in online spaces; consequently, online spaces are diverse and dynamic. In order to further explore how networked field sites shape contemporary qualitative research, it is helpful to introduce the concept of social networking forums. According to Grimes and Fields (2012), **social networking forums** encompass a broad and inclusive range of online social activities, practices, and platforms. They

Spotlight Box 2.2
The Hunger Games and Literacy

Young adults' literacy practices can be supported by their participation in online spaces associated with literature, such as *The Hunger Games*, a young adult dystopian trilogy. Jen Scott Curwood (2013a, 2013b, 2014b) drew on a sociocultural and situated approach to examine how youth create and share **transformative works**, which includes a variety of writing and designing practices that take an original artifact and turn it into something with a new function or expression.

Building on theories of affinity spaces and traditions of online ethnographic research, Curwood constructed case studies of focal participants to understand how online spaces offered youth an opportunity to deepen their content knowledge, participate in social interactions, and develop their creative writing skills. Across various sites and through multiple tools, these young adults produced transformative works by writing fanfiction, creating art, making videos, composing music, and engaging in role-playing games.

Affinity spaces are physical, virtual, or **blended spaces** where people interact around a common interest; these spaces can be accessed by a variety of **portals**, or entry points (Gee, 2004). Magnifico, Lammers, and Curwood (2013) argued that there are three types of portals: (1) root websites specific to *The Hunger Games* affinity space,

including HungerGamesRPG.com and HungerGamesTrilogy.net; (2) archives of creative artifacts that include transformative works from multiple affinity spaces, such as Fanfiction.net and DeviantArt.com; and (3) social media tools that promote interaction within and beyond the affinity space, including Twitter, Facebook, and Tumblr. Within the affinity space, participants traverse across different portals and move within specific portals as they engage with other *Hunger Games* fans. Moreover, each portal offers different interest-driven trajectories, opportunities to learn with others, and paths toward becoming a participant (Squire, 2011).

The methodological approach focused on constructing case studies of focal participants and tracing their literacy practices across time and space. For example, 17-year-old Georgia from Western Australia primarily used Tumblr as a means of role-playing *Hunger Games* characters; the microblogging platform allowed her to write dialogue and share artwork, which can occur synchronously or asynchronously (Curwood, 2014b). On the other side of Australia, 13-year-old Jack was actively involved in online discussion boards related to *The Hunger Games*; here, he critically analyzed the novels, collaboratively constructed a character index, and discussed global issues (Curwood, 2013b). In the United States, 16-year-old Cassie wrote news stories and reviewed books on a popular portal; she also acted in YouTube fan videos and managed a popular Twitter account (Curwood, Magnifico, & Lammers, 2013). By following a person, rather than an object or metaphor (Marcus, 1998), Curwood examined how each specific portal shaped an individual's literacy practices and learning processes. Read against each other, each case study then offers insight into the wider networked field site of *The Hunger Games* fandom.

extend beyond social network sites to include virtual worlds, digital games, and project-sharing spaces; moreover, participation in social networking forums can be both interest-driven and socialization-based.

For researchers, social networking forums offer a place to observe and to participate in various communities. Social networking forums can help reveal how online tools and places shape the ways in which individuals learn from and with one another. As Pascoe (2012) pointed out, this kind of observation can offer insight into social worlds that may not otherwise be available. Social networking forums extend across contexts, platforms, and interactions. Grimes and Fields (2012) argued that social networking forums have four key attributes: forms of communication, personal profiles, **networking residues**, and hierarchies of access. Each of these attributes has clear implications for qualitative research and can be helpful in explicating the content and practices inherent in networked field sites.

To begin, communication is a central aspect of online social networking sites that can be facilitated through posts, comments, messages, and chat options. Personal profiles may feature photos, quotes, and status updates; these also serve to connect users with each other. Networking residues are "the traces of one's social connections to other users on a site" and allow users to "demonstrate their affinity with one another" (Grimes & Fields, 2012, p. 43). Through participating in groups, creating friend lists, and favoriting posts, comments, and projects, users participate in the wider community. Finally, hierarchies of access allow some users more options for participation and more kinds of privileges than others. In this instance, access may be determined by membership, age, or status.

Given the constantly evolving nature of social networking forums, it is not possible to offer a definitive typology. For instance, while Instagram may primarily function as a photo- and video-sharing site, it also serves as a social networking service that allows users to apply digital filters and share their photos and videos to Facebook, Twitter, Tumblr, and Flickr. Just as there is not a clear typology, there are often not distinct boundaries between different social networking forums. However, it is important that researchers know what kinds of online spaces exist and that they consider how such spaces can shape the formulation of research questions, the scope of data collection, and the process of data analysis.

Outlined below are six kinds of social networking forums associated with collaborative learning, social networking, media sharing, microblogging, project sharing, and virtual worlds. These examples offer qualitative researchers evidence of how, when, and why individuals learn as well as how digital culture shapes the learning process. Despite evolving technologies and tools, the examination of current social networking forums can provide insight into the range of norms, functions, and practices that inform, and sometimes govern, meaning making in online spaces. Though it is difficult to predict the contour of future online practices and spaces, the characteristics of these six social networking forums can shed light on the historical development of learning processes.

Learning in Social Networking Forums

Learning within and across social networking forums typically is fluid. Learners often access distinct spaces according to their interests and their needs; consequently, researchers must decide on the aims of their study and the boundaries of their field site. In outlining six kinds of social networking forums, our purpose is not to be restrictive or definitive; rather, we seek to give qualitative researchers ideas about the types of spaces for learning that exist online.

Collaborative learning can be a defining feature of social networking forums. For example, wikis allow individuals to add, modify, or delete content in collaboration with others. Wikipedia has articles written in 288 languages, and it allows individuals to engage in collaborative knowledge construction (see Figure 2.2). While anyone can contribute to Wikipedia, there are hierarchies of access for writers and editors. As of 2015, Wikipedia is the seventh most-visited website worldwide, and it is the best known wiki ("Alexa Top 500 Global Sites," 2015). However, tools such as Wikispaces and Wikia readily allow individuals to construct and share their own wiki. Another tool for collaborative learning is a discussion board, which can be publicly or privately available. Here, users can ask questions, share resources, and engage in dialogue. Many discussion boards include personal profiles, where the post history can show each user's networking residues.

Social network sites, such as Facebook, involve users' public or semipublic profiles, a list of other users with whom they are connected, and an ability to view others' connections. By differentiating between *social networking* and **social network**, danah m. boyd and Nicole B. Ellison (2007) suggested that many individuals use these spaces as ways to connect with people who are already a part

Figure 2.2 Wikipedia

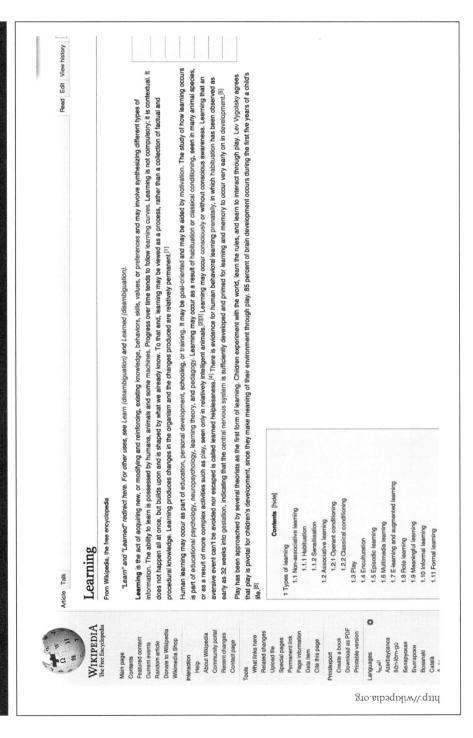

Wikipedia is a free, collaboratively authored encyclopedia that features content navigation and hyperlinks.

of their social network. Founded in 2004, Facebook has 1.49 billion active users ("Facebook Stats," 2015). Other social networks are popular in certain countries, including Bebo in Ireland and Orkut in Brazil. Because most of these social networks restrict access to users over 13 years old, recent years have seen the launch of children-specific social networks, including Scuttlepad and Everloop.

Within each social network site, users maintain personal profiles and engage in various forms of communication, such as writing status updates, sharing photos, and leaving comments. Because such actions can create networking residues, social networks offer researchers an opportunity to trace participation within the site and across other social networking forums. While some researchers may have access to back-end data, such as analytics, often networking residues are traced through front-end data that are more readily accessible and potentially limiting in terms of following navigation pathways and interactions. An analysis of social networking, in this sense, can often offer insight into how, when, and why individuals learn.

Media-sharing sites allow users to readily share photos and videos. While YouTube, Vimeo, Instagram, and Flickr all include video content, the latter two primarily include photography. Meanwhile, **microblogging** sites like Twitter and Tumblr encourage users to share short sentences and resource links. Through the use of descriptions, hashtags, and favorites, media-sharing sites and microblogs encourage users to connect with one another through diverse forms of communication. Very often, one user will access multiple social networking forums, perhaps by uploading a video to YouTube and sharing it via Twitter. This leaves networking residues that qualitative researchers can then trace across multiple spaces and over time. These networking residues may offer evidence of learning; for instance, a young adult interested in photography may learn how to use Photoshop through a YouTube video, connect with other photographers on Flickr, and share his or her work on Instagram.

Similarly, project-sharing sites encourage users to make both the process and the product of their creative work visible to others. Fanfiction.net and Figment.com, discussed in greater detail in the following section, encourage writers to remix popular plots and characters in their fanfiction writing. Other project-sharing sites, like Scratch, encourage programmers to develop their skills through creating games and stories. Project-sharing sites depend on communication between creators and their audience, and many sites facilitate this communication through private messages, public comments, favorites, and groups. Status within project-sharing sites is often obtained through users' length and scope of participation, and there can be hierarchies of access related to leadership roles within the community. Within Fanfiction.net, writers can craft their own profile, with links to their stories and their favorites. As such, the design of the site allows researchers to readily access the related networking residues and trace learning within and across projects.

Some virtual worlds can also be considered project-sharing sites, and they may vary greatly in terms of content and participation. Whereas Webkinz and Club Penguin cater to a younger audience, Second Life is designed for users over 16 years old. With most virtual worlds, users create an avatar and explore the virtual space, which may involve interacting with other users, building objects, and sharing digital work. Other virtual worlds, such as World of Warcraft, are situated around massively multiplayer online role-playing games (MMORPGs). The seven million World of Warcraft players construct an avatar and navigate the virtual world, either individually or as part of guilds. Though Second Life allows users to readily share code, World of Warcraft users need to go to other spaces to engage in project sharing, such as making modifications. Unlike social network sites, virtual worlds encourage users to create a profile for a character rather than themselves. Communication between users is often facilitated through text, audio, and video; moreover, participation in virtual worlds may be supported by related online spaces that offer tutorials, FAQs, and group membership.

Layers of Learning in Formal Learning Spaces

While social networking forums are primarily interest-driven, many schools, universities, and organizations support online spaces known as learning management systems (LMSs). Learning management systems allow instructors to manage an entire class, communicate with students, and share course material in a platform designed specifically for formal online learning (Ellis, 2009; Szabo & Flescher, 2002). Learning management systems make it possible for instructors to document, track, report, and deliver course content to students at any time and from anywhere (Watson, 2007). Most learning management systems coordinate student learning across courses with a landing page, the central location for course information and materials such as deadlines, tasks, emails, and grades.

Some common LMSs include Blackboard, WebCT, Edmodo, Moodle, and Canvas. Additionally, in line with the concept of open access learning, consortia and companies such as Coursera, EdX, and Udemy—all massive open online course (MOOC) providers—often employ the use of LMSs on a global scale, relying on immense systems to manage learning for thousands of students.

For nearly two decades, scholars have been studying how learners interact and subsequently learn within formal, online learning management systems. One model for understanding online learning—the Community of Inquiry (CoI) Model—was developed by Randy Garrison, Terry Anderson, and Walter Archer (1999). The CoI Model is grounded in the work of John Dewey and sociocultural theories of learning, and stresses that good online learning must include overlapping interactions of social presence, instructor presence, and cognitive presence. Since the development of the CoI Model, conferences dedicated to the study of formal online learning such as the Online Learning Consortium (OLC) have promoted CoI as a model for good online instruction. Since its development, multiple studies have been conducted using the CoI Model for understanding learning interactions (e.g., Annand, 2011; Swan, Garrison, & Richardson, 2009; Swan et al., 2008).

Instructors of formal courses often blend learning among several tools and environments. Thus, researchers interested in studying these spaces may find themselves designing studies that draw on a combination of face-to-face classroom discussions, learning management systems, and social networking forums. An instructor may interweave formal learning opportunities with informal social networking forums, such as Twitter and Google Hangout, in order to expand the time and media for course discussions, encourage students to draw on a variety of resources in their coursework, provide an archive, and/or welcome outside individuals to take part in the learning experience.

For instance, Li and Greenhow (2015) examined how the American Education Research Association's conference Twitter backchannel influenced participants' understandings of social media's impact on meaning making. This research showed that at conferences, professional development opportunities, and formal classes, a backchannel can bring the attendees' experiences and insights to individuals who may not be physically or synchronously present in the space. In a university class, an instructor may use WebCT to disseminate course materials, Twitter to foster a backchannel discussion during lectures, and a YouTube channel to share relevant videos. These examples show that learning in a digital age involves the layering of literacies (Abrams, 2015), the intersection of multiple tools and spaces, and the necessity of individual learners' movement across and between multiple components of field sites (see Table 2.1). Researchers interested in such environments must communicate with instructors and students to define the scope of the project, clearly articulate their research questions, and consider how to map these networks.

Mapping Networked Field Sites

Because of the complexity of social networking forums and learning management systems, as well as the rapidly evolving nature of available technologies, qualitative researchers must make deliberate decisions about their field site. Very often, the boundaries of a research project will emerge once a researcher formulates research questions related to the content and scope of the study. As boyd (2008a) noted, "Networked technologies have completely disrupted any simple construction of a field site" (p. 27). Consequently, researchers will need to map their networked field sites and leverage available technologies and networking residues. Not only will this allow them to navigate networked

Table 2.1	Examples of Online Spaces for Learning	
Type	**Learning Space**	**Description**
Social Networking Forums	Wikis	An online tool that allows individuals to create, change, or delete content in collaboration with others. In addition to Wikipedia, Wikispaces and PBWorks are free wikis used to support formal and informal learning.
	Facebook	An online social networking tool; Pages, open or closed groups, chat, and other features can support learning. Founded in 2004 and currently has over a billion users worldwide.
	Twitter	An online social networking and microblogging tool. Tweets are limited to 140 characters and can support learning through the use of content, hyperlinks, and hashtags. Created in 2006 and has over 340 million Tweets each day.
	Instagram	An online social networking tool that supports the sharing of photos and videos, including on Facebook, Twitter, Flickr, and Tumblr. Founded in 2010 and acquired by Facebook in 2012.
	The Sims	A life simulation videogame series launched by Electronic Arts in 2000. The sandbox game has sold over 175 million copies worldwide.
	Webkinz	Toy stuffed animals with a virtual counterpart; Webkinz World was founded in 2005 and allows users to own a virtual version of their pet for online gameplay.
	Minecraft	A sandbox indie game released in 2009; now also available on Xbox 360 and mobile devices. MinecraftEDU, an independent entity, supports its use in the classroom to foster students' literacy and numeracy skills.
	Whyville	An educational website launched in 1999. It aims to educate children in topics related to science, art, and business and has over seven million users.
	Figment	An online community and self-publishing platform for writers founded in 2010 and acquired by Random House in 2012. Similar to Fanfiction.net in that it supports the creation and distribution of transformative works. It also encourages writing through groups, comments, and reviews.
	DeviantArt	An online community that showcases artwork, including photography, film, digital art, and traditional art. Since its inception in 2000, it now has over 25 million members.
Learning Management Systems	Blackboard	An online learning management software primarily used within higher education; fee-based.
	Moodle	A free online e-learning platform used within secondary and tertiary education.
	Edmodo	A free social learning platform generally used within secondary schools.

field sites, but it will also offer a way for them to reflect on what these links and pathways mean for those involved (Hine, 2008).

The Internet can be seen as a tool, a place, and a way of being; moreover, each aspect offers different methodological choices (Markham, 2003) and supports different research questions (see Chapter Three). For example:

- If researchers focus on online spaces as tools, their studies will likely address how the specific designs of social networking forums privilege certain kinds of learning processes. In this instance, learning may be mapped within and through tool use, such as Scratch programming or fanfiction reviews.

- In contrast, if researchers conceptualize online spaces as places, they will seek to understand how interactions within a social networking forum shape the ways in which individuals learn. Here, they may bound their study by the place itself; for instance, they may focus on how children learn within a specific virtual world.

- Finally, if researchers emphasize online spaces as ways of being, they will likely focus on how individuals learn across multiple social networking forums. To do so, they will map how an individual accesses diverse tools and participates within multiple spaces.

Each metaphor offers insight into how researchers can conceptualize and map field sites, which is closely related to what they decide to ask, what parts of online spaces they privilege, and how they seek to understand learning in online spaces.

In a recent study, Lammers, Magnifico, and Curwood (2014) argued that Fanfiction.net, a fanfiction writing community, and Scholar, a classroom web-based technology for writing and peer review, leverage technology to encourage developing writers to actively engage with their audience. They used Markham's (2003) description of the Internet as a tool, a place, and a way of being as a framework to analyze both Fanfiction.net and Scholar (see Chapter Three for more about Scholar).

As tools, both Fanfiction.net and Scholar connect writers with an audience and serve as writing repositories. Each space provides multiple tools, such as drag-and-drop functionality and author notes that allow writers to readily communicate with their audience. Lammers and colleagues (2014) suggested that these technology-mediated writing contexts can exemplify the tool metaphors of conduit, extension, prosthesis, and container that Markham (2003) described. In addition, Steinkuehler and her colleagues (2005) reinforced this notion that an understanding of the tool must be contextualized within each space. In other words, reviews and feedback are tools that shape writing in each of these contexts, but writers employ such tools differently in each context.

As places, these technology-mediated writing spaces are "sociocultural places in which meaningful human interactions occur," and exchange between participants "does not only require a sense of architecture, but also requires a sense of presence with others" (Markham, 2003, pp. 6, 8). In defining Fanfiction.net and Scholar as places, Lammers and colleagues (2014) recognized the "fuzzy boundaries" (Steinkuehler, Black, & Clinton, 2005, p. 98) and noted that all of the interactions with audience and all of the writing may not happen solely within the technology-mediated writing space. Lastly, as ways of being, Fanfiction.net and Scholar establish patterns and practices that fundamentally shift what it means to be a writer in these spaces. In particular, these technology-mediated writing spaces encourage participation that is self-directed, multifaceted, and dynamic (Lammers, Curwood, & Magnifico, 2012). Markham (2003) noted that the way-of-being metaphor encourages us to see that "the self's relation to Internet technologies is much closer and one can begin to see a collapse of the distinctions that separate technology, everyday life, self, and others" (p. 9). By understanding the Internet as a tool, a place, and a way of being, qualitative researchers can begin to map learning within and across multiple spaces.

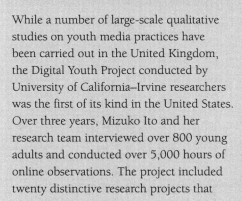

Spotlight Box 2.3
Living and Learning With New Media

While a number of large-scale qualitative studies on youth media practices have been carried out in the United Kingdom, the Digital Youth Project conducted by University of California–Irvine researchers was the first of its kind in the United States. Over three years, Mizuko Ito and her research team interviewed over 800 young adults and conducted over 5,000 hours of online observations. The project included twenty distinctive research projects that were framed by four main areas: homes and neighborhoods, institutional spaces, online sites, and interest groups. They drew on qualitative methods to gain insight into young adults' social, cultural, and digital practices that move across and in between online and offline spaces. The research project particularly focused on how media was situated within their lives, which included their relationships with family and friends, their involvement within the

(Continued)

(Continued)

local community, and their engagement with society. For this reason, data were also collected from fifty events such as conventions, ceremonies, and summer camps.

The Digital Youth Project found that contemporary youth culture is inextricably linked to the availability of mobile devices and the accessibility of social networking tools and media-sharing sites. Moreover, young adults are often coming of age in a world that offers new opportunities for play, creativity, and communication. At the same time, these tools and spaces may present challenges to the development of their identity and expression of their autonomy. One particular focus of the study was learning in informal spaces.

Rather than seeing these spaces as inconsequential or detrimental to formal schooling, the researchers conceptualized young adults' social and recreational activities as opportunities for peer-based learning. They argued:

Our cases demonstrate that some of the drivers of self-motivated learning come not from institutionalized "authorities" setting standards and providing instruction, but from youth observing and communicating with people engaged in the same interests, and in the same struggles for status and recognition, as they are. Both friendship-driven and interest-driven participation rely on peer-based learning dynamics, which have a different structure from formal instruction or parental guidance. (Ito et al., 2010, p. 11)

In this three-year project, the researchers found that if they wanted to understand the role of new media in youth lives, they needed to spend time in both online and offline field sites. Learning, in particular, is an interest-driven practice. Rather than being defined by school institutions, young adults learn more through intentional affiliations and as a result of meaningful peer relationships.

Conclusion

Online spaces are porous and malleable, offering researchers various opportunities to study meaning making as it unfolds in, across, and through online spaces. While social networking forums might be spaces where learners engage in informal learning, learning management systems are deliberately designed educational opportunities that merge traditional learning—whether face-to-face or within learning management systems like Blackboard—with social networking sites, like Twitter backchannels, or Google Hangouts. Because of the protean nature of these spaces, researchers must be specific in how they plan to bound their sites of inquiry, whether they focus on online spaces as digital tools, or online spaces as digital places, or online spaces as ways of being. The possibilities for conducting research on online learning are limitless, but researchers must be conscious about their purposes for conducting research.

CONNECTING TO YOUR WORK ─────────

In this chapter, we have explored how to conceptualize field sites and have discussed contemporary research into learning in online spaces and through the use of digital tools. To move your own research forward, here are some questions to consider:

- Within your field, what online spaces exist?

- How do networked field sites shape the ways in which individuals learn?

- How can learning be mapped within and across diverse online field sites?

- How do social networking forums and learning management systems shape learning processes?

- How does digital culture shape how, when, and why people learn?

Guiding Questions for Chapter 3

- How does learning occur, particularly in online settings when learners have little direct contact with teachers and with each other?

- How does learning differ across settings with accredited teachers and informal online or blended groups?

- What conditions are necessary in order for people to learn?

- How can researchers identify and understand how learning occurs within a particular space?

CHAPTER

How Do We Conceptualize Learning in Online Spaces?

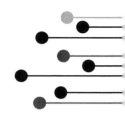

Introduction

In a book about research methods for understanding learning in online spaces, one of the important tasks is to establish what researchers mean by learning and how different theoretical frameworks recognize and describe it in various settings. Over the course of the past century, theorists and researchers have established several positions on learning that have affected the ways teachers and students engage in learning, as well as the ways in which learning spaces are designed. This chapter examines several of these learning theories, providing a general overview of behaviorist, cognitive, and **social accounts of learning**. Then, it explores how these various frameworks inform current investigations into online, media-rich learning spaces. Depending on a researcher's perspectives on learning, the answer to the overarching question for this chapter—how to conceptualize learning in online spaces?—may look rather different. It is important to keep in mind that various theoretical frameworks provide distinct lenses for examining and understanding learning, and that these lenses are themselves rooted in traditional and contemporary understandings of learning.

Using Learning Theory as a Tool for Research Design

This chapter outlines several learning theories (focusing on behaviorist, cognitive and sociocognitive, and sociocultural frameworks) that may be appropriate and useful lenses for designing methods for studying learning in online spaces. The relationship between theory and method is one of the central issues that researchers should consider as they design a new study that includes face-to-face, blended or online spaces. As researchers think about an initial design for learning about an online space, whether they are considering a series of observations, an initial survey, or another kind of study, it is important to consider what the learning looks like. How do researchers know that participants are learning? How might they craft measures to capture evidence of that learning? Such questions begin with determining beliefs about the learning that naturally occurs in that space.

If the learning seems to be mostly individual, with participants downloading particular resources and using them to learn on their own, then the evidence of learning likely appears different from a social space where learners test theories and build knowledge together. In resource-based sites such as Khan Academy, where learners progress individually through sequenced content and exercises, researchers might examine rates of video-watching or trace participants' movement across site areas. On more social sites where multiple users record evidence and refine theories, like Wikipedia's model of collaborative content generation and editing, for example, researchers might trace the diffusion of concepts and conversations as members negotiate and adapt their language. In either case, researchers might additionally interview participants about how offline activities like reading or talking with others face-to-face contribute to online participation.

While developing any research questions about learning and online spaces, it is useful to think about the theories that align best with the forms of learning that are most apparent. What theories seem to provide good insight into that learning? Are there particular methods that align with such a description of learning? For instance, a study focusing on learners' responses to incentives like badges or rewards would align well with a behaviorist framework, whereas a study examining how article revisions are shaped by the discussions on Wikipedia talk pages could take on a more social lens. In this way, researchers' own beliefs about and theories of learning, as well as their beliefs about useful methods for capturing evidence of learning, can become useful tools for initially approaching a new online space. Using learning theories as tools for seeing and interpreting the activities of an online space from the beginning helps researchers to align their study's design, goals, theory, and methods—which subsequently streamlines writing and data collection as the questions and findings evolve over time.

It is important to note here, however, that this perspective itself mirrors a common qualitative, anthropological strategy of letting observation and understandings of social activity (and how it leads to learning) inform researchers' analysis. Online spaces are often in flux, emerging and evolving with participants' interactions, beliefs, and goals. During participation, observation, and data collection, researchers' understandings of meaning making and how to theorize happenings are unstable, too. As such, remaining rooted in various participants' perspectives on what is happening, and why, is vital to the project of building a reasonable account of learning.

Complementary and Contradictory Theories of Learning

Learning is inferential. Learning changes people's actions, behaviors, uses of tools, and reports about knowledge over time, but it is nearly impossible to directly see this learning happen. Instead, researchers must observe learners, collect evidence of their work, and use these traces to build models of their learning activity, which they can then use to inform further data collection and measurement. It is possible that learning seems at its *most* inferential in virtual spaces where learners are interacting at a distance from each other. In these circumstances, when even direct observation may be difficult, thoughtful data collection and measurements of learning evidence are especially crucial.

Crafting such measures often begins with how researchers think about what learning is and how they might observe it. Researchers should always bear in mind, too, that different kinds of useful insights about learning may arise from diverse studies, from a teacher's action research investigation into her or his own students' use of an online space to an experimental design that aims for **generalizability** by testing several groups. As Sandoval and Bell (2004) pointed out in a discussion of design-based research methods for studying learning in context, "There is a tension between the desire for locally usable knowledge on the one hand, and scientifically sound, generalizable knowledge on the other" (p. 199). As noted in Chapter One, philosophical paradigms for understanding learning tend to draw distinctions among valid and reliable approaches for capturing evidence of learning. Making a decision about employing a particular paradigm may be tied to researchers' own understandings of learning—all people, including the authors of this book, have experienced learning and developed biases about how learning occurs—as well as in the types of measurements they hope to use in a study.

We might label the two extremes as a **psychological orientation to studying learning** and an **anthropological orientation to studying learning**, although theorists such as Sylvia Scribner and Michael Cole (1981), as well as Edwin Hutchins (1995), have cautioned against wholly separating these views from each other. As Cole, Gay, Glick, and Sharp pointed out in a 1971 reaction to a tradition of scholarly work that tests people from non-Western cultures using Western intelligence tests, all cultures create coherent systems of thought, as well as ways of passing down this intelligence. These systems, however, do not always agree with each other about what content is important to learn and teach.

- Many psychologists are interested in studying the generalized roots of cognition and response. Learning research that occurs in this discipline often values studies with large populations whose learning may be measured mathematically, using statistics to note whether or not the learning phenomenon in question is generalizable to a larger group. Much of the research on learning motivations, such as Dweck and Legget's (1988) work on goal orientations, falls into this category and seeks to describe how students' theories about their own learning broadly affect their classroom behaviors.

- Many anthropologists are interested in studying the particular behaviors, customs, and cultures of specific groups of learners. Instead of aiming for generalizability, learning research in this discipline often takes a more descriptive form, where researchers spend long periods of time documenting the particularities of learning spaces and practices, focusing on how the learning of a certain group works, and how it is useful and distinct. For instance, Lave, Murtagh, and de la Rocha's (1984) study of grocery store cognition shows how different shoppers' problem solving is situated not only in the supermarket environment and its cultural norms, but also in each particular shopper's own goals and purposes.

As mentioned in Chapter One, researchers may draw from multiple paradigms depending on the questions under study. Some researchers draw on both psychological and anthropological paradigms in their work, examining what works in existing learning spaces and how these insights might be applied to designing and redesigning new learning spaces. The approach, taken up by many **learning scientists**, is pragmatic in terms of the ways in which learning is theorized and studied, drawing on multiple research traditions and methods. Greeno, Collins, and Resnick (1996) explain that this framework is also practical in its focus on design, seeking to analyze the individual, social, and environmental factors in current learning environments and to design new alternatives. In many ways, this discussion is parallel to the mixed methods and multimethods discussion of pragmatism, as mentioned in Chapter One. While many are compelled by the new insights and designs that may become possible when paradigms are combined, others are uncomfortable with mixing fundamental philosophical stances on learning. A pragmatic choice may also be one that privileges a particular paradigm or worldview, as Johnson's (2008) work on how the selection of certain models or methods can alter findings and measurements reveals.

In this book, we focus on theories and methods that are largely drawn from a more anthropological tradition of studying learning. The first books describing how videogames might be taken seriously as learning environments were published a decade ago (e.g., Gee, 2003; Prensky, 2006; Salen & Zimmerman, 2004), and in the intervening years, a new academic discipline has arisen to make sense of learning in a variety of informal and formal online spaces (cf. Abrams, 2009a; Barab, Thomas, Dodge, Carteaux, & Tuzun, 2005; Shaffer, 2006; Squire, 2006; Stevens, Satwicz, & McCarthy, 2008). In that time, technology has changed, too. Online environments have come to allow massive action and collaboration, which is a learning context that is not only very different from typical educational metaphors for learning (such as student/ teacher or master/apprentice), but also evolving quickly.

For any study, researchers must be careful not to assume a static understanding of how such contexts are seen, used, and defined by learners. As Bloome and his colleagues remind us, "What counts as a story [or, they add later, an instance of learning] depends not on an a priori definition but on what is inside of the boundaries of the storytelling as constructed by the participants" (2005, p. 18). In other words, if researchers hope to accurately interpret instances of online learning, then they need to understand the contexts, interactions, and learners' own visions of the meanings that result from their actions in various spaces. Thus, we often find theories of online learning that are **situated**, or based in naturalistic views of participants' own actions and interpretations, most useful as we design studies, gather data points, analyze interactions, and interpret results. We will discuss several contemporary theories of learning in online groups—participatory cultures, connected learning, affinity spaces—in the latter part of this chapter.

Theories of Learning

Before considering these lenses that affect how researchers perceive and study learning spaces, it is important to examine several significant learning theories on their own merits and in terms of their own histories. Despite the focus on online and blended learning environments and, thus, contemporary organizations of participants and resources, researchers must think about these spaces as historically situated products of theory. Particularly, designers of online spaces that are explicitly constructed for educational environments are deeply influenced by the ways in which learning has been traditionally understood and designed. Researchers, too, bring their own theoretically grounded perspectives to how learning unfolds. It is, thus, important to begin any research project by reflecting on various ideas about learning and considering how they may and may not apply in new spaces.

Behaviorist Theories of Learning

One significant learning theory that captured the imaginations of many learning researchers in the early part of the twentieth century was the idea of **behaviorism**. Philosophically, this position states that humans and animals are fundamentally similar in that we engage in inner, thought-based activities that lead to learning, but only the activities—the behaviors—are visible. As such, researchers cannot know, infer, or measure thoughts and cognitions. Even while the workings of the mind take place in an unknowable "black box," however, those interested in learning can observe and reinforce direct behavioral patterns. Providing various **stimuli**, like food or praise, when a subject produces a desired behavior **reinforces** that behavior. Conversely, when a behavior is ignored, it slowly becomes extinct.

Behaviorist scholars believe that because behaviors are objectively visible, they are useful teaching tools. As teachers praise students for completing actions like hand-raising and correct answers, the students associate behaviors with particular rewards. Consequently, this conditioning strengthens or discourages students from acting in specific ways. These kinds of designs for learning, however, often leave out the question of meaning making. Skinner famously criticized "mentalism," arguing that understanding behaviors is more important than understanding thoughts. When people attribute reasons or results to internal thought or emotion, Skinner (1976) noted that "investigation is brought to an end," even while it might be possible to more clearly trace actions to environmental stimuli (p. 16). As previously mentioned, manipulating the environment in order to elicit responses from students is a common technique in many learning environments, but the ways in which students make sense of these experiences needs greater exploration.

While this theory informs the design of many learning environments, behaviorist learning can be difficult to trace online. In many online spaces such as forums and message boards, the environment is observable but users' responses and behaviors are not. Instead, evidence of learning is constituted by people's reports of their behaviors. For example, pulling a website's slot machine for virtual coins or completing missions to gain achievements are actions designed to condition people to keep playing and learning from a game.

Deterding, Dixon, Khaled, and Nacke (2011) noted that "gamification," or "the use of game design elements in non-game contexts" (p. 10), has become a key way for designers of learning spaces to encourage engagement in various tasks or topics. For example, many teachers use the learning management system Edmodo to create reward badges for students' successful achievement of course objectives, or Class Dojo (see Spotlight Box 3.1) to condition students' positive classroom behaviors and consequences. In some ways, these systems are digital sticker charts, where students receive items that they favor (such as stickers or small prizes) in return for exhibiting behaviors their teachers want to reinforce. Along these lines, Bogost (2011) declared gamification "exploitationware" and explained that page clicks and rewards, rather than learning or play, are the true goals of such designs.

Several researchers have examined situations where gamification and other behaviorism-based technologies like Class Dojo can support learning effectively. Gerber (2014) has posited that in order for gamification to move beyond "exploitationware," game designers and educators must work together to reexamine what constitutes learning, play, and collaborative interactions. Otherwise, she argued, gamified educational experiences will continue to develop learners' isolated skills rather than effectively broadening or connecting concepts. Consortia such as Mozilla Open Badges Initiative (2012) have advocated for such systems to create openings for encouraging, rewarding, and

Class Dojo (online at http://www.classdojo.com/about) is a classroom behavior management tool for use by teachers and schools. Whereas many learning management systems, such as Blackboard or Edmodo, focus on and reward the outcomes of students' actions with grades or badges, Class Dojo instead focuses on reinforcement of lower-level behaviors. Students select monster avatars to represent themselves, and teachers choose the positive and negative behaviors that are particularly important to them—for example, task persistence and class participation on the positive side, or interrupting or tardiness on the negative side. Then, as they observe their students' work over the course of a class, teachers can award positive or negative points. Thus, students can see the direct consequences of the actions that they take, both positive and negative. The application also traces students' behaviors over time, and teachers can share this history with students and their parents by providing an access code.

The designers of the Class Dojo system recommend that students and parents have this access to the ongoing chronicle of their behavior. For example, teachers might review the students' behavior records with their parents during conferences, or project the full class's progress chart via smartphone app or LCD projector. As such, teachers are provided with very direct ways of motivating student compliance with classroom norms, and students can see how their own behaviors (as well as those of their classmates) affect teachers' ongoing evaluations of their work.

In these ways, Class Dojo explicitly draws on behaviorist theories of learning. Teachers reward students' actions as they occur, and students are thus conditioned to value and perform positive classroom behaviors. On the website, many teachers have written testimonies about how students' immediate access to this information about their ongoing class performance has helped them to set better goals and achieve greater success in their schoolwork overall.

measuring specific skills and competencies that are difficult to tease out from students' grade reports or course completions. Just Press Play at the Rochester Institute of Technology, for example, overlays an achievement system that closely aligns with course and program goals on undergraduate education (Martinez et al., 2012). Participation encourages behaviors that support student success, such as attending office hours and forming "study clubs" with other students. Further, some adaptive technologies can promote self-directed learning and collaborative problem solving, something Abrams and Walsh (2014) found when studying online and offline gamified vocabulary approaches.

There still is much work to be done at this juncture of learning, behavior analysis, motivations to participate, and the design of online spaces. As Morford and his colleagues highlighted (2014), many researchers in this tradition have rarely collaborated with game or learning designers, but an interdisciplinary effort to build conceptual structures that unify gamification design principles and behavior analysis might lead to better designs and learning outcomes.

Currently, unless researchers have face-to-face access to participants themselves, or to tools that approximate real-time activity by mining back-end data about participants' achievements and time spent on various tasks, they must rely on self-reports of activity and resulting learning that may or may not be entirely reliable. As such, a behaviorist framework may be a difficult lens to work with when solely researching online spaces. Message board posts, game runs, and submitted solutions to problems can certainly serve as evidence of learning behavior, but quite a bit of social activity, solitary thinking, or other activities may elapse in the spaces between these actions—and these behaviors may comprise vital learning activity, whether or not the learner is aware of it. Thus the conditioning of participants' behaviors and responses often may simply be too veiled in typical online researchers' data. As always, when beginning a new research program, researchers must consider their research questions and how they will align with available data and existing frameworks for studying participants' learning.

Cognitive and Sociocognitive Theories of Learning

Both humans and computers are capable of following algorithms that can solve various kinds of problems. Both can be taught to recognize patterns, conduct searches, and transfer knowledge to different problems or areas of expertise. Although computers must be programmed to "think" in ways that are natural for humans, an analogy can be made between human thinking and information processing. Work in the field of **cognitivism** often follows this brain-as-computer metaphor.

Theories about learning from this tradition tend to see cognition as an individual achievement. When people achieve successful solutions for various problems, their brains store this information for later access (and, perhaps, modification), when similar problems arise. As such, what is known as **prior knowledge**—as well as clear indications of where that prior knowledge might be valuable—is an important component of learning environments. People learn new concepts and actions in the context of what they already know, which means that based on our current knowledge, new experiences or concepts are slotted into existing frameworks. Particularly if this new information proves useful, it becomes part of a durable schematic, or **schema**, within the brain that can be modified and extended as more is learned (cf. Bartlett, 1932/1995; Piaget & Inhelder, 1969).

Chi, Feltovich, and Glaser (1981) showed that while undergraduate physics students tended to sort solving physics problems by focusing on the features of the problem (e.g., the problem involves an inclined plane), doctoral students approached the same problems by citing deeper structures and principles (e.g., "the problem can be solved by Newton's Second Law," p. 127). Novice and expert physicists sort the same problems differently, and the categories that they create vary with experience. It might be expected that if the undergraduate physicists continued their study, their problem categorizations would gradually come to resemble the experts' work. Dreyfus and Dreyfus (1986), along with many others, have stated that learning how to see a problem's structure quickly is a central part of developing expertise. Experts, in short, see and interpret in unique ways as a result of their more complex body of prior knowledge, which has been learned and honed through both didactic learning and active experience.

Many expert learners easily recognize how they try to solve a particular problem. This kind of **metacognitive** reflection—or, as Schön puts it in his 1995 discussion of expert thought and teaching, "reflection on action"— helps learners to recognize when they need to consider a new approach to a particular situation or seek out new, related information. Metacognition assists in knowledge **transfer**, which is often seen as the root of today's typical focus on liberal arts education. If students learn in a broad-based way, then they will be better workers and more informed citizens. While Broudy's (1977) work revealed that students often forget the specific facts and formulas that they learn in school, transfer is not a hopeless proposition. Rather, Bransford and Schwartz (1999) have shown that while direct transfer is difficult, helping students to envision uses for their knowledge—to understand their active "preparation for future learning" (p. 68)—aids them in both retaining information and in making conceptual shifts over time.

Finally, sociocognitive factors, which are learners' beliefs about themselves and their learning, can affect learning and transfer. Whereas behaviorism posits that learners' main actions are reflexive responses to social or environmental stimuli, sociocognitive work shows that people respond to internal beliefs as well. Learners set goals and motivations, refine techniques, make inferences from experiences, and modulate their own cognition.

Work on motivation shows that learners' goals are central to their actions. The studies of Dweck and Leggett (1988) and Ames (1992) show that students whose goal is to learn or master content are more willing to persist in difficult situations. Students who want to perform well (e.g., get good grades), however, choose to avoid solving difficult problems when they can. If teachers reward students' successful problem-solving efforts by praising their intelligence, students often respond by shifting their goals toward good performance rather than thorough learning of the concepts at hand. Such an example demonstrates that goal setting, and learning as a result of goal setting, is a product of *both* external contextual and internal cognitive interactions. Learners' self-monitoring internal cognitions combine with stimuli within educational environments to produce specific attitudes toward learning, which then loop back to affect how well students develop new schemata and transfer their learning to new situations.

Such theories are central to learning about learning, but how are these cognitive concepts useful in considering online and virtual environments? If understanding cognition largely rests on individual knowledge "in the head," is it possible to see traces of this learning in virtual environments?

Many learning environments expect teachers to break complex concepts into simpler building blocks, an approach that follows from a cognitive schema metaphor for knowledge building. As Coopman's (2009) design analysis of Blackboard discusses, the default settings of Blackboard's learning management system, for example, would split "course content" into week-by-week topics. As a result, achieving a holistic view of the topics, or remapping them later on, would have been difficult for users. Additionally, by offering structures that mirror classroom structures like quizzes and achievement badges, the current architecture of Blackboard seems to expect individual learning.

Collaborative tools do exist, such as threaded discussion interactions and videoconferencing, both of which make it possible for classes and small groups to converse. Still, as Coopman (2009) acknowledged, many of the settings and features framed students as users of a teacher's preset learning structure. These user interface elements suggest a view of knowledge where complex concepts are stable and typically built up through constrained week-by-week interaction. These designs may allow for Bransford and Schwartz's (1999) call for active "preparation for future learning," but in a proscribed, teacher-led way. Even while collaborative assignments exist, an individual, cognitive, guided view of learning predominates. A similar critique of many MOOCs (massive open online courses) and other "virtual courseware" experiences is that they are not courses, which require student partnership and active engagement, but high-tech, video-and-Internet-enabled textbooks (e.g., Bombardieri, 2014; Drake, 2014).

Gee (2003) suggested that one of the significant things that virtual environments can do differently from teacher-led spaces—and that games, specifically, *often* do differently—is to allow for players' direct, leveled action. Whereas a textbook often introduces new knowledge to learners by explaining a basic concept, videogames place new learners into a situation where they need to accomplish a task. Early levels provide opportunities for practicing basic skills, such as jumping or using a new magic spell, whereas later levels combine these tasks or require the player to learn how to use them in a new way. Similarly, in their aforementioned discussion of gamified vocabulary, Abrams and Walsh (2014) identified how adaptive features of an online program supported self-paced and iterative learning. High school students "leveled up" and earned points and badges as they mastered vocabulary in a variety of contexts. Thus, just as Gee contended, players actively build on their own skills, and often use those skills in multiple ways in order to make progress in the game.

Even though the traces of these individual cognitions may not be readily apparent outside of experimental contexts, there are techniques available for capturing evidence of such learning. Abrams's (2009a, 2009b, 2015) work shows how researchers can use **stimulated recall** in conjunction with other qualitative data collection methods to understand gamers' thinking and decision making in particular contexts. More specifically, Abrams video-recorded videogame play and then asked participants to immediately watch the video and describe the actions they took and the decisions that they made during the activity. Abrams explained that for time-constrained situations that involve complex interaction, stimulated recall procedures (Lyle, 2003) were necessary to elicit participants' reflection and critique of their gaming sessions. Such methods are similar to **think-aloud protocols** (Ericsson & Simon, 1980), in which people complete tasks while verbalizing their processes, revealing at least some of the complexities of the schemata that they are employing in order to solve a problem. However, as Abrams explained, think-aloud protocols can be problematic because often gamers do not like to suddenly and artificially stop gameplay to discuss moves; additionally, most games require such concentration and complex tasks that talking and gaming often are difficult to do, resulting in partial-to-no participant feedback.

Similarly, analyzing learning environments (such as the Coopman Blackboard analysis above) or participant-written tutorials (text-based or video-based), a common genre in online forums, may provide evidence of individual schemata or thought processes. While these techniques are indirect ones, they may provide windows into participants' conceptual understandings in settings where researchers believe that individual, schema-based learning is central to successful learning and participation.

Sociocultural Theories of Learning

Sociocultural theories of learning, which focus on learning as a cultural experience that occurs in situ and in practice, collectively represent perhaps the most common frameworks for examining online learning. This "social turn" in learning research largely occurred in the 1980s and 1990s, and its constructs include situated cognition (e.g., Brown, Collins, & Duguid, 1989), distributed cognition (e.g., Hutchins, 1995; Wertsch, 1991) communities of practice (e.g., Wenger, 1998), situated learning (e.g., Lave & Wenger, 1991), and New Literacy Studies (e.g., New London Group, 1996).

Much of this work, however, draws on Russian traditions that examine learning and development as fundamentally social accomplishments. The work of Lev Vygotsky (1978), for example, was conducted in the 1930s but not translated into English until the 1970s. Vygotsky's central insights focus on how language and social interaction enable learning. When children work alongside of others—particularly "more capable peers" (p. 86)—they learn quickly and effectively, developing common language, tools, and norms for looking at particular problems through discussion, testing, success and failure, and retesting. He described this social extension of an individual's capabilities as a "zone of proximal development" that would solidify into actual learning and development as the child matured (p. 86). Vygotsky pointed out that even when we are learning nominally by ourselves (e.g., when we are reading or thinking alone), we continue to consider others' perspectives in an internalized, but still social, way. The voices of our teachers, mentors, or favorite authors accompany us and remind us of the directions, ideas, or techniques that we have been taught in earlier situations.

Instead of seeing learning as a primarily individual, cognitive, "in the head" accomplishment, sociocultural theories take an anthropological, cultural perspective in which the structures of environments and co-participants play important roles in the learning that occurs. Jean Lave and Etienne Wenger (1991), and later, Wenger (1998), described one of the most widely known sociocultural lenses as "situated" study of "communities of practice." Under this research paradigm, they found key insights in the examination of communities themselves, the ways in which they structured activities around particular goals, such as maintaining efficiency in a large office or mentoring alcoholics into sobriety, as well as the methods by which full members mentored new members into participation. Descriptions of such processes, as well as the changes that occur in people who become members, help researchers to understand how learning occurs. Such accounts reveal that learning is bound to culturally important actions and is often very different from learning in formal and didactic learning environments.

More broadly, sociocultural theories stand in opposition to behaviorist and cognitive theories, giving very different accounts of how cognition and learning are accomplished by people in a variety of situations. While, as this chapter has outlined, behaviorist and cognitive accounts of learning focus on the individual as the center of such activity, sociocultural perspectives focus on how cultural and environmental structures, language, sociality, and communication with others mediate learning. In short, learning is made possible by interactive and social situations, such as those enabled by the Scholar environment, as shown in Spotlight Box 3.2. Learners construct knowledge from experiences in the world and with other people.

Such views of learning fundamentally transform typical structures of formal learning. An understanding of learning as active, cultural, historic, and social enables, particularly, a different view of literacy. In schools and other formal learning environments, literacy is traditionally seen as a collection of general skills, such as reading and writing, that are disconnected from specific social practices or settings. In this view, literacy learning inherits elements of practice and design, which means that writers and composers must consider not only how to articulate a particular meaning, but how to use different modes or a combination of modes (e.g., text, image, sound) to express this idea (e.g., Cope & Kalantzis, 2000; Kress & van Leeuwen, 2001). In the project of creating and sharing meanings toward various social ends, many kinds of literacies (e.g., literacies of print production, image production, web page coding) are available and important.

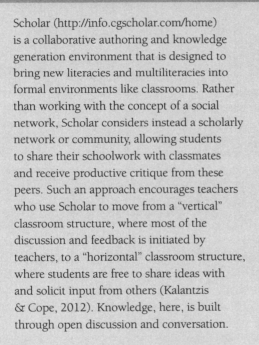

Spotlight Box 3.2
Scholar

Scholar (http://info.cgscholar.com/home) is a collaborative authoring and knowledge generation environment that is designed to bring new literacies and multiliteracies into formal environments like classrooms. Rather than working with the concept of a social network, Scholar considers instead a scholarly network or community, allowing students to share their schoolwork with classmates and receive productive critique from these peers. Such an approach encourages teachers who use Scholar to move from a "vertical" classroom structure, where most of the discussion and feedback is initiated by teachers, to a "horizontal" classroom structure, where students are free to share ideas with and solicit input from others (Kalantzis & Cope, 2012). Knowledge, here, is built through open discussion and conversation.

Scholar relies on a publishing metaphor, reimagining teachers as publishers of students' work and students as authors and editors, all working together to publish related sets of multimodal work. Teachers are Publishers who set up each assignment in a Publisher application; then, students, who are Creators, compose their work in a variety of media in the Creator application (see Figure 3.1). When classroom assignments are complete, teachers or students may publish their work more broadly in a variety of web-friendly formats as well, enabling sharing beyond the classroom. Teachers and students within one class can also share their work, as well as status updates and links, in a protected Community application.

Bill Cope and Mary Kalantzis, lead designers on this project, describe several key "openings" or "affordances" for the transformation of education that Scholar helps to make possible (Cope & Kalantzis, 2013, p. 333): enabling ubiquitous learning anytime and anyplace; drawing on the collaborative intelligence inherent in a classroom or scholarly space; allowing for differentiated instruction; encouraging metacognition; focusing on multimodal, active knowledge production; and requiring formative as well as summative assessment.

In these ways, Scholar explicitly draws on sociocultural theories of learning and takes seriously the building of social, interactive, formative knowledge communities within classrooms. Instead of serving primarily as students' evaluators, teachers who use Scholar help their students to see knowledge work as a social act that requires feedback, drafting, and the interplay of many ideas.

Figure 3.1   Scholar's Creator

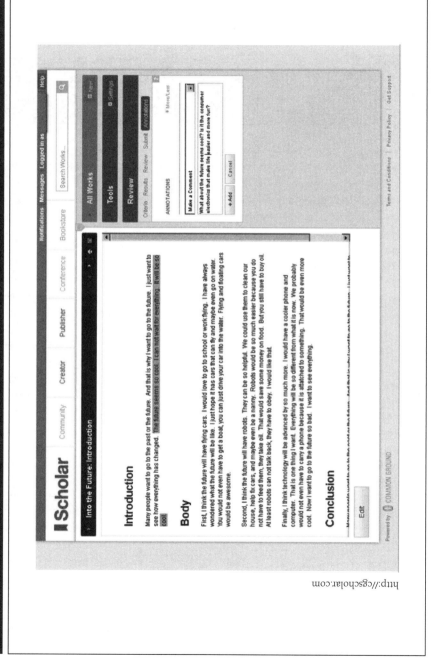

Learning in Online Spaces

Sociocultural theories of learning are fruitful frameworks to guide research in online spaces because they focus on the idea of learning as participatory, active, and dependent on interaction. In addition, sociocultural work focuses on social context and notes that researchers must develop an understanding of context in order to make good hypotheses about how learning occurs. In other words, if learning is a matter of moving toward fuller participation, then a researcher might pay close attention to how a new member moves toward competence and, eventually, expertise (cf. Dreyfus & Dreyfus, 1986).

In online environments, simultaneous expertise in several practices and literacies is often required for a participant to become a central member, and, as such, "constellations" have become common metaphors in analyses of this kind of learning. Steinkuehler (2007), for example, has described the "constellation of literacy practices" in massively multiplayer online gaming, thereby identifying the cohesion of in-game texts and the development of literacy practices, while Martin (2012) noted how players may seek "a constellation of information," or online and offline game-related information resources that are necessary to complete specific in-game tasks. Further, Abrams and Gerber (2014) examined the "constellation of connections" that youth make as they collaboratively encounter cross-disciplinary texts online and offline.

The typical structure of formal educational environments has an expert or teacher leading novices explicitly through a series of activities designed to hone particular kinds of individual valued skills (see Chapter Two for more on learning management systems). Many online spaces, however, lack this formal structure, instead focusing on the "common endeavour" (Gee, 2004, p. 85) of group knowledge building. Thus, in order to understand community norms and how learners become effective central participants, researchers must investigate and document the social-learning structures that do exist.

Initially, a substantial amount of research on online learning and online communities imported a framework influenced by situated learning research. While this work is valuable to understanding online communities because it captures and investigates multiple ways in which learners gain expertise, many of its insights are based in environments where settled trajectories of mentorship, participation, and learning exist (even while these trajectories are often radically different from each other). For example, in one case study developed by Jordan (1989), and quoted extensively by Lave and Wenger (1991), girls who become apprentices in Yucatec midwifery—almost always descended from expert midwives—first travel with their mothers as they attend to pregnant women. As they grow, they begin performing tasks such as carrying messages or fetching supplies, and begin assisting their midwife mothers or grandmothers only after they birth their own children. These kinds of **legitimate peripheral participation** describe paths of progressive growth into full expertise (Lave & Wenger, 1991).

Squire (2002, 2006) has argued that videogame play and experience with simulated activity can help students develop legitimate conceptual knowledge over time, even if this participation does not mentor them into real-world communities of practice. For instance, Squire pointed out that when combined with historical study, playing Civilization can help students answer questions about world resources, such as why European settlers colonized North America and Africa. Shaffer, Squire, Halverson, and Gee (2005) advanced this idea and showed that games such as Full Spectrum Warrior provide occasions for players to learn about real military tactics, terminology, and related information. Games may be simulations, but they are fully capable of immersing players in practices, epistemologies, and ways of seeing and doing.

In many online spaces, however, researchers have increasingly observed that participants may take multiple legitimate paths to participation (Gee, 2004, 2005; Hayes & Duncan, 2012; Lammers, Curwood, & Magnifico, 2012). There is, in other words, no primary learning trajectory. Instead, participants in these informal learning settings are often described as learning complex literacies across multiple media (e.g., Cope & Kalantzis, 2000) or sets of practices that add up to a Discourse (e.g., Gee, 2008). Importantly, this kind of knowledge is acquired rather than learned, which means that it is accomplished chiefly through social participation and action.

While there may be some explicit norms and instruction (e.g., "chat rules" or codes of conduct for forum participation, described in Lammers, 2013), participants largely develop expertise by exploring and contributing to the space according to their own interests, perhaps not even realizing how much they have learned in the course of doing so.

As research in online spaces begins to mature into its own field, theorists have begun to examine the ways in which members accomplish learning and participation, and how these actions and activities may be distinct from formal learning in face-to-face spaces. Perhaps the most important facet of theorizing in this field involves capturing and articulating *what* people learn as they wade into and begin to parse and participate in these large, general spaces, as well as how they navigate these spaces when so many possibilities and conversations occur simultaneously. Though each online space is structured slightly differently, and participants develop esoteric ways of navigating them, commonalities do exist, and researchers have much to learn about information gathering and learning as a result.

Three significant frameworks for describing and theorizing this kind of learning have gained traction in the research literature: participatory cultures (Jenkins,

Clinton, Purushotma, Robison, & Weigel, 2006; Jenkins, Purushotma, Clinton, Weigel, & Robison, 2007), connected learning (Ito et al., 2010, 2013), and affinity spaces (Gee, 2004; Duncan & Hayes, 2012). Even though each of these bodies of work has been built around similar settings—people's interactions with media and online spaces, as well as how participants in them learn by building knowledge and community contacts—each body of qualitative research and resulting theory emphasizes a somewhat different facet of this kind of participation and learning.

Participatory Cultures

As long as literature has existed, consumers of narrative have been participating in it by reading and telling, sharing, and remaking stories in their own ways. Biblical characters and stories were reimagined as morality plays and allegories such as *Everyman* and *Pilgrim's Progress*. While the Brothers Grimm set out to collect German folktales, they later adapted these stories for family telling, and the tales have been readapted with shifting children's literature conventions. The work of playwrights such as Shakespeare has been modernized through the ages; for instance, *Romeo and Juliet* became *West Side Story* in the mid-1950s, as well as *Warm Bodies* in 2013. And, of course, people retell, reenact, and debate their favorite dramas in backyards, pubs, and family room theaters.

Although media consolidated substantially as a result of the twentieth century's large movie, television, and music studios, the Internet has considerably eased the time and cost of writing and distributing such fan and audience creations. As Verba's 2003 history of *Star Trek* fandom suggests, mid-1960s Trekkie zines contained some of the first published writing that we now would call "fanfiction," even though the circulation of these materials was limited. FanFiction.net, the Internet's largest and most diverse fanfiction archive, contained over six million titles in the year 2010, as reported by Sendlor's FFN Research blog (2011). (The full blog can be found at http://ffnresearch.blogspot.com/)

Henry Jenkins (2006) has perceived these phenomena as integral parts of our media systems becoming increasingly participatory and, perhaps, democratic, as indicated in Chapter One. Internet fanzines, forums, archives, videos, and role-playing games allow media consumers to interact directly with each other, even though much work on media (such as ratings) suggests passive consumption. Convergence, Jenkins (2006) said, represents "the flow of content across multiple media platforms, the cooperation between multiple media industries, and the migratory behavior of media audiences who will go almost anywhere in search of the kinds of entertainment experiences they want" (p. 2). Television, cinema, theatre, radio, and Internet sources all now coexist in a vast mediascape, and while many of these media held much more centrality and prominence when they were first introduced, they can now reinforce or challenge each other's roles in people's lives.

This kind of convergence also requires a shift in culture. Viewers and listeners who were previously seen as passive are now recognized as active participants who are likely to seek out additional information about their favored media, share it across their social networks, or even produce related content in response. In his 2006 book, Jenkins labels this set of behaviors as activity in "participatory cultures," although he notes that all participants are not equal, seeing as corporations hold much of the power in this mediascape. Later, in 2007 and 2012 white papers written with several colleagues, Jenkins suggested the potential for young people's learning and media production in participatory cultures. In these works, he pointed out that formal learning environments like schools are useful places for students to learn about and reflect on the new norms of communication, production, and political participation enabled by Internet cultures. As such, teachers still play key roles in students' learning about new media: "Educators need to learn the social and cultural logics that are shaping the new communication systems" (Reilly, Vartabedian, Felt, & Jenkins, 2012, p. 12).

Social networking and online creation of creative arts texts such as stories, photographs, and artworks have become common activities for teens and young adults, both in formal and informal learning environments. Wide-ranging access to the Internet in home, school, and mobile environments has granted young writers and creators the ability to share their creations, solicit feedback from others, and publish their work in a variety of media on a variety of sites. For example, Rosa, one of the participants in Magnifico's (2012) study of Neopets, created outfits, settings, and customized code for each of her Neopets' lookups, so that people who navigated to her profile would understand her pets as full-fledged, coherent characters (see Figure 3.2 for an example of some of these artifacts). Over time, she submitted longer (~2,000- to 3,000-word) stories about these characters to the Neopian Times online newspaper as well. Lenhart and her colleagues' work at the Pew Internet and American Life project demonstrated that such practices are widespread. Their studies (Lenhart, Madden, Smith, & Magill, 2007; Lenhart, Purcell, Smith, & Zickhur, 2010) showed that 93 percent of teens and young adults use the Internet regularly, 73 percent use at least one social network, and 64 percent engage in online content creation. These percentages are likely to be even higher today.

The participatory cultures framework for researching and understanding these activities focuses on the artifacts that participants make and share, as well as the media that they use to accomplish this creation. Jenkins, Purushotma, Clinton, Weigel, and Robison (2007) noted that a "participatory culture is a culture with relatively low barriers to artistic expression and civic engagement, strong support for creating and sharing one's creations with others, and some type of informal mentorship whereby what is known by the most experienced is passed along to novices" (p. 9). Thus, Jenkins and his colleagues focused on the vast number of young people who create and share content online, building a fanbase as well as, often, a group of collaborators who assist with the making, editing, and critique

Figure 3.2   Neopets

fyre

this is the way you wish your voice sounds / handsome and smart

I live my life according to a strict code of chivalry, honour and personal hygiene.
I write down every thing I say, becaues I know it will be invaluable to future generations.

I'm featured in the NT!

"After I started writing I started making up different stories for all my pets with the idea that they would then be written... for example I gave my pet Fyre this delightfully egotistical personality... which was so much fun to think of that I just had to write a few stories about it."
—— Rosa (interview)

Fyre has a Petpet!

Phinny the Whinny
(569 days and 10 hours old)

www.neopets.com

Screenshot of Rosa's customized pet lookup, as well as her explanation of the design. This screenshot has been altered to create a pseudonym for this Neopet.

of this work. A participatory cultures perspective, in other words, addresses media consumers as potential and actual content producers who are eager to express themselves creatively and talk with others about the work that they want to do in shared online or blended spaces.

Citing Livingstone (2003), Jenkins and his team (2007) noted that these participatory cultures may serve to help youth become engaged in civic projects as well, and that they build social capital through acts of creative production. The Harry Potter Alliance, for example, is a group of fans who use J.K. Rowling's characters as inspiration to act in their own communities: "We're changing the world by making activism accessible through the power of story. Since 2005, we've engaged millions of fans through our work for equality, human rights, and literacy" ("Harry Potter Alliance," 2015). Such projects involve members' development of deep real-world knowledge about problems and potential remediation, and require substantial, situated learning and action on members' parts. This project is one case of Internet fandom enabling real-world design, learning, and activism. Somewhat similarly, Halverson (2013) called for researchers to make a shift from representing and documenting "participatory cultures," in situ in spaces like Fanfiction.net and the Harry Potter Alliance, to designing "participatory media spaces" as deliberate learning environments for young people interested in the media arts and in how they might become more effective content producers.

Affinity Spaces

Initially theorized by Gee (2004) as spaces where "newbies, masters, and everyone else" work together and socialize around a "common endeavor" (p.85), the idea of an affinity spaces framework recognizes changing notions of participation and learning that emerge in online and blended spaces. Affinity spaces might be said to be the online, in-person, and blended spaces of members of participatory cultures.

While the situated cognition-based framework of "communities of practice" often describes learning communities with settled trajectories of participation and leadership, as well as a strong social structure in which members form tight bonds (Lave & Wenger, 1991), Gee's work problematized the notion that these assumptions can be generally applied to learning settings in which participants gain expertise informally. Many members of affinity spaces—from in-person spaces like kayaking clubs, to blended (online and face-to-face) spaces like the Harry Potter Alliance, to fully online spaces like Internet message boards—do develop significant "community" ties, but not all do. Thus, describing affinity space settings as "learning communities" or "communities of practice" by default paints an idealized picture of cohesion among contributing members' values, actions, and goals that may not exist (Hayes & Duncan, 2012).

Perhaps the most significant difference between formal learning spaces and affinity spaces is the presence of multiple kinds of participants, activities, and goals. Descriptions of affinity spaces often emphasize multiple legitimate paths to membership that are directed by such factors as how different groups of participants use the space according to their interests and their values. For example, Gee (2004) noted that Age of Mythology Heaven, a fan site for the game Age of Mythology (AoM), includes multiple forums where participants can read and contribute to topics relating to game news, technical help, strategy guides, and building mods for the game. Figure 3.3 shows a view of the front page of these forums. Similarly, Lammers (2013) explained that on The Sims 2 Writer's Hangout, a message board for players of The Sims who enjoyed writing stories about their various game characters, contributors participated in a variety of activities including story writing, proofreading, graphics creation, and getting to know each other in "off-topic" chat. In other words, participants' own desires for information, particular activities, or social connections led them to take action in various "portals" (Gee, 2004; Lammers, 2014; Lammers, Curwood, & Magnifico, 2012).

As affinity spaces have expanded in the ten years since Gee's (2004) initial articulation of this framework, one of the most significant changes in the spaces

Figure 3.3 Age of Mythology Heaven Forums

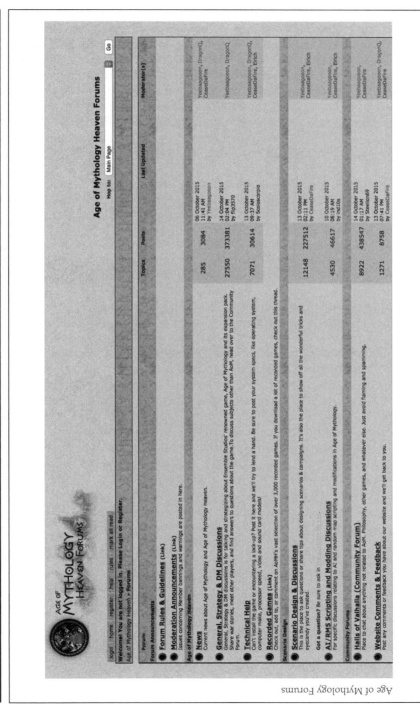

themselves has been the expansion of possibilities for connection, sociality, and action. While early-2000s affinity spaces were often centered on single sites, such as a particular forum or website, they have now grown much more diverse. As indicated in Chapter Two, many affinity spaces now comprise root websites that represent the central, content-focused spaces of participants' interactions (e.g., the AoM Heaven forums, WoWWiki); fandom websites that collect multimodal creative work that is related to several fandoms (e.g., DeviantArt, FanFiction.net); and social networking tools (e.g., Twitter, Tumblr, Facebook) (Magnifico & Curwood, 2012). All of these portals have porous, fuzzy boundaries, and many of them share posts and can be used in ways that suggest multiple categories.

Affinity spaces increasingly comprise online and face-to-face portals, as well, each of which contributes to the "common endeavour," as Gee (2004) explained, without participating in a formal learning trajectory. Fields and Kafai (2009), for example, used the method of "connective ethnography" (cf. Leander & McKim, 2003; Magnifico, Lammers, & Curwood, 2013) to document an online (in the virtual world Whyville) and face-to-face "computer clubhouse" where students explored the virtual world and shared information that they learned both online and in person. Grimes and Fields (2012) additionally pointed out that social networking residues such as "likes" and "reblogs" may be traced on many sites, providing additional information about users' actions and interactions.

Significant challenges persist, however, in capturing comprehensive pictures of affinity space activity. For one thing, as mentioned previously, different participants' interactions with affinity spaces may look quite different depending on their particular interests. Additionally, capturing evidence of learning across multiple online and face-to-face portals is difficult when researchers lack face-to-face contact with participants and data sets that include artifacts like browser histories and screen recordings (cf. Leander & Lovvorn, 2006). At the same time, participants often lack this kind of access to *each other*, so it seems important to the research community's understanding of these spaces to attempt to replicate and learn from such interactions, partial and incomplete as they are.

Connected Learning

A more recent significant framework for researching and understanding online cultures is that of **connected learning**. Developed and led by Mizuko Ito and her team (2010, 2013), this work moves away from defining spaces of interaction or labeling individual participation, and toward what they term "genres of participation" (Ito et al., 2010, p. 36). These genres, primarily labeled as "hanging out," "messing around," and "geeking out," broadly describe how people participate across a variety of media and activities without fixing them in particular categories.

Connected learning research recognizes that media users have differing expertise or skills that may or may not be brought to bear in differing areas, and does not assume that experts in any one particular area or activity will be able to easily cross over into a new space. That is, expert videogame players may—or may not—be expert fanfiction writers, digital artists, or video diarists. They might "geek out" and attain a high degree of expertise in their current favorite game, but play other games or share media on social networks in a more casual "hanging out" manner when friends are also engaged. As Salen (2008) put it: "Born into a world where concepts like copyright, mastery, civic engagement, and participation are seamlessly negotiated and redefined across highly personalized networks spanning the spaces of Facebook, Yu-Gi-Oh, and YouTube, today's kids are crafting learning identities for themselves—hybrid identities—that seemingly reject previously distinct modes of being. . . . [W]e now just call them *kids*" (p. 2, emphasis in original).

Connected learning thus aims to bridge existing frameworks and understand ecologies of and connections across media use, rather than placing focus on isolated instances or practices. This work draws together situated learning and situated cognition frameworks—which push back against individually based, cognitive science accounts of learning and examine how thinking occurs deeply embedded within social contexts—with identity development and media studies work. Such research as Brooker and Jermyn's (2003) collection, which highlighted audience studies work from the field of communication arts, showed how media that are traditionally considered passively consumed offer opportunities for active response and engagement.

Recent descriptions of media use often focus on youth cultures, largely because young people have begun using and expanding these technologies in ways that are much less common for adults. boyd's (2006, 2008b) ethnographic work that explored teens' social media use and understanding of their own "networked publics" shows that many young people have become physically disconnected from each other because parents, schools, and regulators of public spaces have become less tolerant of groups of unorganized, unsupervised teens. Thus, online and offline "third spaces," such as clubs, Facebook and Google Hangouts, and online MMO games have become important places for young people. There, they can "hang out" in less-structured ways, being together while getting to know each other, watching television or YouTube, listening to music, or playing games. Qualitative research conducted by Gutierrez (2008), Ito and her team (2010), and Steinkuehler and Williams (2006) has also highlighted young people's hanging out in various third spaces. Connected learning describes hanging out practices as largely "friendship-driven," in that much of the associated media use and developing expertise is related to making and maintaining social connections. Interactions around media, such as conversations about particular songs, television series, or books, provide friends with things to do together in person or online.

The frequent use of such media spaces, though, may lead to "looking around" and "messing around" genres of participation, where participants begin to seek out deeper specific information or develop their expertise in a particular area. Ito and her colleagues (2010) described, for instance, teens' learning of coding techniques in order to modify their social networking profiles or Photoshop tools to retouch photos of friends. While some of them had explored creative writing or digital art before, others started to participate as a result of social connections—they enjoyed hanging out online and reading each others' stories.

These kinds of behaviors may become more "interest-driven" (Ito et al., 2010) as participants begin to delve deeper into information gathering and skill learning. As Hidi and Renninger's (2006) research described it, while "situational interest" may be initially triggered by an emotional event such as love for a new band or positive response to a friend's post, participants' knowledge of and value for a particular topic deepen as interest develops. "Individual interest" develops and is sustained over time through continued engagement and growing expertise with a topic. This kind of interest overlaps with the Connected Learning Network's "geeking out" participation genre, in which users develop significant expertise and often engage in active, regular activity or content production in their site or topic (see Figure 3.4). Chen's (2012) ethnographic research, for instance, provides a window into the lives of a group of World of Warcraft players who met online regularly, practiced together, and crafted strategies and norms for working collaboratively to conquer the most difficult monsters in that game.

Figure 3.4 The Connected Learning Network's Venn Diagram of Typical Spheres of Youth Learning and Their Confluences

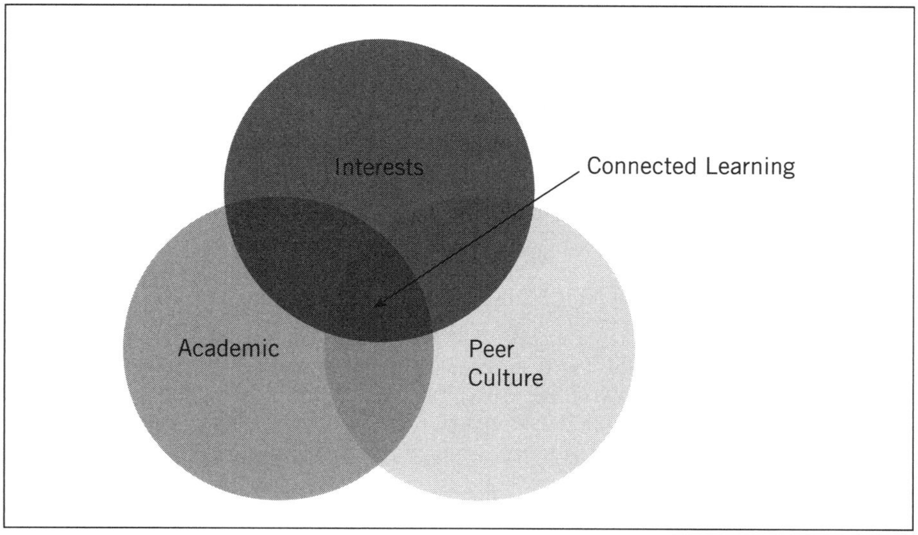

Source: Ito et al., 2013. Connected Learning Research Network.

Centrally, the Connected Learning framework highlights the effectiveness of learning that occurs at a juncture within and among young people's ecologies of personal interests, academic skills and knowledge, and peer cultures.

As this work progresses, many proponents have begun to use this principle to describe and design "third space" programs that offer youth from diverse backgrounds mentorship as they develop skills that align with their own interests. Halverson and Sheridan's work (2014) highlighted Makerspaces, which primarily support young people's engineering skills, but draw in academic knowledge and personal needs to motivate designs. Gutierrez's (2008) Migrant Student Leadership Institute, which supports immigrant students as they recognize, make sense of, and make art from their own complex lives, similarly brought together personal and academic identities. The theoretical framework of participation genres additionally has pushed theory forward, providing researchers with a way to think about young people's learning as not individually transferable (as Bransford and Schwartz's 1999 paper, cited in earlier sections, might highlight), but valuable across multiple loosely related groups and communities. As Halverson (2013) explained, "Learning happens no matter what we do. However, learning *something* [emphasis in the original] is an entirely different matter" (p. 244). Connected learning shows us that these "somethings" can often be relevant and useful across settings.

Conclusion

• •

This chapter explores the idea of *learning*, and the anthropological and psychological frameworks that theorists and researchers have used to understand students' (or, more broadly, participants') progress through and participation in a variety of online and blended settings. Three longstanding frameworks—learning as behavior, cognition, and social interaction—provide bedrock ideas for thinking about mechanisms of learning, as well as implications of taking on these diverse views. In addition, this chapter discusses how researchers might begin to analyze the behaviorist, cognitive, and cultural components of various spaces and explains why many studies of online spaces incorporate a strong situated, cultural component.

CONNECTING TO YOUR WORK ——————

As you begin your research study of learning within online space(s), it makes sense to use your ideas about how this particular space(s) envisions or enables learning. Consider keeping track of the ways in which you see individual and collective learning in process, and use the questions below to help you contemplate your study's design and your understanding of this space. For instance:

- How do participants use the space(s)? Are there particular activities or tools that encourage new or ongoing participation?

- How do participants inhabit the space and interact with others? Do they choose pseudonyms? Do they design profile pages, as in social networks or creative archives? Do they create character avatars, as in many MMO games? Do these ways of defining identity seem to influence participation?

- How is the particular online space designed? Is there any explicit discussion of learning, collective goals or projects, or the like?

- Does the space seem to place emphasis on individual goals? Do members need to contribute on their own, or are there obvious, legitimate ways to collaborate with others?

- Does the space seem to place an emphasis on collective goals? Are there spaces where multiple members are working together to articulate theories, test knowledge, or engage in other kinds of knowledge building?

- Does the space share similar features with an affinity space, participatory culture, or connected learning space?

Guiding Questions for Chapter 4

- How do qualitative traditions apply to the research of online spaces?
- In what ways does the online component complicate the researcher's role?
- What affordances and constraints might researchers anticipate in designing qualitative studies of learning?
- What online and offline contexts might researchers need to consider when designing a study?

What Does It Mean to Be a Qualitative Researcher of Online Spaces?

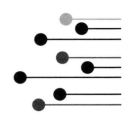

Introduction

Contemporary qualitative research has included the co-presence of researchers and participants. Though qualitative traditions apply to research of online spaces, the dynamic and static components of online spaces complicate the role of the researcher. Predetermined design structures may guide and control aspects of the online space and activities, but users can move within and across sites and devices according to their own discretion; they create their own traveling practices (Leander & Lovvorn, 2006). Online activities include, but are not limited to, planned and exploratory site visits and searches, as well as voyeuristic "lurking" or "creeping" in which one assumes a purely observational (not interactional) stance.

For researchers, these factors can complicate the study of meaning making, as it may be difficult to trace interaction and online presence. Conversely, the archival component of some online documentation can connect an artifact to a particular point in time, helping the researcher to situate the meaning-making activities and artifacts. There also are networking residues (Grimes & Fields, 2012) that inherently tie users to their online activity, and with the ability to download information or take a screen capture, researchers can accumulate an offline repository of online data in the form of images, videos, voice memos, or written text (for more on data collection, please see Chapter Five). This chapter focuses on what it means to be a qualitative researcher of online spaces, specifically addressing the role of the researcher by exploring the researcher-as-tool, researcher positioning, and the development of **research questions** in light of qualitative inquiry that includes online spaces.

Aspects of Researching Online Meaning Making

The discussion of learning in online and offline spaces as separate entities helps to highlight features of both environments that support and abate opportunities to develop in-depth and multifaceted perspectives of the research. Though some (Bowker & Tuffin, 2004) have called attention to extant research that has addressed online and offline activities as distinct practices, such a perspective is not presented in this text. Likewise, there is no conscious attempt to privilege one space or to view the offline and online worlds as disassociated entities. The insights of Mizuko Ito and colleagues (2010), who were "not interested in establishing a boundary between online participation as distinct from offline" (p. 366), as well as the suggestion that the research of online interaction not exclude offline components, inform this discussion. This is not to deny meaning making that begins and continues within the online space; rather, it is to recognize the multiple entry points to meaning making that "are largely a mirror and extension of" offline behavior and contexts (Ito et al., p. 366). When researchers design a study of online meaning making, the congruence between the methodology and guiding questions is essential. Researchers need to be mindful of the potential myopia related to the term *online* and account for the offline component, be it in the research design or in the limitations of the study.

In addition, researchers of online spaces need to consider how the design structures of websites, applications, and programs can regulate and normalize behavior (Abrams & Rowsell, 2011), which also harkens back to the discussion of learning management systems in Chapter Three. Users are guided and influenced by textual and hyperlinked infrastructure, and this "architecture or code of Cyberworlds" (Williams, 2007, p. 13) provides pathways to activity. Consider, for example, how one might traverse the social networking site Facebook. As noted in Chapter Two, there are a number of options for a user to participate directly or indirectly on the site. For instance, one could post on his or her personal timeline, private message a Facebook friend (one who has accepted the connection), view or respond to a newsfeed (a list of others' posts), and read the timelines of others whose privacy settings grant access to this content. When users select a hyperlinked post, the "outside" content is displayed in a new tab, enabling users to view the content without exiting the Facebook site. In other words, users may have a number of paths they can traverse—and they can even visit outside Facebook via hyperlinks—but, when they are within Facebook, they are confined to the paths available to them.

Privacy settings can restrict access to others' content, and users can display and modify content according to the site's design and capacities for modification. Access to content, therefore, can be immediately limited by the degree of content one is willing to share publicly in general, or with the researcher in particular. Further, evolving technology translates into program updates, and sites may provide advance notice or suddenly "push" or deploy changes that can modify the structure and rules of the space. Thus, the architecture of an online space and users' inhabitation of a space can create opportunities for and barriers to observation and participation. Researchers of online spaces "must work within these restrictions as would an observer work with physical restrictions in an offline setting" (Williams, 2007, p. 13). As such, there are differences between the online and offline world that can complicate research and enrich understandings of multidimensional and multidirectional learning.

Unlike the offline world, where removing oneself from a space may be contingent on multiple factors, such as the rules of the space (one cannot simply leave school) and transportation needs, online users have the ability to leave a site, sign off the Internet or close a digital device; they can remove themselves from the online world with relative ease. Many times, users place their online activity on hold to attend to offline necessities, such as caring for pets, eating a meal, or addressing personal care; but they resume their work in the virtual world when they return to their device. Martin and her colleagues (2013) found this to be true for twenty-five-year-old Jaea, who would break from his videogaming to address offline responsibilities and then continue his gaming. Whereas Martin and her colleagues observed Jaea's behavior in person, a researcher viewing behavior solely online may not be able to explain seemingly erratic or unpredictable participant behavior; one moment participants might be digitally active, and the next moment they might not. What is evident—and what extant research suggests—is that though the online space is separate from its offline counterpart, the inhabitation of an online space is not completely bereft of offline connections (see Spotlight Box 4.1). These are important points scholars must account for as they design and conduct investigations.

Spotlight Box 4.1
Investigating Collaboration In and Beyond Minecraft

Cathy Burnett and Chris Bailey (2014) called attention to the connection between online and offline meaning making when they examined the collaboration of eighteen ten- and eleven-year-old children as they played Minecraft during lunchtime in school. Bailey introduced and oversaw the Minecraft Club, and, noting "the entwined nature of on/offscreen activity (Hine, 2000)" (p. 53), the researchers discovered that the "Minecraft Club was a hybrid between Minecraft, the classroom and Bradborough" [the online Minecraft world the children created] (p. 54).

Burnett and Bailey designed their study acknowledging that meaning making could span online and offline spaces. Data collection included observation of gameplay, and video and field notes of on- and off-screen interactions. Though Burnett and Bailey (2014) attempted to talk to the youth as they played, they found that such an approach changed the nature of student participation. "Children slowed down and shifted into teaching mode as they guided us . . . around and explained what they had done and why they did it. This stopped them from talking with others in the class, interrupting the kind of collaboration we were interested in observing" (p. 54). As a result, they relied primarily on observation and used video to inform their understanding of meaning making.

(Continued)

(Continued)

The researchers and children were physically present together in the offline school environment as Burnett and Bailey investigated collaboration by examining the ways the students learned about Minecraft. They observed students looking at others' screens and listening to publicly announced instructions and gameplay. Additionally, the researchers noted how the students drew on a number of resources, which they defined as "what was available on screen but also other children, objects, locations, and immaterial resources such as memories, preferences and prior experiences" (p. 52). In this way, the students were layering their literacies (Abrams, 2015) as they called on a variety of experiences and resources to make meaning. Burnett and Bailey (2014) acknowledged how "(im)material relationships have particular implications for the use of digital technologies, where individuals' actions and intentions materialise 'virtually' on screen but of course are always enabled and experienced in physical locations" (p. 51).

Burnett and Bailey's (2014) highlighted work is part of a burgeoning line of research that not only has begun to address how offline behavior may be tied to online stimuli and interactions, but also has provided insight into learning and applying information across porous spaces (Abrams, 2011, 2015; Burnett, 2011; Burnett & Merchant, 2014; Lynch 2014). In other words, when it comes to studying online learning, researchers must be mindful not to treat the online space as a hermetically sealed experience.

Being a Qualitative Researcher of Online Spaces

Just as we advocate for the consideration of offline components, so too do we call attention to the application of traditional and multimethod qualitative approaches, to studies of online meaning making. At the heart of all qualitative research is the investigation of people, culture, artifacts, and meaning making *across* diverse settings, including online spaces.

> In the social and behavioral sciences, [qualitative] approaches to research are often used to explore, describe, or explain social phenomenon; unpack the meanings people ascribe to activities, situations, events or artifacts; build a depth of understanding about some aspect of social life; build "thick descriptions" (see Clifford Geertz, 1973) of people in naturalistic settings; explore new or under-researched areas; or make micro-macro links (illuminate connections between individuals-groups and institutional and/or cultural contexts). (Leavy, 2014, p. 2)

Such a broad definition of qualitative pursuits leaves room for the expansion of methods and the reshaping of research to account for epistemic shifts (Marcus, 1995). Established qualitative protocols for researching offline environments, cultures, artifacts, and ways of being include an extensive amount of **researcher reflexivity**, and thick, rich description (Creswell, 2013; Geertz, 1973). The level of rigor and documentation necessary for traditional qualitative studies is just as necessary when using multiple methods to investigate learning in online spaces. Though ethnographers have been criticized for "making rather than reflecting culture" (Clifford & Marcus, 1986; Flewitt, 2011), the dangers of myopia can impact any study. Like Flewitt (2011), we underscore the importance of examining multimodalities, such as sound, image, positioning, and structure (Kress, 2010; Kress & van Leeuwen, 2001) in researching online cultures and meaning making.

Whereas some tools can help support the collection of accurate, verbatim data, all research has limitations. The protean nature of the online world, we argue, suggests that a researcher's role needs to be open, flexible, and adaptable. The researcher needs to be sensitive to the affordances and limitations of online and offline techniques and willing to adapt methods to accommodate the participant and the research. Androutsopoulos (2008) suggested that this type of "guerrilla ethnography" involves "seizing the opportunity to use whatever methods are possible under the circumstances of each particular context" (p. 9), an approach that seems rooted in pragmatism and opens possibilities for using multiple methods. In relation to qualitative inquiry in general, although one needs to have a thorough methodology established, a researcher also needs to embrace the exploratory ethos of qualitative inquiry and be willing to consider the online world from multiple perspectives and approaches.

Inhabiting an online space includes an agency that often is not associated with restrictive school-based culture (Black, 2008; Gee, 2007). Choice and self-direction are key components as users select and move within and about online sites. As many programs and sites become increasingly available across multiple platforms, users have the ability to access sites at their discretion, on a whim, and certainly beyond the confines of the home or school. Mobile devices enable users to enter online spaces, engage with others, and post thoughts, often responding to immediate stimuli they encounter both online and offline, offering researchers a window into a particular activity or social context. As noted in Chapter Two, research into social networking forums has revealed a spectrum of participatory social practices. The sharing of private lives in public spaces enables the researcher to be privy to situated meaning making that he or she otherwise may not have had access to. For example, a person takes a selfie or a photo of friends at a party or a sports game and immediately uploads it to Instagram, Snapchat, or even Facebook, following with tweeting updates on Twitter. If the person has made his or her settings public, has posted to a public site, or has provided the researcher access to a private account, the researcher then gains additional insight into the following information:

Offline Environments   If one posts a picture at a party, then the researcher can examine the setting, which includes the physical space (and objects within it), the people in the space, and the ways the people present themselves (e.g., dress, gesture, objects).

Online Interaction   Most social networking sites have a running record of recent posts, "likes," and "friends" or "followers," and these networking residues (Grimes & Fields, 2012) can help researchers trace users' interactions with others and their involvement within and across spaces. Many networking sites note the time and location of the image (if geo-settings are enabled). Even if the communication is through email and not a website, then the researcher has a time-stamped record of the communication.

Movement and Artifacts   Participation, socialization, and literacy development take place in affinity spaces (Knobel & Lankshear, 2007), and the various multimodal portals support activity within and across sites (Curwood, Magnifico & Lammers, 2013). Artifacts link online and offline culture, history, and context (Pahl & Rowsell, 2010), and discussions of materiality and immateriality highlight the tangible features and the intangible experiences that are part of artifact production on and off the screen. Burnett and Bailey (2014) suggested that the interplay of these material and immaterial artifacts can be conceptualized as interwoven relationships "rather than seeing the material and immaterial in terms of binary distinctions between on/offscreen or on/offline" (p. 51). Further, the layering of literacies, practices, and experiences also stems from participants' movements within and across texts, practices, and spaces and the confluence of experiences that are part of overall meaning making (Abrams, 2013, 2015).

Though there are tools to capture these online movements, interactions, and texts, researchers need to be mindful of the situated nature of learning; meaning making is not relegated to one particular screenshot or site. Additionally, as indicated in Chapter Seven, researchers must pay special attention to ethics, namely how they access and report data from public and private contexts.

Kendall and McDougall's (2013) study of adolescent male gamers in England purposely included Facebook as a research site and tool. In Spotlight Box 4.2, the discussion of the researchers' approach sheds light not only on the online-offline connection, but also on how social sites and participatory practices can become part of the research design.

In their study of adolescent male gamers' interactions with videogames and the co-construction of literacy practices, Kendall and McDougall (2013) selected eight sixteen- to seventeen-year-old, self-identifying players of the action-adventure videogame Grand Theft Auto 4 (GTA4), which often has been maligned for its violent and sordid content. Given the controversies surrounding the GTA series, the researchers sought to "contribute to the debates around protectionist accounts of media literacy" and not only found GTA4 to be a unifying component for participants, but also recognized that the game "represents the most significant example to date of a mass market, narrative-based game with detailed, complex, and open-ended location to explore online alongside or even outside the mission-based storyline" (p. 91).

The researchers created a Facebook group specifically for their study as a means to facilitate conversation among the gamers. Though participants received instructions for joining the group and protocols for participation, there was an open-ended prompt to discuss their gaming experiences and freely respond to others' posts. Additionally, the researchers followed up with a semi-structured interview with each player. Kendall and McDougall (2013) noted that there were three reasons they used the Facebook group as a tool:

- They chose a space that was familiar to the participants.

- They perceived the interaction on Facebook as a means to support agentive literacy practices.

- They found Facebook "offered a 'transliteracy' bridge from playing to talking" (p. 92).

The authors noted that they needed to provide participants "plenty of guidance on the technicalities of how to participate," which included joining the Facebook group and the frequency of posting (p. 92). Though the participants were prompted to share their GTA4 gaming experiences, they had the freedom to respond to others' posts as they felt necessary. Kendall and McDougall explained that they did not contact participants individually; instead they used whole-group messages to relay reminders to their participants. In other words, though it was a research-based Facebook group that the researchers guided, the participants had a degree of autonomy in their interaction during the established two weeks of reporting. Not only did this approach help to uncover the adolescents' perceived differences between the game world and "real life," but also it supported a level of metacognition that informed the participants' discussions of identity and participatory learning.

Research of affinity spaces helps to inform our understanding of dynamic learning. In their discussion of affinity space methodology, Lammers, Curwood, and Magnifico (2012) built on Gee's (2004) theory of affinity spaces and portals to theorize adolescents' evolving literacies and participation in online spaces, such as the aforementioned social networking and microblogging sites. They suggested that the often-multimodal portals, or pathways that support presence and involvement, typically include self-directed meaning making, and call attention to how "self-directed participation requires an affinity space researcher to look for new portals and examine participants' motivation for engaging in various literacies within and across portals" (p. 48). Therefore, qualitative inquiry of online learning must account for movement and connections within and beyond specific online and offline spaces.

Positioning the Researcher as a Research Tool

In addition to knowledge of and access to online and offline meaning making, researchers must consider their own role of **researcher as a research tool**. This starts with researchers' familiarity with qualitative methodology and their willingness to be thoughtful and reflexive. Matthew B. Miles and A. Michael Huberman (1994) identified four characteristics that are necessary to assess the trustworthiness of the human instrument: (a) the degree of familiarity with the phenomenon and the research context; (b) a strong interest in theoretical knowledge and the ability to conceptualize large amounts of qualitative data; (c) the ability to take a multidisciplinary approach; and (d) investigative skills, which are developed through literature review, course work, and methodological experience.

These four traits may have been established prior to the widespread public and global use of the Internet, but they have direct applications to the examination of online learning and spaces. Further, knowledge of the context is multifaceted. It is not enough to be familiar with the website or program. As Kafai and Fields (2012) noted in their study of Whyville, despite access to log files, chats, and videos of interaction, there can remain gaps in the data. Given that only consenting participants' work was reviewed, "reading the logs was often like listening to one-sided telephone conversations. . . . [They were] left to guess at what others were saying, and when they switched from talking from one person to another" (p. 271). In other words, though Miles and Huberman's (1994) characteristics may address trustworthiness, the multiple layers of an online context can mean that familiarity with it may not be enough to contribute to trustworthiness. Rather, a transparent approach to reviewing and understanding the data from multiple sources not only will help researchers accurately report their positioning, but also will highlight the affordances and limitations of their study and underscore the trustworthiness of the research.

Additionally, in all qualitative inquiry, the researcher is the preeminent research tool (Wolcott, 1975), and often there is a tension between subjectivity and objectivity.

"Because all data are filtered directly through the eyes of the data collector, results are considered to be too intuitive, personal, and individualistic" (Borman, LeCompte, & Goetz, 1986, p. 43). Conversely, too much objectivity may lead to a certain detachment that can impede data collection. For these reasons, personal discipline is instrumental in qualitative research, and it can allow researchers to avoid excessive subjectivity (Borman et al., 1986). Without proper reflection and care, researchers may inadvertently interject personal biases and interpretations by using language with positive or pejorative connotations or privileging one aspect of the research (e.g., an experience, text, mode, case) more than another.

Transparent and logical rationales, as well as active self-reflection, can help researchers to mitigate excessive subjectivity. Furthermore, just as research paradigms and inquiry design need to be carefully appropriated and applied (for more, see Chapter One), researchers need to adopt a "disciplined subjectivity" (Erickson, 1973) that involves rigorous examination for each decision in the research process, from the construction of research questions to relationships with participants. Qualitative researchers can also engage in "intersubjective understanding" (Erickson, 1973) in order to both embrace and explicate the subjective nature of the study.

As researchers grapple with levels of objectivity and subjectivity, they can actively seek external criticism and engage in critical self-reflection. Borman, LeCompte, and Goetz (1986) argued that researchers can assume an insider-outsider role by "stepping outside their involvement with subjects while still in the field, or they may actually take a vacation from the field to regain perspective" (p. 44), both of which should be part of the study design. Researchers can also seek out feedback from colleagues and mentors, which can enable them to develop research questions, clarify theoretical concepts, and refine methodological approaches. Such peer examination can enhance the trustworthiness of the study's findings.

In addition to peer debriefing, member checking and triangulation can confirm, clarify, or challenge researcher beliefs and perspectives, and, thus, help support the trustworthiness of the data (Creswell, 2013; Creswell & Miller, 2000). Because member checking involves participants providing feedback on "parts of the polished or semi-polished product, such as the major findings, the themes, the case analysis, the grounded theory, the cultural description, and so forth" (Creswell, 2013, p. 201), the researcher not only enables the participants' voices to emerge across the various stages of the study, but also allows for misinterpretations to come to the fore. During such a process, participants can provide insight into their intentions, suggest alternate interpretations, and inform revised or expanded analyses and understandings.

Just as researchers should look to others for feedback, they also need to engage in reflexive practice. When researchers engage in reflexivity, they consider the influence of their own background, interests, and beliefs on the process of qualitative research. There is a crucial distinction between reflection and reflexivity. As Chiseri-Strater (1996) explained, "To be reflective does not demand an 'other,' while to be reflexive demands both an other and some self-conscious awareness of the process of self-scrutiny" (p. 130). This process requires that researchers account for their own personal history and assumes that there is no neutrality in their fieldwork. As such, researcher subjectivity is an inherent part of qualitative inquiry, and researchers must both accept and explicate that "how knowledge is acquired, organized, and interpreted is relevant to what the claims are" (Altheide & Johnson, 1994, p. 486). To that end, Pillow (2003) suggested four reflexive strategies—reflexivity as recognition of self, reflexivity as recognition of other, reflexivity as truth, and reflexivity as transcendence—that work together to cultivate researchers' self-awareness.

In addition, researcher reflexivity is supported by the maintenance of personal memos, which include reflections on "assumptions, beliefs, and biases" (Creswell & Miller, 2000, p. 127). The use of thick, rich description in such writings can "transport readers to the setting and give the discussion an element of shared experiences," which reveals **researcher positioning** and perspective, and supports validity (Creswell, 2013, p. 202). Further, the researcher should be "submerged or engaged in the data collection phase over a long enough period to ensure an in-depth understanding of the phenomenon (Merriam, 2002, p. 26). The study's length and depth help to validate not only the findings, but also the role of the researcher as the research tool.

In positioning the researcher as a research tool, the concept of bricolage also is helpful. Bricolage suggests that "poetic making do" (de Certeau, 1984, p. xv) is integral to qualitative inquiry. Here, the qualitative-researcher-as-bricoleur uses diverse aesthetic and material tools, deploys multiple strategies, and initiates new approaches (Denzin & Lincoln, 2013). To better "interpret, criticize, and deconstruct," Denzin and Lincoln (2000) called for bricoleurs to employ "hermeneutics, structuralism, semiotics, phenomenology, cultural studies, and feminism" (p. 3). For contemporary qualitative inquiry, such an interdisciplinary approach is vital. Kincheloe (2001) argued, "Given the social, cultural, epistemological, and paradigmatic upheavals and alterations of the past few decades, rigorous researchers may no longer enjoy the luxury of choosing whether to embrace the bricolage" (p. 681). Bricoleurs recognize the limits of a single method and embrace multiplicity, creativity, and diversity, thereby also supporting a pragmatic approach to research. Moreover, they understand that the object of inquiry is concomitantly a part of multiple contexts and processes; it is culturally inscribed and historically situated (Kincheloe, 2005).

Researcher Positioning in Online Settings

Researcher positioning sheds light on the researcher's proximity and accessibility to participants, methodological and theoretical dispositions, and personal biases and limitations. Inhabiting an online space can be critical to the examination of participants' social behavior and meaning-making experiences. For example, Rebecca Black's (2008) ethnographic research of adolescents' literacies online involved inhabiting Fanfiction.net, posting online, and interacting with others, all which informed her understanding of the culture and practices of the Fanfiction site. Black was not covertly observing from afar; rather, she situated herself within the space and among its inhabitants.

Similarly, other researchers have immersed themselves in an online space, partaking in the same activities as their participants as a means to understand social behaviors and literacies. For instance, Lange (Ito et al., 2010), who studied the social behavior of video bloggers, also became a video blogger herself, thereby engaging in and receiving feedback from others within the space. Likewise, as Ito and Bittanti (2010) noted, Cody (2010) became part of a Final Fantasy XI end-game "linkshell," or guild, a process that involved gaining approval by lead guild members; once part of the linkshell, Cody gained insight into the norms of the guild, namely the social structure and the "pressure . . . to be 'perfect' . . . and not make mistakes" (Ito & Bittanti, 2010, p. 219). In this way, we can see how researchers positioning themselves as an active part of a site, contributing in ways that others do, can deepen their understanding of the online site-as-research-space, as well as the complex literate practices that are an inherent component of such inhabitation.

When researchers become actively involved in a site, they must be mindful of their positioning in the space. More specifically, they need to acknowledge how their role as researcher (i.e., an investigator of learning) and their decision to join a site (as opposed to building on an extant involvement) may influence and perhaps privilege their perspective of the data. As Grimes, Fleischmann, and Jaeger (2010) explained, "While at times a researcher may fulfill the role of a user, they cannot divorce themselves from ethical responsibilities. . . . Researchers should not lose objectivity and [should] resist the urge to 'go native' in virtual world research" (p. 88). In other words, as with any qualitative inquiry, a researcher's heightened awareness of biases and positioning will help to reduce subjective reporting. This includes, but is not limited to, remaining keenly mindful of researcher participation in activities and longitudinal involvement in online sites, which support the development of an insider's view of the particular environment and its inhabitants, as well as offer insight into successful methodologies.

There are studies, too, in which researchers examine online activity while also inhabiting the online *and* offline spaces with participants. Merchant's (2010) study of primary school children's interactions and literacies in the virtual world Barnsborough included his coinhabitation of participants' online and offline spaces (see Spotlight Box 4.3). More specifically, Merchant (via his avatar) joined the students in the online world, Barnsborough. In this space, he conducted

Between 2006 and 2008, Guy Merchant from the United Kingdom worked with a design team both as a consultant and a researcher to assist and study nine- to eleven-year-olds' interaction in the immersive world known as Barnsborough. During this time, Merchant coinhabited the space with the participants and interviewed the students while in Barnsborough. These data were then complemented by offline observations of the youths' online practices.

As Merchant (2010) explained, students entered Barnsborough, a town that "had been hurriedly and mysteriously abandoned by its inhabitants," and the students' roles revolved around problem solving as they began "collecting evidence available in-world in a number of media and textual forms" (p. 138). Such evidence included "environmental print" found on buildings or in advertisements,

program-generated assistive "tool tip clues," "hyperlinked text" that led to additional multimedia texts, and "interactive chat" bubbles that were the primary form of in-world communication.

In addition to forty- to sixty-minute observations that involved "over the shoulder" examination of students' in-world interactions, as well as archived chat logs of avatar conversations, Merchant "negotiated follow-up in-world interviews with groups of pupils," which hinged on a combination of simultaneous presence and absence. The students were "co-present in the classroom or computer suite at the time of the interview," and thus were together in both online and offline spaces (2010, p. 139). During the avatar-to-avatar group interviews, Merchant may not have been in the same room as the students, but he was co-present with them in Barnsborough.

observations and interviews; however, Merchant also engaged in offline "over the shoulder" observations of the students and their avatars. Other data sources included a final teacher questionnaire, archived chat logs, and field notes.

Williams (2007) explained that researchers can achieve a "graphical pseudo-presence" (p. 12) through the embodiment of the avatar and the successful "immigration process" (p. 13) of gaining access to a particular space or group. In the online space, researchers can find that the interaction with participants' avatars can be very rich. In fact, connecting with others through the avatar medium "can be said to provide a more immersed interaction than is found in text-only environments. . . . The use of avatars enrich the communicative process . . . [and] avatar positioning, appearance and performance combine to create online identity" (p. 12). Additionally, when researchers are co-present with participants in a text-only space (e.g., a chat space, text messages), there may be access to spontaneous conversation and artifacts of literate behavior and meaning-making activities (Domokos, 2007; Taylor & Harper, 2003), but participation can be inconsistent. Lapses in response time, as well as abrupt silence or incongruent texts, can complicate the researcher's role and underscore the importance of reflexivity and member checking (Abrams, 2010).

As noted in Spotlight Box 4.3, the combination of online and offline interaction with the participants supported researcher-participant rapport. It also underscored Merchant's (2010) role as the researcher, especially given that the primary school children knew what he looked like as an avatar and a human. Finally, given that the participants were sitting next to each other at adjacent computers while inhabiting the online world, Barnsborough, they were making meaning across and within both contexts. However, Merchant noted a disconnect between the online and offline worlds because of the ways the students viewed the practices and spaces: "In some cases, this use of the virtual world met with resistance from the pupils who enjoyed exploring Barnsborough and the literacy practices embedded in it, but were unwilling to transfer this enthusiasm into conventional literacy" (p. 146). This suggests that although **co-presence** can offer a different perspective and experience for the participant (and the researcher), there are a host of social, cultural, economic, curricular, and political factors that can shape meaning making. Thus, when researchers consider the affordances of their positioning, they also need to account for the constraints beyond their biases and their role as researcher; they need to examine and address the contextual fabric within and beyond the online space, as well as note what contexts they could not anticipate or did not account for in the study's design.

Ethical Considerations

Though explored in greater detail in Chapter Seven, ethics remain of key concern for researchers, especially as they consider their role in the collection of data in online spaces. In addition to the aforementioned components of researcher reflexivity and bias, there are the issues of disclosure and presence. For instance, Spotlight Box 4.2 focused on Kendall and McDougall's (2013) use of a Facebook group as a conduit to research adolescent videogamers. In the Facebook space, they met and interacted with participants. At all times, the participants were aware of the researchers' intended use of the space; there was no surreptitious data collection. Similarly, as noted earlier in this chapter, there have been other researchers (Black, 2008; Ito et al., 2010; Merchant; 2010) who have been co-present in an online space with participants, namely as cocreators in the space.

In the cases of Merchant (2010) and Burnett and Bailey (2014), there was an offline data collection component, and, thus, participants inherently knew of the researchers' presence. However, in other instances, such as Rebecca Black's ethnography of online fanfiction, attention is drawn to the ethics of online research, especially in spaces that are considered public. Despite the public nature of the online site, Black (2008) noted how she felt "obligated to obtain traditional forms of consent from authors whose work I focus on in my research" (p. 23). Similar to Black's research, Cody's (2010) and Lange's (2010) work in a public online space also involved interacting with youth. Their research, reported in *Hanging Out, Messing Around, and Geeking Out,* included collective discussion of data collection and the obfuscation of participant identity. Although not specifically linked to Cody's and Lange's work, in the text there is an acknowledgment of interviews being conducted under the "constraints imposed by our universities' institutional review boards" (Pascoe, 2010, p. 121). This leads researchers to consider some important ethical questions when considering their own positioning within the study:

- How will the participants know and interact with the researcher: as a researcher, as a fellow inhabitant/participant, or both?

- What additional ethical concerns might a researcher need to consider when investigating learning in online spaces as a coinhabitant of the space?

- How might a researcher's co-presence support or limit data collection?

Designing Research Questions

Researchers' consideration of ethics is inherently part of their research design and their access to and interaction with possible participants. Additionally, an understanding and inhabitation of a space can directly impact the research design, which includes the conceptual and methodological frame, as well as the guiding research questions. Given that online spaces for learning continue to change and evolve, the theoretical frameworks and methods that researchers use to study these spaces should change and evolve as well. As with all research settings, different kinds of research questions may be more or less difficult to study online. Necessary precursors to a data analysis plan include a sound rendering of a researcher's understanding of the particular space and a clearly articulated rationale, logic of inquiry, and methodological framework for the study. It also may be useful for a researcher to consider *how* to plan and carry out particular facets of the inquiry and to identify potential difficulties up front.

Some research questions may be relatively easy to study in an online environment, especially in light of the archival component of digital spaces. For example, if a researcher were interested in an online space where gamers interact by sharing machinima or game-based fanfiction artifacts, it is likely that such evidence would be archived on sites of interest. Archival data informed the study by Viegas, Wattenberg, and McKeon (2007), who considered how rules and dialogic social structures arose by examining the Talk pages of Wikipedia. Similarly, Jamison (2013) examined the social nature and complexities of the Internet's many hypertextual archives of fanfiction. In fact, Jamison questioned why some practically canonical fics (short for fanfictions) are impossible for readers to find when archives have been carefully maintained by legions of fans around the world. The archival impulse of many Internet users makes such questions viable areas of research and opens up immediate free access to decades of historical record. In addition to archives of texts, videos, and images themselves, almost all contemporary websites are designed with some kind of social component whereby users and readers can reveal their presence by leaving comments, reviews, or other evidence of interaction (for more, see Chapter Two and the discussion of Grimes and Fields's [2012] concept of networking residues).

A content analysis that maps current trends and trends over time, or a discourse analysis that explores the kinds of roles that participants take on and how they mark these roles linguistically, could both be viable research strategies for research questions that unfold in spaces like these. Such analyses fit well with mental models of studies (as indicated in Chapter One) that value how online contexts shape online actions and build knowledge from participants' interactions with each other. Kafai, Fields, Roque, Burke, and Monroy-Hernández (2012) have taken such work into a qualitative-quantitative, mixed methods sphere by first observing and documenting the activities of a smaller number of advanced Scratch users, then using back-end algorithmic techniques in order to answer the question of how these roles play out across a site that hosts over one million accounts created. These studies may still be descriptive in nature, but **massively descriptive** (Kafai & Peppler, 2011) in a way that distinguishes their questions from ethnographies that focus on a small number of individuals. While work and research questions like these may seem initially to present fewer barriers to design and entry because of this all-online quality, Jamison (2013) asserted that even the most carefully maintained sites may vanish if their owners lose interest, let their sites lapse into unusable legacy technologies, or allow domain registrations to lapse. Though vast amounts of data may be present right now, various components may also be lost without warning.

Other questions, however, may be very difficult for researchers to answer using online spaces as sole sources of information. As discussed in Chapter Five, studies designed to answer various questions may need to incorporate artifactual data from online spaces as well as various kinds of interviews. danah boyd (2014), for example, explained that teens' activation and deactivation of their Facebook accounts and their tendency to text instead of talk may be in response to their feelings of being surveilled by parents and other authority figures. Such insight would have been impossible without incorporating face-to-face interviews into the data collection, since the teens in question often appeared not to maintain profiles on social media sites. Abrams's (2009a, 2009b) investigation of videogaming practices and decisions included stimulated recall. As noted in the previous chapter, this required video-recorded gameplay followed by immediate, face-to-face reflective interviews because it is nearly impossible for gamers to play and verbalize the decisions that they are making simultaneously, as in a think-aloud protocol. Cognitive overload sets in too soon. Further, Abrams used other methods, such as extensive classroom observations, individual and focus group interviews, and participant shadowing, to gain a robust understanding of the gamers' literacies.

Finally, research questions may change over time. Magnifico's (2012) initial research questions indicated interest in how Neopets players collaborated with and learned from each other when they wrote articles for the Neopian Times site newspaper. Magnifico used a connective ethnography design to fully explore young writers' talk and writing across several different settings and modes of communication (Fields & Kafai, 2009; Leander & Lovvorn, 2006). When the participants used on-site group message boards to discuss their stories, talk about the stories was readily accessible on the Neopets site—although the site purged public message boards periodically, which sometimes led to lost data. Interviews, though, revealed that much more often, participants used private sites to discuss their writing plans: on-site private email, instant messaging programs, and Skype, primarily. Thus, it became impossible for Magnifico to gather *all* of their conversations about collaboration. She became dependent on participants to save the off-Neopets texts, drafts, and conversations. While many initially indicated willingness to do so, several barriers including simple forgetfulness, file corruption, and computer viruses meant that a full set of collaborative communications could not be gathered. Detailed discourse analysis became impossible, and Magnifico instead reworked her research questions to focus on topics where case study and interview analysis methods were appropriate—the young writers' motivations to write and impressions of reader interactions.

As described in this section, research questions and logics of inquiry should be inherently aligned. At the beginning of any study, researchers should begin by identifying areas of interest and hone these areas to formulate research questions. What kinds of activity are interesting? Why? How might various practices indicate learning or processes of enculturation or membership? Such questions need not follow established patterns; researchers may, in fact, be making space for new kinds of meaning by examining esoteric corners of online spaces. Once the inquiry itself becomes clearer, it is helpful for future phases of the study to begin identifying and documenting answers to questions such as:

- How does this learning become visible?

- What kinds of data might demonstrate it?

- What contextualized factors might contour the inquiry?

- What initial and shifting perspectives have shaped the inquiry?

- What kinds of analysis might be productively employed to further teach the researcher about the phenomenon that she or he noticed?

If researchers follow these steps, they may discover that they are also making a commitment to **emic research** and to documenting participants' activities, as much as possible, in a way that represents participants' points of view. Too often, researchers believe that they already know something about how formal learning occurs and that, therefore, online learning spaces may be studied as if they were equivalent to face-to-face learning spaces. The emic research cited in this section, however, argues for understanding the contributions of multiple approaches and diverse data collection and analyses.

Conclusion

This chapter addresses the ways online spaces can complicate the design and implementation of qualitative research. The discussion of qualitative traditions reveals how contemporary examinations remain rooted in established conventions; however, there is room for a blended approach, not only including a variety of research methods, but also involving online and offline data collection. Overall, this chapter underscores the need for flexibility and care. Research questions and methodological approaches may need to be reconsidered in light of shifting or unanticipated contexts.

CONNECTING TO YOUR WORK

This chapter challenges you to consider how researcher positioning might influence your understanding of online spaces. The following questions about researchers' roles and perspectives will help you to design a study:

- When thinking about yourself as a researcher of online learning, what are some preconceived notions you have about the online space? The participants within the online space? Your role in the online space?

- Consider how you will design your study to include questions that address the specific aspects of learning you wish to explore. How, if at all, will you account for (or simply acknowledge) contexts within and beyond the online space that impact participant meaning making?

- Finally, how, if at all, will your research involve offline components that inform your understanding of online practices?

Guiding Questions for Chapter 5

- What strategies can researchers use to establish the trustworthiness of their findings?
- What techniques demonstrate rigor within online qualitative research?
- What data sources are available for qualitative inquiry in online spaces?
- What tools can assist researchers in the collection and organization of online data sources?

What Methodological Tools Are Available for Data Collection?

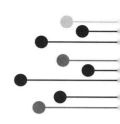

Introduction

As Chapter One discussed, qualitative research is "a particular tradition in social science that fundamentally depends on watching people in their own territory and interacting with them in their own language, on their own terms" (Kirk & Miller, 1986, p. 9). Pragmatic frameworks can be especially useful in territories that are constantly changing and evolving. By selecting theoretical perspectives and methodological tools that are suitable to the context, researchers are able to gain insight into their research questions. To that end, this chapter begins by considering **trustworthiness** and rigor in online qualitative research. Today's digital tools and online spaces offer researchers the opportunity to connect with participants around the world and trace learning practices across sites, modes, and texts. However, researchers must make critical decisions about their guiding research questions, the boundaries of their study, access to participants, and data sources. For qualitative researchers who venture into online territories, this means that they must investigate the cultural practices, specialist languages, and tacit expectations of particular groups. From writers and artists to programmers and gamers, each group has its own history, its own rules, and its own culture.

In this chapter, we emphasize the importance of culture in shaping how, when, and why people learn in online spaces. As Nancy Baym (2000) pointed out, "Online social worlds are accessible to researchers in ways that few other worlds are. If we want to understand them, we need to look with rigor and detail" (p. 198). Very often, learning in online social worlds is self-directed and collaborative. Sometimes, a learner's practices leave traces in and across a variety of spaces that are readily accessible to researchers. Other times, learning happens behind the scenes, perhaps in private conversations between two Civilization modders or through a Wattpad writer's drafts. In such instances, it is vital that researchers understand the complexity of networked field sites, define the boundaries of their study, and establish relationships with research participants to gain access to data sources that may otherwise be unavailable. This chapter considers how data collection in online spaces draws on a rich history of qualitative research, as well as how it is impacted by specific tools and spaces. It outlines key data sources, explicates how they can inform qualitative inquiry within online spaces, and suggests digital tools to support the collection and organization of data sources in online research.

Establishing Trustworthiness

Since the introduction of naturalistic inquiry into the field of education, questions have been raised about the rigor of qualitative research. Scholars have critically considered how to judge the trustworthiness of qualitative research and have debated whether the terms and frameworks from quantitative research can (or even should) be applied to qualitative research. Often, qualitative research has been judged against the positivist criteria of validity and reliability, and consequently found to be insufficient (Anfara, Brown, & Mangione, 2002). For positivists who believe that the social world can be studied in the same way as the natural world (Mertens, 2005), the product of qualitative inquiry is fiction rather than science, and qualitative "researchers have no way to verify their truth statements" (Denzin & Lincoln, 2000, p. 8). Consequently, researchers must create a logic of inquiry (see Chapter One) that links their theory to their methodology. For instance, scholarship in the learning sciences has shown that it can be advantageous to think about learning from both cultural and cognitive perspectives.

To ground the subsequent discussion on data collection, we will first explore the nature of rigor within qualitative research, which involves making "data and explanatory schemes as public and replicable as possible" (Denzin, 1978, p. 7). Then, we will discuss strategies to ensure the trustworthiness of qualitative methods. Traditionally, four criteria were applied to quantitative research: internal validity, external validity, reliability, and objectivity (see Table 5.1). In the 1980s, Guba and Lincoln argued that naturalistic inquiry must move away from the language of experimental inquiry (Guba & Lincoln, 1981, 1982; Lincoln & Guba, 1985).

Norman K. Denzin and Yvonna S. Lincoln (2000) characterized this period in the development of qualitative methods as a "triple crisis of representation, legitimation, and praxis" that challenged qualitative researchers to engage in a "serious rethinking of such terms as validity, generalizability, and reliability" (p. 17). They consequently suggested trustworthiness criteria, which include credibility, transferability, dependability, and confirmability (see Table 5.1). In later work, Guba and Lincoln (1989) proposed a fifth criterion, authenticity. Lincoln (2001) has since reflected that this scholarship was "rooted in the concerns of positivist inquiry, but were not certain how to proceed with breaking free of those mandates" (p. 34). Nevertheless, their seminal work offers a framework to understand the nature of trustworthiness within qualitative research.

For scholars, it is critical to establish the trustworthiness and rigor of their qualitative research (Seale, 1999). This begins with the design of the study, which includes the "logic that links the data to be collected (and the conclusions to be

Table 5.1	Scientific and Naturalistic Terms Related to Trustworthiness	
Scientific Term	**Naturalistic Term**
Internal validity	Credibility
External validity and generalizability	Transferability
Reliability	Dependability
Objectivity	Confirmability

drawn) to the initial questions of the study" (Yin, 1994, p. 18), often involves simultaneous data collection and analysis to generate categories and build theories (Creswell, 2013; Merriam, 2009), and continues with the representation of the findings that are disseminated within the research community.

For qualitative researchers examining meaning making in online spaces, this has specific implications for the collection and analysis of data. First, their study must be rooted within learning theory, as discussed in Chapter Three, and they must be forthcoming about how theory shaped the design, implementation, and dissemination of their study (Trainor & Graue, 2014). Second, while some data sources may be readily accessible and publicly available, others may depend on building relationships with participants and asking them to share information (such as chat logs and writing drafts) that otherwise would be unavailable. Therefore, transparency is vital, especially in terms of methodological approaches and ethical considerations. Finally, positionality and reflexivity are essential for qualitative researchers, as noted in Chapter Four. In particular, "researchers maintain an appropriate balance when acknowledging their positionality, articulating sufficient detail to reveal relevant personal and professional identities and their significance while avoiding overshadowing the participants' voices and related data" (Trainor & Graue, 2014, p. 271). Taken together, these three aspects allow qualitative researchers to demonstrate rigor and establish trustworthiness.

In a review of the literature, John W. Creswell and Dana Miller (2000) identified eight verification procedures. These include: (1) prolonged engagement and persistent observation, (2) **triangulation**, (3) peer review or debriefing, (4) negative case analysis, (5) clarifying researcher bias, (6) member checks, (7) thick description, and (8) external audits. Creswell (2013) suggested that qualitative researchers engage in at least two of the eight in any given study. If qualitative researchers aim to understand how learning takes place within online spaces, then they must establish the trustworthiness of their findings. The verification procedures noted above may occur before, during, or after data collection, and they are directly linked to the credibility, transferability, dependability, and confirmability of the study.

Credibility

To establish **credibility**, Sharan B. Merriam (2009) argued that researchers must ask, "How congruent are the findings with reality?" According to Lincoln and Guba (1985), "The most crucial technique for establishing credibility" is member checking (p. 314). As discussed in Chapter Four, member checking may involve asking participants to read transcripts and ensure that their words match with what they intended to say. It may also include a researcher sharing emerging theories with participants; given their involvement in the study, participants may be able to offer insight into certain patterns or themes noted by the researcher. Since online research may involve a large number of participants, some of whom may be anonymous, member checking may not always be feasible. An alternative is for qualitative researchers to establish relationships with focal participants and share emergent themes, theories, and findings with them, to solicit their thoughts and opinions. However, it is important that researchers acknowledge their **sampling** procedures, and clarify whether their focal participants are typical or exceptional cases within the online space.

Based on the same principle as member checking, peer examination involves the researcher discussing the research process and findings with impartial colleagues who have experience with qualitative methods. As previously addressed in Chapter Four, peer examination can be one way to keep the researcher honest while encouraging deeper reflexive analysis (Lincoln & Guba, 1985). Given the growing number of scholars within the humanities and social sciences interested in online research, peer examination can be initiated through electronic mailing lists (such as the one maintained by the Association of Internet Researchers) and supported through collaborative tools (such as Google Docs). For research to be credible, it must be congruent with reality; since reality is always based on our own subjective perspectives, member checking and peer examination encourage qualitative researchers to consider alternative experiences and interpretations. Other strategies to ensure credibility may include sustained field experiences, field journals, and triangulation.

Triangulation involves "using different methods as a check on one another, seeing if methods with different strengths and limitations all support a single conclusion" (Maxwell, 2013, p. 102). Denzin (1978) proposed four types of triangulation: (1) the use of multiple methods, (2) multiple sources of data, (3) multiple investigators, or (4) multiple theories to confirm emergent findings. While triangulation should be applied throughout a study, it is primarily associated with the data collection phase. Yin (2011) suggested, "The ideal triangulation would not only seek confirmation from three sources but would try to find three different kinds of sources" (p. 81). In the following chapter, for instance, Spotlight Box 6.1 explores the use of multiple data sources in a study of Figment.com as a multi-sited writing space. With qualitative research, triangulation reduces the risk that the conclusions reflect the biases of a single method and contributes to the trustworthiness of the findings.

Transferability

Transferability in qualitative research refers to the extent to which the findings of one study can be applied to others. Shenton (2004) argued that it is vital that researchers convey the boundaries of the study: (1) the number of organizations taking part in the study and where they are based, (2) any restrictions in the type of people who contributed to the data, (3) the number of participants involved in the fieldwork, (4) the data collection methods that were employed, (5) the number and length of the data collection sessions, and (6) the time period over which the data were collected. Other strategies may include the use of a nominated sample and the comparison of a sample to demographic data. For researchers interested in learning within online spaces, transferability may be difficult to establish, namely because the age, gender, language, interests, and practices of learners may vary widely from one space to another. However, by clearly conveying the boundaries and aims of their study, researchers can provide opportunities for others to investigate learning in the same or similar spaces.

Dependability

There are close ties between credibility and **dependability**. As Lincoln and Guba (1985) argued, a demonstration of the former can be instrumental in ensuring the latter. Related strategies may include a rich description of research methods, triangulation, peer examination, and replication. This is why it is critical that qualitative researchers are explicit about the methods. As explained in Chapter One, not only should others be able to understand the logic of inquiry (Gee & Green, 1998) that links the research questions, theory, methodology, and findings, but also other researchers should be able to replicate the study. Online research is dependable when the researchers have taken care to explicate the research design and implementation, to detail the process of recruiting participants and collecting data, and to check with participants and colleagues alike on the study's emergent findings.

Confirmability

Finally, **confirmability** is the degree to which researchers disclose their predispositions (Miles & Huberman, 1994), which may include sharing the beliefs that underpin their methodological decisions. Since no researcher can be truly objective, confirmability depends on how a researcher reflects on and discloses the subjective nature of qualitative inquiry. For those interested in how learning occurs within online spaces, this may mean sharing why they chose to collect certain forms of data and not others as well as how they engaged in data analysis; it may also include a discussion of the relative affordances and constraints of methodological decisions. Other strategies may include triangulation and reflexivity.

Trustworthiness and Analytic Openness

A key part of establishing trustworthiness involves the public disclosure of decisions made during the research process. This includes demonstrating the methods and processes "by which raw data were collected and the processes by which they were compressed and re-arranged so as to be credible" (Lincoln, 2001, p. 25). In particular, Anfara, Brown, and Mangione (2002) argued that the public disclosure of processes is not sufficiently addressed in qualitative inquiry. They return to the core elements of classical science, refutability, and replicability. Because one of the challenges of qualitative research is that it is often not strictly replicable, Anfara and colleagues (2002) recommended analytic openness based on refutability and freedom from bias.

Rather than freedom from bias, qualitative researchers should instead strive to acknowledge their biases and reflect how they may impact methodological decisions. As noted in Chapter Three, learning may not be predictable or replicable. For example, connected learning scholarship often crosses multiple portals within an affinity space, and learners' trajectories may be complex, nonlinear, and multi-sited. Consequently, trustworthiness must be established in other ways, and analytic openness is a crucial part of the process.

Constas (1992) added, "Since we are committed to opening the private lives of participants to the public, it is ironic that our methods of data collection and analysis often remain private and unavailable for public inspection" (p. 254). Moreover, the absence of the opportunity for public inspection may result in "suspicion, naive acceptance, or outright dismissal" (p. 266) within the research community. While scholars may not always be successful in fully disclosing their research decisions, Altheide and Johnson (1994) suggested that there should be clear evidence that indicates an attempt has been made. With online research, this may include hyperlinks to research contexts, screenshots to illustrate data collection, or examples of coding schemes used with print-based and multimodal data sources. However, researchers must take care that direct links, quotes, and examples do not jeopardize the confidentiality of research participants and that such use of data sources aligns with the ethics approval for the study (see Chapter Seven for more on ethics).

Data Sources

At its core, data collection involves asking, watching, and reviewing (Merriam, 2009). To establish trustworthiness, researchers must embrace interdisciplinary reflexivity and transparency, and qualitative inquiry in online spaces often involves the triangulation of multiple data sources. As expanded on in Chapter Four, some of these data sources may be online and some may be offline, depending on the study design and focus. Orgad (2009) argued that online and offline data cannot be separated, and she asked:

> Do we necessarily need offline information to be able to adequately account for online meanings and experiences? Or can we produce high-quality, persuasive, and grounded qualitative research of an Internet phenomenon that draws merely on online data? . . . If the Internet is treated as simply a means of communication that is used in an everyday social context, can it therefore be studied as such—that is, merely by using methodological procedures in offline contexts, without any online data? (p. 37)

In a qualitative study, the breadth and depth of data sources are closely linked to the research questions. Creswell (2013) explained, "Qualitative research questions are open-ended, evolving, and nondirectional" (p. 138). Consequently, researchers need to consider how their research questions shape the nature of data sources and the duration of and approach to data collection.

As explored in Chapter Four, research questions typically begin with *what* or *how*, rather than *why*, to explore a central issue. In Jackson's (2013) study of elementary students' use of the virtual world, Adventure Rock, her research questions included: "What did the children think of Adventure Rock? How did it compare with other virtual worlds for the children?" To answer these and other questions, she relied on "Creative Methods" (Gauntlett, 2007) that hinged on participants' use of various modalities, such as drawing or video, to communicate their thoughts. In addition to video recording workshop sessions, Jackson examined children's media diaries and questionnaire responses, and she juxtaposed qualitative data with the quantitative information that the BBC Television Centre shared with her as part of a larger study of production. Though most of the data collection occurred face-to-face, some of it was online. Consequently, questions of when, why, and how data are collected within a qualitative study are directly informed by the study design, guided by the research questions, and linked to data analysis.

For researchers interested in online learning, multiple options exist for data collection. Depending on the study design, including the research questions, context, and participants, all data collection may occur in online spaces. For instance, Constance Steinkuehler and Sean Duncan's (2008) study of scientific habits of mind in virtual worlds involved the analysis of 1,984 posts made within a World of Warcraft (WoW) discussion forum. Their findings indicated that WoW players demonstrated deep learning through social knowledge construction, systems-based and model-based reasoning, and the use of evidence and counterarguments. Because their research questions specifically focused on how players engaged in scientific habits of mind within a discussion forum, their data collection consisted solely of forum posts.

In other studies of learning in online spaces, data collection has spanned real-world environments and online spaces. Glynda Hull, Amy Stornaiuolo, and Urvashi Sahni's (2010) study of cultural citizenship, identity formation, and communication involved youth in South Africa, India, Norway, and the United States. To understand how young adults and their teachers engaged in Space2Cre8 online, data sources included: quantitative surveys and skills questionnaires, records of online participation through the use of a website history tracking system, digital artifacts, and audio- and video-taping of face-to-face group interactions and semi-structured interviews. Notably, research staff members at each site were fluent in both English and the respective local language. For researchers interested in studying learning in online spaces, data collection may need to take place in multiple physical and virtual spaces.

It is important for researchers to consider the various types of **sampling**, as well as examine four key types of data available in online research: observation, interviews, questionnaires, and artifacts. Each type will be discussed in detail, and relevant examples from contemporary research will be highlighted in spotlight boxes. Building on Chapter One, the remix framework and multimethod approach can be pragmatically applied to data collection and data analysis. Notably, researchers can bring multiple data sources and diverse methodological approaches together within their studies. By being reflective and transparent, they can make their logic of inquiry evident and can promote the trustworthiness of their findings.

Sampling

Many qualitative studies have more than one level of data collection. Yin (2011) described the nested arrangement that often includes a broader level (such as a field setting) that contains a narrower level (like a participant within the setting). He explained that the broader level generally includes a geographic, organizational, or social entity. In the previous examples, the broader level in Steinkuehler and Duncan's (2008) study consisted of the World of Warcraft forum; the narrower level involved individual gamers who posted to the forum. The study by Hull and her team (2010) was more complex and involved a broader level defined by geography as well as by social participation in Space2Cre8; the narrower level included the students as well as the teachers.

Once a researcher has identified the number and nature of levels of data collection, important decisions need to be made related to sampling.

Specifically, the sample needs to be selected either before data collection begins or while the data are being gathered. The challenge is to ensure that data collected from each level directly relates to the research questions and allows for triangulation. In the aforementioned Space2Cre8 study, for instance, surveys and artifacts were collected at the broader level, while interviews were conducted at the narrower level. Because their study design involved classrooms from multiple countries, it increased the trustworthiness of their findings.

The two main types of sampling are probability and nonprobability sampling. Probability sampling, such as simple random sampling, allows researchers to generalize findings from the sample to the population from which it was drawn. Merriam (2009) argued that nonprobability sampling is the method of choice for most qualitative researchers, as probabilistic sampling is often not necessary or even justifiable. The most common kind of nonprobabilistic sampling is called purposeful sampling, which is based on "the assumption that the investigator wants to discover, understand, and gain insight and therefore must select a sample from which the most can be learned" (Merriam, 2009, p. 77). Guided by the study's research questions, samples are likely to be chosen in a deliberate manner. Moreover, the rationale and power of purposeful sampling depends on the qualitative researcher choosing information-rich cases for study in depth (Patton, 2002).

Other main types of sampling common in online research include convenience sampling and snowball sampling as well as a sampling that leads to typical, intense, or extreme cases. Convenience sampling involves the selection of data sources based on their availability; Yin (2011) argued that this can produce an unknown degree of incompleteness and an unwanted degree of bias. In online research, convenience sampling can provide quick access into specific spaces and offer researchers initial insight into the cultural practices.

Snowball sampling involves selecting new data sources as an offshoot of an existing one. In an online study of fanfiction writers, for instance, it may involve asking research participants to share the names of their collaborators. It is important that snowballing is purposeful. If the study seeks to understand how beta readers shape fanfiction writing, then it is entirely appropriate to seek to interview fanfiction writers' reviewers who read their stories, offer feedback, and collaborate on joint creative work. Table 5.2 outlines other types of sampling strategies.

Observation

Once qualitative researchers have considered their approach to sampling, they must then decide how various data sources will offer them insight into their research questions. Observation is a cornerstone of qualitative inquiry (Adler &

Table 5.2 Sampling Schemes

Type of Sampling	Purpose
Maximum variation	Documents diverse variations of individuals or sites based on specific characteristics
Homogenous	Focuses, reduces, simplifies, and facilitates group interviewing
Critical case	Permits logical generalization and maximum application of information to other cases
Theory-based	Finds examples of a theoretical construct and elaborates on and examines them
Confirming cases	Elaborates on initial analysis, seeks exceptions, looking for variation
Snowball or chain	Identifies cases of interest from people who know people who know what cases are information-rich
Extreme or deviant case	Learns from highly unusual manifestations of the phenomenon of interest
Typical case	Highlights what is normal or average
Intensity	Involves information-rich cases that manifest the phenomenon intensely but not extremely
Politically important	Attracts desired attention or avoids attracting undesired attention
Random purposeful	Adds credibility to sample when potential purposeful sample is too large
Stratified purposeful	Illustrates subgroups and facilitates comparisons
Criterion	All cases that meet some criterion; used for quality assurance
Opportunistic	Follows new leads, taking advantage of the unexpected
Combination or mixed	Triangulation, flexibility; meets multiple interests and needs
Convenience	Saves time, money, and effort, but at the expense of information and credibility

Source: Miles and Huberman (1994); Kuzel (1992); Patton (1990).

Adler, 1994). Guided by research questions, observation may entail watching physical settings or online environments to gain insight into the interplay of individuals, activities, texts, and interactions. Observation can offer critical insights into the learning process. Participants may report certain learning practices in an interview, but an observation of how they engage within an online space may offer a more nuanced, or even a contradictory, perspective. For instance, an avid Minecraft player may report minimal use of cheat codes, but an analysis of her gameplay may reveal otherwise.

Angrosino (2007) explained, "Observational researchers traditionally have attempted to see events through the eyes of the people being studied. They have been attentive to seemingly mundane details and to take nothing in the field setting for granted" (p. 732). As discussed in Chapter Three, qualitative inquiry in online spaces requires researchers to consider their conceptualization of learning as well as how, when, and why learning occurs in online spaces. Rather than entering into a field site with assumptions and biases, observational research encourages researchers to engage in "thick description" (Geertz, 1973). Often observation will be the first approach to data collection, and it will later allow researchers to triangulate their data.

Historically, naturalistic observation should not interfere with the people or activities under observation. However, more recent scholarship recognizes that a lack of interference does not equate to objectivity. Depending on the research questions, qualitative researchers may take more active roles as observers and participants. Adler and Adler (1994) discussed a range of membership roles in observational research. These include: (1) peripheral member researchers who seek to develop an insider's perspective without directly participating in group activities; (2) active member researchers who participate in activities without fully committing themselves to the group's values and goals; and (3) complete member researchers who study spaces in which they are already a member or ones that they become fully affiliated with in the course of their research.

Observations can be "rendered as descriptions either through open-ended narrative or through the use of published checklists or field guides" (Angrosino, 2007, p. 730). Patton (2002) argued that skilled observers must pay attention, write descriptive field notes, and know how to "separate detail from trivia . . . using rigorous methods to validate observations" (pp. 260–261). With research of learning in online spaces, observation may take many different forms. For instance, it may involve observing individuals in a physical setting as they engage in digitally mediated learning, or it may involve observing individuals in an online setting. Similarly, observation may occur synchronously or asynchronously. In Black's study of literacy within the Webkinz, Club Penguin, and Barbie Girls virtual worlds, she developed an online observation protocol (see Figure 5.1). This allowed Black and her undergraduate research assistants to track specific types of texts, artifacts, and literacy practices (Black & Reich, 2011).

Figure 5.1 Online Observation Protocol From Black's Research

Literacy	Webkinz	Club Penguin	Barbie Girls
Grade level of texts			
Environmental print: "familiar print found in the surroundings, such as logos, labels, and signs"			
Functional print: "print for a purpose, such as informational signs or texts, directions, greeting cards, lists, letters, and messages"			
Receptive language development/ meaning making: reading, listening, decoding images			
Expressive language development/ meaning making: writing, speaking, drawing, moving avatar			
Literacy artifacts			
Literacy-related games			
Outside-of-game literacy/meaning making			

Source: Unpublished figure courtesy of Rebecca Black.

Real-time observations in online spaces can offer researchers the opportunity to watch the learning process unfold. Through the use of field notes or checklists, researchers can immediately take screenshots, note time stamps, and describe the interactions, texts, and tools evident within the space (see Spotlight Box 5.1). While a peripheral member researcher is limited to what is visible to the entire group, active and complete member researchers can develop relationships with participants and gain access to data that may be private. For many researchers who conduct qualitative studies in online spaces, online research offers archives of previous discussions and interactions (Lammers et al., 2012).

Rather than limiting their data collection to the present day, researchers can look to online spaces for historical records that go back many years. However, it is important to note that this may not always be a complete or accurate record. In Lammers's (2012, 2013) study of The Sims Writers' Hangout, an online space dedicated to Sims-based fanfiction, the site offered her rich archival data; however, the entire space was eventually deleted. For researchers, the Internet can alternatively be ephemeral or perpetual, often when it is most inconvenient.

Wendy Hsu
@wendyfhsu

I caught a cold & heat exhaustion in near tropical Taipei. Suction and moxa treatment. #fieldwork

🐦 10 MONTHS AGO   ↩ REPLY   ↻ RETWEET   ☆ FAVORITE   +

Nakashi Sightings: Live House, Street, Youtube Performances

Fortuitously, I encountered many performances that pertain to the notion of Nakashi. While some of these performances displayed a redefinition of the term in other genre, specifically experimental noise, performance art, and indie rock, I found did encounter living nakashi musicians who were renown within the original scene in Beitou. These "performances" take a variety of form, ranging from busking to experimental noise and rock music shows, and Youtube video. I'm happy that my experiences of the nakashi phenomenon in Taipei were so rich and diverse.

www.beingwendyhsu.info

At an experimental karaoke-inspired performance art show at the Wall:

Some researchers have used blogs as a form of electronic field notes. The image above provides an example of Wendy Hsu's blog related to her research of Nakashi, a Taiwanese performance, infused in everyday life. Hsu provides a running record of these notes in her "hypermedia documentary" of her field research (https://storify.com/wendyfhsu/wendy-s-fieldwork-in-taiwan-2012). Unlike the traditional paper-based document, the blog can provide more than an archival component. Examining researcher Wendy Hsu's blog (http://beingwendyhsu.info), one can see that in addition to having automatic time and date stamps, a researcher can benefit

(Continued)

(Continued)

from blogging and receiving input of others. The researcher can gain additional context and perspective on the data from global positioning software applications that can be connected to one's camera. Hsu explained that she used a "two-phase method" that involved gathering online data, filtering it using a program she designed, and then mapping that data using geospatial visualization:

> Phase 1 is web-scraping, the process of mining data from the Internet. This process entails first, locating a source of useful geographic data, and then harvesting this information programmatically. I was interested in two sets of data, specifically: the physical location of the band's performance tours; and the self-reported (physical) location of the friends in an online community. . . . Phase 2—geospatial visualization—is the process of turning the harvested data into a meaningful visualization. Using OpenLayers, an open-source mapping program, I created a dynamic map containing all the points of the physical locations of the band's MySpace friends and performance tours. To contextualize the reading of the physical points, I added various map layers. For example, I added a Google Street Map layer to label the visualization with the proper name of countries and cities. The rest of my efforts were spent to refine the map, to make it readable and meaningful. (http://beingwendyhsu .info/?p=432)

What comes to the fore is that with ever-developing technologies, there are increasing possibilities to track and trace layers of meaning making. Hsu's work appeals to the online-offline connection and the ability for researchers to view data from different vantage points, something that also is highlighted in the upcoming discussion about databases.

Interviews

In qualitative studies, interviews offer researchers insight into what is "in and on someone else's mind" (Patton, 2002, p. 341). Though observation can provide vital information related to learning practices in specific contexts, it typically does not elicit or reveal an individual's thoughts, beliefs, and intentions. Consequently, an interview is "a process in which a researcher and a participant engage in a conversation focused on questions related to a research study" (deMarrais, 2004, p. 55). Maxwell (2013) made the important distinction between research questions and interview questions, calling attention to the purpose: "Your research questions formulate what you want to understand; your interview questions are what you ask people to gain that understanding" (p. 101).

Creswell (2013) suggested that researchers first decide what questions will be answered by interviews, and then identify participants who can best answer these questions based on one of the purposeful sampling procedures. He then argued that researchers should determine what type of interview will be most practical and result in the most useful information, such as a telephone interview, a focus group interview, a one-on-one interview, or an online interview. He emphasized the use of adequate recording procedures and the design and use of an interview protocol that includes five to seven open-ended questions that have been refined through pilot testing. Yin (2009) recommended a pilot test to develop clear lines of questions and refine data collection procedures; pilot cases are often selected on the basis of convenience and access.

Qualitative inquiry may involve synchronous interviews that occur face-to-face, over video chat, or via instant messenger; or it may involve asynchronous interviews that take place over email (see Spotlight Box 5.2). In addition, the choice of interview format may be dependent on what is permitted by individual ethics review committees. Hewson and Laurent (2008) noted that online communication is primarily text-based, which tends to lead to a reduction in the amount of information available from extralinguistic cues in face-to-face communication. Whereas this may constrain online research and result in ambiguities and misunderstandings, it may also offer heightened levels of anonymity and perceived privacy, which in turn may increase research participants' candor and self-disclosure. Similarly, researchers must decide whether interviews will take place synchronously or asynchronously in online spaces. Flick (2009) posited that online chat rooms come the closest to face-to-face communication, given the real-time nature of the exchange; unlike in-person interviews, however, there may be additional limits due to participants' multitasking, typing speed, or time zones. Hanna (2012) argued that video chat can allow participants to be interviewed at the time and location of their choice, but technical difficulties can be problematic.

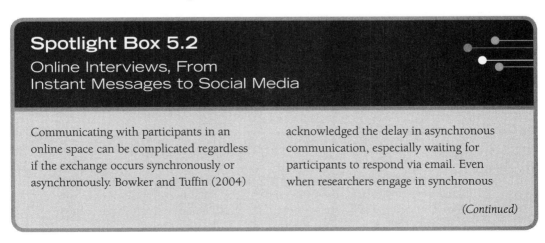

Spotlight Box 5.2
Online Interviews, From Instant Messages to Social Media

Communicating with participants in an online space can be complicated regardless if the exchange occurs synchronously or asynchronously. Bowker and Tuffin (2004) acknowledged the delay in asynchronous communication, especially waiting for participants to respond via email. Even when researchers engage in synchronous

(Continued)

(Continued)

communication, there can be unpredictable behavior or delayed responses. Abrams (2010) had similar experiences when she used text messaging to communicate with adolescents at their discretion, and some participants began and ended the conversations unexpectedly. Though Hewson (2014) noted that with Internet-mediated research, asynchronous methods have been more prevalent than real-time approaches, synchronous interaction with participants has proven to be beneficial for collecting data within sites that rely on internal messaging.

For instance, Merchant (2010) looked to in-world chat logs to capture internal chat between participants in the virtual world of Barnsborough. Chat logs, as well as other forms of static documentation, provide a "textual format of naturalistic data" that supports thorough data collection, namely the absence of transcription bias (Bowker & Tuffin, 2004, p. 230). Snapshots of discourse also can extend to researcher-to-researcher text message jottings, which provide immediate reflections that are collaboratively deliberated and expanded, supporting the refinement of semi-structured interview questions and the codevelopment of inductive analyses (Abrams & Gerber, 2014).

One qualitative study may combine different design elements. For instance, in Curwood's (2013a, 2013b, 2014b) study of the Hunger Games fandom, she began with email-based interviews with young adults about their literacy practices. This allowed her to save time and transcription costs while quickly accessing research participants from around the world. Subsequent interviews then occurred over Skype and allowed her to build rapport with participants.

In other studies, the nature of interviews has been dictated by participant preferences, research decisions, or study aims. Hewson and Laurent (2008) stated, "Asynchronous approaches allow respondents to participate at times convenient to themselves, to potentially engage in greater levels of reflectivity and reflexivity, and to consult external documents and sources" (p. 68). However, they also noted that this approach to interviewing does not allow for conversational flow or for quick interactions between researchers and participants. Kazmer and Xie (2008) added that asynchronous approaches, such as email interviews, may increase participant attrition since there are multiple points when participants can be lost. These times include when the researcher ends the call for participation, requests the consent form, sends the list of initial interview questions, and shares follow-up questions.

In qualitative inquiry, interview questions may be highly structured, semi-structured, or unstructured (see Table 5.3). Notably, "an interviewer's questions and interviewing style shape the context, frame, and content of the study" (Charmaz, 2003, p. 317). Charmaz argued that "framing questions takes skill

Table 5.3	Interview Structures	
Highly Structured	**Semi-Structured**	**Unstructured**
Predetermined wording and order of questions	A mix of more and less structured questions; no predetermined wording or order	Open-ended questions, similar to a conversation
Interview is the oral form of a written survey	All questions are used flexibly	Flexible and exploratory
Usually used to obtain demographic data	Usually specific data is required from participants	Used primarily in ethnography and case study approaches

Source: Adapted from Merriam, 1998.

and practice" and emphasized the need to ask questions that "both explore the interviewer's topic and fit the participant's experience" (p. 315).

Depending on the focus of the study, interview questions often include the following three categories: (1) introductory questions, which are neutral and seek background information on participants; (2) questions that directly relate to the study; here, researchers may explicitly ask for more information, reformulate participant statements, ask for examples and counterexamples, and point out contradiction; (3) closing questions, which ask participants to "either supplement earlier talk or introduce something that is relevant but has not really been addressed earlier in the interview: ideas, reflections, suggestions for further work" (Alvesson, 2011, p. 55). However, this structure is not prescriptive; a qualitative study may begin with open-ended interviews to learn more about the group as a whole in order to narrow down what to study and how to focus the inquiry. Alternatively, the study may start with highly structured questions to identify key themes that are then followed up during later in-depth interviews (Alvesson, 2011).

Michael Patton (2002) suggested six types of interview questions: (1) experience and behavior; (2) opinion and values; (3) feelings; (4) knowledge; (5) sensory; and (6) background and demographic. Patton recommends against asking *why* questions, as they may lead to speculation about causal relationships and to dead-end responses. In Lammers's (2012, 2013) study of Sims fanfiction writers, she used semi-structured interview questions to investigate writers' backgrounds and their experiences with fanfiction writing and multimedia content creation. Her follow-up questions targeted their participation within fanfiction writing communities to gain insight into their learning processes and literacy practices (see Figure 5.3). In line with Patton's (2002) typology of interview questions, Lammers asked a variety of questions to gain a holistic understanding of fanfiction writers' beliefs and practices.

Alvesson (2011) noted that any interview involves "an interplay between two people, each with their own gender, age, professional background, personal appearance, and ethnicity, [which] puts a heavy imprint on the accounts produced" (p. 80). Researchers should remember that interviews will be shaped by any number of factors, from their own identity to how the questions are posed to participants. For this reason, researchers must take time between interviews to reflect on what worked well, what can be improved, what questions to add, and how the interviews addressed the study's research questions (see Figures 5.2 and 5.3).

Surveys

The main purpose of a survey is to gather information about a population. Like interviews, surveys involve collecting self-reported information from individuals. According to Marshall and Rossman (2006), "In deciding to survey a group of people, researchers make one critical assumption—that a characteristic or belief can be described or measured accurately through self-reporting. In using questionnaires, researchers rely totally on the honesty and accuracy of participants' responses" (p. 125). For this reason, surveys and questionnaires—which Wolcott (2008) delineates as more formal and standardized (surveys) and less formal and semi-structured (questionnaires)—often serve as tools for triangulation in studies with multiple data sources. In online research, surveys and questionnaires cannot offer substantial insight into complex social relationships or intricate patterns of interaction, but they can be instrumental in collecting quantitative and qualitative data as well as in identifying typical or exceptional cases for further study. For example, Hargittai's (2010) survey of college students established that even those generationally labeled "digital natives" have a wide range of Internet expertise. This work revealed a need for small and in-depth studies of Internet sites to examine this diversity of experiences.

Online surveys can offer significant improvements over traditional pen-and-paper surveys (Vehover & Manfreda, 2008). This is evident in terms of the design, such as self-administration, question skips and filters, randomization of answers, and inclusion of multimedia resources, as well as the fact that answers are immediately stored in a database. This can save time and costs while reducing the likelihood of transcription errors or lost data. There are a number of free and cost-effective websites that qualitative researchers can use, including SurveyMonkey, SurveyGizmo, or SurveyMoz. Depending on the study's ethics protocol and the focal website's terms and conditions, researchers may elect to distribute information about the survey through an online, publicly accessible post or private communication with prospective research participants.

Depending on the study's research questions and sampling procedures, surveys can be a useful way to gain insight into learners' beliefs and practices in online spaces. In terms of the survey design, researchers can take a cross-sectional measurement at a single point in time or longitudinal measurements at several

ONLINE INTERVIEW PROTOCOL

I appreciate your time in providing responses to the following questions. Please type your responses below each question, and use as much space as you need. Thank you!

Some General Questions about You

- How would you describe the area where you live: urban, rural, or suburban?
- What grade or year are you in school?
- What is/are your most favorite subject(s) in school?
- What is/are your least favorite subject(s) in school?
- What are your future plans for education? What are your future career plans?

Start of Your Sims Activities

- When did you first start playing The Sims? What prompted you to start playing?
- When did you first starting visiting fan sites? What sites did you visit, and what prompted you to look at them?
- When did you start creating stories, and what got you started?
- What were the first kinds of stories you created?
- What other Sims activities have you done/do you do? (For example, create custom content, create Sims movies, etc.)

Your Current Sims Activities

- What versions of The Sims (including expansion packs) do you have?
- How much time do you typically spend per week on playing The Sims, creating content/writing stories/etc., and participating in Sims fansites?
- What has motivated you to participate in these activities over time?
- When do you fit your Sims activities into your schedule?
- Where do you host your Sims creations? (For example: Do you have a Sim Page on the EA site? A Flickr photostream for your Sims images? Your own website/blog that you use to display your Sims creations?)

Learning to Create Sims Content

- What have been the most valuable resources in helping you learn to create content/write stories/other?
- What software tools do you use?
- What have you learned most recently?
- What has been the most difficult thing for you to learn? How did you overcome this challenge?

(Continued)

Figure 5.2 (Continued)

- What computer-related skills have you learned from creating Sims content?
- Have you used what you have learned from making Sims content in any other area of your life? If so, please describe.
- [Prompt (if needed): Have you used what you've learned in school? Has anything you've learned in school been helpful in your Sims content creation?]

Figure 5.3 Follow-Up Online Interview Protocol Used by Lammers (2012, 2013)

FOLLOW-UP ONLINE INTERVIEW

I appreciate your time in providing responses to the following questions. Please type your responses below each question, and use as much space as you need. Your responses will help clarify some of the activities you mentioned in your responses to the first set of questions. Thank you!

The Sims fan communities

- When did you first discover the __(insert website name here)__ fan community? What made you want to be a part of this community?
- How did you figure out how to participate in __(insert website name here)__? Did you read their rules? Did you spend time reading what others had posted?
- What parts of the site do you visit most frequently? Has your use of the site changed over time? How?
- (If staff member) How did you become a staff member for the site? What is your role?

Interaction with other Sims fans

- What forms of communication do you use with other people on The Sims fan sites (such as writing in guestbooks, posting in forums, blogging, participating in chat events, email)?
- How do you communicate with other Sims fans beyond the fan site (if at all)?
- How often do you give others help and advice on content creation/story writing/other? Can you provide a recent example?

Learning

- If you use online tutorials, what makes a tutorial particularly helpful or useful for you?
- Could you name (and provide links to) one or two of the tutorials that you've found most helpful?
- Is there any one approach that you find yourself doing first when you try to learn new content creation/want to learn how to do something for writing stories/other?
- Was there anything that you tried to learn related to Sims content creation/story writing/ other, and weren't able to do?

- Can you tell us about any kind of content creation/story production technique/other that you haven't even considering pursuing? Why haven't you chosen to pursue this?
- Is there anything that you would like to learn to create, but haven't yet? What might you need before your pursue this?

Computing skills

- How would you rate your own computer skills in relation to other people you know? Please mark your self-rating on the following scale:

1	2	3	4	5
Basic	Average	Intermediate	Advanced	Superior

- How confident do you feel about your ability to learn new computer-related skills?
- How often do people in your life ask you for advice or help with computers or software?

We have just a couple of other questions.

- What do others in your life think of your Sims activities?
- To what extent do you consider yourself a "gamer"? Do others consider you to be a gamer? Why?

Source: Unpublished protocols courtesy of Jayne C. Lammers.

different times. While the former offers insight into how various individuals learn, the latter provides information about how these learning practices may change over time. Groves (1989) outlined common errors in survey design, which often occur when some part of the population is not included within the sample (see Table 5.4). When surveys are administered online, it reduces the likelihood of measurement errors; however, it is the researcher's responsibility to ensure accurate coverage, informed sampling procedures, and response rates.

With online research, quantitative data can be useful in shedding light on qualitative data. For instance, Biddolph and Curwood (in press) used a survey at the beginning of their study to understand how secondary school English teachers used social media as part of their professional learning. This allowed them to gain insight into specific Twitter chats and hashtags that teachers frequently used and also offered them a way to recruit interview participants. Surveys may contain open-ended questions where participants formulate their own response; for instance, "How do you use Khan Academy to improve your mathematics knowledge?" They may also contain closed-ended questions with single or multiple responses. For example, a Likert-type scale question may ask participants to respond to the following statement on a scale from 1 (strongly disagree) to 5 (strongly agree): "Khan Academy has improved my mathematics knowledge." Compared to paper-based surveys, online surveys offer a range of response options, including plain-text typed entry, typed entry boxes, check boxes, radio buttons, pull-down menus, and graphical rating systems (Best & Krueger, 2008).

Table 5.4 Sources of Survey Error	
Type of Error	**Definition**
Coverage	The failure to give any chance of sample selection to some persons in the population
Sampling	Heterogeneity on the survey measure among persons in the population
Nonresponse	The failure to collect data on all persons in the sample
Measurement	Inaccuracies in responses recorded on the survey instruments

Source: Groves, 1989.

Artifacts

Online field sites offer researchers ample data. One of the key challenges with data collection involves capturing, organizing, and accessing multiple forms of data. In addition to observations, interviews, and surveys, artifacts can be an important data source for online qualitative inquiry. Pahl and Rowsell (2011a) proposed that an artifactual approach examines "objects and their meanings in everyday life" as well as "the situated nature of texts in places and communities" (p. 130). In this light, artifacts are instrumental to meaning making and inextricably linked to contexts and interactions. Contemporary researchers have found that video screen captures, screenshots, and still images are instrumental in capturing artifact data and tracing learning within online spaces. Given the impermanence of online data, these approaches allow researchers to collect artifacts before they are modified, archived, or deleted.

Blogs are reminiscent of online journals, enabling users to enumerate their reflections and insights in a space with a relatively "organic and unstructured format" (Williams & Jacobs, 2004). In this way, blogs began with a seemingly unidirectional component; the author would write a blog, and others would read. The comment function, however, allows for others to provide feedback and contribute to the conversation, and the "like" and "share" features suggest that blogs can be distributed and assume a potentially unknown trajectory. Though blogs are often seen as journal alternatives, they also are spaces for chronicling site-specific insights and activities, and they "may arguably be treated as either a document or an ongoing social interaction" (Hewson, 2014, p. 435). Lammers (2012) reported how some Sims participants blogged to capture what they were learning and doing with The Sims 2. Notably, these websites were part of a developing infrastructure hosting Sims-related content.

Like the Sims posts, blogs in general are written for specific audiences and "enable dialogue and even co-production between authors and readers"

(Hookway, 2008, p. 96). Because blogs often provide public access to a user-generated text, researchers can have relatively easy access to longitudinal chronicles of participants' practices. Though some may question the veracity of blog content, as authors may post fictitious information, Hookway (2008) reminded us that regardless if what is posted is "true," the important question to ask is "whether a researcher is looking at how blogs work to produce particular effects or whether they are looking at how blogs correspond with an 'offline' reality" (p. 97). In either case, the content of the online posting typically is related to the author's purpose and audience, and shades of truth or deceit may be connected to online or offline cultures, identities, or constructs.

Video screen captures are a useful tool to show how individuals navigate online spaces and interact with the virtual environment. Though screen capture software can record moving images and mouse/controller/cursor movements, recording on-screen observations may not be simple, especially when the researcher is not online and/or the activity is taking place through a medium that does not have screen capture capabilities (e.g., some older gaming consoles). Additionally, as Gerber (2008) found in her study of adolescent males' gaming and literacy practices, screen capture software programs can slow down the computing power for participants who are engaging in games that run heavy programs on their computers, thus interfering with both gameplay and data collection. Video recording the on-screen activity with an external camera can be a good alternative.

Recording on-screen behavior is similar to taking a screenshot of a particular artifact; however, the dynamic nature of moving images also enables the researcher to home in on and replay specific data points, as Abrams has in her research of videogaming (see Figure 5.4). Marsh (2010, 2012) examined the children's Club Penguin gaming from an offline stance. She visited children in their homes and recorded their on-screen movements. Simultaneously, she observed students as they played, examining gaze directionality. Walsh and Simpson (2013) used photos and video to capture children's creation of digital texts on "touch pads" in the classroom. As noted in Chapter Three and in Spotlight Box 5.3, Abrams (2009a, 2009b, 2015) recorded adolescents' on-screen videogame play. She immediately followed it with a stimulated recall technique (Lyle, 2003) to understand videogaming behavior, namely players' on-screen decisions, interactions, and movement.

In addition to video screen captures, screenshots can provide a static (as opposed to moving) image of the screen at a particular point in time. Researchers have relied on this feature to record chat logs, emails, text messages, instant messages, and online forms, to name a few. Often facilitated using tools available on most computers (e.g., the snipping tool on most PCs; command-shift-4 or command-shift-5 on Macs), the static image can prove helpful in the analysis of written artifacts created in an online space. For example, Wargo (2015) provided screenshots of participants' Snapchat photographs, as well as physical maps

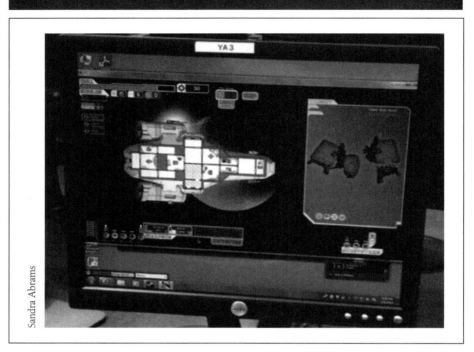

Sandra Abrams

Spotlight Box 5.3
Capturing Dynamic Learning With Stimulated Recall

Though useful for tapping into the ways people read and write, think-aloud protocols have been found not to be helpful for measuring the cognitive processes of time-constrained situations that involve complex interaction (Lyle, 2003). Abrams (2009a, 2009b), therefore, applied the stimulated recall method to elicit student reflection and critique of their gaming sessions.

Upon commencement of participants' videogame play, Abrams (2009a, 2009b) recorded the screen (in a similar fashion to the example in Figure 5.4), using a tripod to keep the recording device steady. She noted the time stamps of moments when players made particular moves or voiced comments or concerns to each other or to themselves. At the end of a set period of time she had agreed on with participants (e.g., twenty-five minutes or three rounds of gameplay), she replayed the footage on a monitor. She asked the adolescent gamers to explain their moves and feelings about their gameplay, and, when necessary, she paused the video when she reached a particular time stamp to ask participants specific questions about their actions and reactions. All the while, Abrams audiorecorded the stimulated recall interview session.

This technique provided the researcher a window into the adolescents' decision making and the experiences that influenced their moves. It also privileged gamer knowledge and honored game space practices. Offline recordings of participants' use of online tools can provide insight into the offline behavior associated with online endeavors (Abrams, 2011). Additionally, the recordings can call attention to how the environment and physical infrastructure (e.g., the positioning of the technology in the room, the presence of wires) contribute to or interfere with online activities (Flewitt, 2011).

of where those images were produced, to illustrate the Snapstories that they composed (see Figure 5.5).

Research of online meaning making often hinges on participants' self-selected data, which typically honors a co-constructed understanding of participant-generated texts. The use of participant-generated photos has been used in research of young children to investigate and depict physical space

Figure 5.5 Wargo's (2015) Visual Representation of a Participant's Snapstory

Snapchat images overlaid on a Google Map of the story's physical space.

and participant reflection (Cappello & Hollingsworth, 2008; Einarsdottir, 2005). Barton's (2012) content analysis of adults using Flickr 365 included the examination of participants' self-uploaded photos to the image-hosting website. He found that the photos supported the generation of reflection and feedback. Turner, Abrams, Katic, and Donovan's (2014) examination of teens' digital discourse (also known as Digitalk) stemmed from teens' self-selected samples of their communication from a variety of sources, including social networking sites, emails, and text messages.

In online qualitative research, some artifact data is publicly available and readily accessible; at other times, access is contingent on participant cooperation. Given that participants' perception of data (and the data they *think* researchers want) can influence the artifacts they provide, multiple sources are especially important. Thus, as in the aforementioned studies, participant-selected data works in concert with researcher-driven techniques, such as observation, interview, and surveys.

Conclusion

For researchers, it is essential to understand and account for trustworthiness and rigor. Throughout the process of data collection, they are guided by their theoretical framework, their research questions, and their logic of inquiry. Contemporary digital tools and online spaces offer researchers access to a variety of data sources. They must decide how a combination of observations, interviews, surveys, and artifacts can offer insight into learning practices across sites, modes, and texts. As noted earlier, learning in online social worlds often allows for agency, self-direction, and collaboration. By tracing learning within and across networked field sites, and collected multiple data sources, contemporary researchers can gain significant insight into the practices and process involved in meaning making.

CONNECTING TO YOUR WORK ──────

As a researcher interested in studying learning in online spaces, you will need to consider what types of data will allow you to address your research questions. Depending on the boundaries of your field site, and the access that you have to online spaces and research participants, you might collect multiple data sources to strive for trustworthiness in your research. Consider the following questions:

- Given your field site, what kinds of data sources can you collect?

- What features of the field site might make data collection challenging?

- What data sources will allow you to best answer your research questions?

- What digital tools can facilitate data collection?

- As a researcher, how can you ensure the rigor and trustworthiness of your findings?

Guiding Questions for Chapter 6

- What types of data analysis are available to researchers in online spaces?
- How should qualitative researchers in online spaces conceptualize their tools for data analysis?
- How can researchers assure that the data they collect will be appropriate for the kind of data analysis in which they hope to engage?
- How can researchers in online spaces begin to formulate a plan for data analysis from the beginning of their studies?

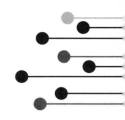

What Analytical Approaches Are Available for Data Analysis?

Introduction

In this chapter, we offer a description of several analytical methods that are useful when designing open-ended, qualitative research studies. Beginning with a philosophical discussion of data analysis plans for research studies, this chapter offers several analytical frameworks that work well for studies that rely on naturalistic data sources. These methods may be used alone or remixed in creative ways to allow researchers to ask more complex research questions or examine multiple facets of participants' learning experiences. The chapter focuses on thematic analysis, grounded theory, discourse analysis, multimodal analysis, and artifactual analysis. It also examines studies that use multimethod approaches and quantitative methods to describe the learning and participation that happens in large online sites, such as Scratch (e.g., Kafai, Fields, Roque, Burke, & Monroy-Hernández, 2012), as well as sites of mass collaboration, like Scratch and Fanfiction. net (e.g., Kafai & Peppler, 2011; Magnifico, Curwood, & Lammers, 2015).

Moving From Data Collection to Analysis

As researchers begin to think about choosing site(s) for understanding particular forms of online learning, writing their research questions, and crafting general approaches to data collection, it is also useful to consider how such decisions will shape the approach to data analysis. Though at first it may seem premature to identify a beginning analytic approach before any data have been collected, it is useful to do so to maintain clear ideas about the logic of inquiry (Bloome, Power-Carter, Christian, Otto, & Shuart-Faris, 2005; Gee & Green, 1998) of the overall study, as mentioned in Chapter One of this book.

The remainder of this chapter focuses on presenting analytical methods that online researchers have often found useful, and it pays particular attention to the ways in which the analysis of data gathered in online spaces may be distinct from data gathered in face-to-face spaces. It is important to remember, however, that no single analytical approach is predictable or universal. Researchers, especially those who are interested in studying learning in online spaces, are often working with research situations and research questions that are fluid (for more on fluidity in these spaces, see Chapter Two and Chapter Four). Researchers may find themselves immersed in capturing a variety of facets of learning and communication because the context of their study is not yet clearly defined by prior research.

For instance, many scholars seek to understand how online learning is similar to or different from face-to-face learning of similar topics. What do students gain when their school makes a course available online? What do they lose? How can these changes be documented? In situations like these, a researcher's initial predictions about her or his questions, perspectives, or findings may shift significantly as data are collected and analysis begins. This flux can be frustrating, but, at the same time, it may mean that valuable knowledge is in the offing.

As Jennifer Greene (2007) noted in *Mixed Methods in Social Inquiry*, maintaining a pragmatic and dialectical approach to mixing methods and theoretical orientations can allow researchers to open up a broad conversation in which it is possible to generate new insights about learning that might be impossible to see from the perspective of a single tradition. Constructing mixed method or multimethod (Creswell, 2015) studies may help researchers to view online learning and participation in new, creative ways. As online spaces for learning continue to change and evolve, the theoretical frameworks and methods that researchers use to study these spaces should change and evolve as well.

In the next sections, we describe several analytical methods that are open-ended, typical to qualitative research in online spaces, and likely to be useful components of the analytical framework for a new study: thematic analysis, grounded theory analysis, discourse analysis, multimodal analysis, and artifactual analysis. It would, however, be impossible to explore fully all of the facets of qualitative data analysis in the short space of one chapter (or even in one text). Many excellent complementary texts have been written, both about individual methods and about qualitative research more broadly. Greene's (2007) *Mixed Methods in Social Inquiry,* cited earlier in this section and in Chapter One, offers a very readable guide to thinking about how building mental models of inquiry and using various methods together can help researchers to make and triangulate meanings within a study.

In addition, Graham Gibbs's (2007) *Analyzing Qualitative Data* and Matthew B. Miles, A. Michael Huberman, and Johnny Saldaña's (2014) *Qualitative Data Analysis: A Methods Sourcebook* are broad, seminal texts that offer insight into the fundamentals of qualitative data analysis. Finally, Johnny Saldaña's (2013) *The Coding Manual for Qualitative Researchers* presents a paradigm- and method-neutral description of several approaches that researchers can take to coding, which usually represents the first phase of any data analysis. Single-method guides and guides to software designed for qualitative analysis (e.g., Atlas.ti, Nudist, NVivo, QDA Miner), too, provide important detail and supplementary reading once a method and approach have been selected.

Considering Data Analysis
in Networked Field Sites

It is important for researchers to consider designs of and uses for research in online spaces. Because the information and interactions to which researchers can gain access in online spaces are constantly evolving, interpretive methods of meaning making are particularly useful tools for building understanding. Designers and users of online spaces have the ability to change and innovate in a variety of ways, and they often do so to modify their online surroundings. Even designers of established sites may redesign or modify their practices when various situations change, such as the availability of new web technologies, social networks, or kinds of access to each other (e.g., groups of users who find themselves in the same physical location, such as Coursera MOOC study groups who use Meetup.com to organize local face-to-face meetings).

In such places where designs, conversations, and modes of learning may remain unsettled throughout a research study, qualitative and naturalistic methods for understanding learners' contexts, practices, and actions are particularly useful. As explained in Chapter Five, the reality of "life online" (Markham, 1998) presents significant challenges for study design, data collection, and data analysis. How is it possible for researchers to develop a clear data collection and analysis plan when they might not be confident about the stability of the online cultural context that lies at the center of the study?

One thing that is important to remember about data analysis in online and blended spaces (see Chapter Two for more on conceptualizing online spaces as networked field sites for studying learning) is that like the spaces themselves, techniques for conducting such analyses have changed rapidly over a short number of years. It has now become expected that data points gathered from online spaces will include multimodal components. Whether or not researchers choose to give equal focus to all of the modes employed in an online environment (for instance: page layout, images, text, audio, and various kinds of video), all of these modes are likely to be present as meaningful forms of online communication.

For example, to think carefully about how different modes contribute to users' (and researchers') meaning making, Steinkuehler, Black, and Clinton (2005) considered how several digital, multimodal environments provided new opportunities for website users and videogame players to develop literacies. Examining three different and common ways of interacting online—using sites based on alphabetic text like Fanfiction.net, massively multiplayer online games (MMOs) like Lineage or World of Warcraft, and single-player games like Grand Theft Auto or Prince of Persia—they explored how Markham's (2003) tool, place, and way of being metaphors for the Internet could also describe three ways of becoming "literate" in diverse digital spaces.

Research on literacy in MMOs might involve the examination of how play reflects "participation in a multimodal and digital textual place, one with fuzzy boundaries that expand with continued play" (Steinkuehler, Black, & Clinton, 2005, p. 98). Research on single-player videogames, on the other hand, might include documenting players' online identities as they are projected into new worlds and avatars. Black's related work (2008, 2009) focused primarily on her participants' written texts and how they used tools such as genres and media. She showed how written modes of communication were most important for young fanfiction authors, even while they interacted in a multimodal space (see Spotlight Box 6.2). Researchers today often have more leeway in what to analyze—increased data storage space, for instance, has made screen recording a more viable data collection strategy—but may make similar choices to focus their research questions and data collection on modes that seem most central to learning or participation.

As discussed in Chapters Four and Five, current online spaces often become networked field sites in qualitative research studies—complex mixtures of social networking, archived contributions, and topic-focused content. Researchers may need to draw on a variety of data sources and think about how to combine analytical methods in a multimethod approach (Creswell, 2015) to make meaning from these complex research situations. Traditionally, many qualitative researchers have thus taken up a "bricolage" framework for research, bringing methods together and considering how such combinations strengthen the researcher's analytical lens (Denzin & Lincoln, 2000; Kincheloe, 2001). Similarly, mixed methods researchers often have referred to pragmatic frameworks to focus on data collection and analytical methods that most closely correspond to the research questions (Johnson & Onwuegbuzie, 2004; Morgan, 2007).

Researchers' beliefs, as well as their research questions and knowledge of current contributions, are the clearest guides to developing data collection and data analysis protocols, as discussed extensively in Chapter Four. Different kinds of research questions may be more or less difficult to study online, and necessary precursors to a data analysis plan include a sound rendering of researchers' understandings of the particular space and a clearly articulated rationale, logic of inquiry, and methodological framework for the study. It also may be useful for researchers to consider how they plan to articulate and implement particular facets of the inquiry and to identify potential difficulties up front.

Thematic Analysis

As mentioned in Chapter Five, online and face-to-face observation and interviews are key components of data collection when researchers are interested in qualitatively capturing and understanding the ways in which participants become engaged in learning environments. These data are particularly useful in networked field sites where participants, sites, modes of interaction, or research questions may shift over time (as many online environments do), and they lend themselves to methods of data analysis that leave space for member checking and evolving interpretations. Given that researchers do not always enter into new studies with hypotheses about participants' activities or the learning that results, more open-ended investigation methods are both useful and appropriate.

Thematic analysis is one such approach. This kind of analysis is an open-ended qualitative technique that can be useful for flexibly sorting and grouping initial findings. Once a researcher has completed initial coding, a thematic approach can help to organize these codes into larger patterns and interpretations. As Saldaña (2013) indicated, "A theme is an outcome of coding, categorization, and analytic reflection, not something that is, in itself, coded" (p. 175). Even while working across data points that include online conversations, patterns of interactions or activities, interviews, and screenshots, themes can unify and identify groups of codes that belong together as parts of a pattern of recurring or common experiences. Because individual codes or pieces of data might be too small to have analytic power alone, bringing them together under the rubric of a theoretically (or experientially) generated theme helps to give them meaning and make sense of the larger setting (Boyatzis, 1998; DeSantis & Ugarizza, 2000).

Many articles and books have discussed the utility of thematic analyses. Researchers who wish to pursue this method may find it useful to do further reading on the different ways in which it has been conceived and used, including the following:

- Saldaña (2013): *The Coding Manual for Qualitative Researchers*

- Guest, MacQueen, & Namey (2012): *Applied Thematic Analysis*

- Braun & Clarke (2006): "Using Thematic Analysis in Psychology"

- Boyatzis (1998): *Transforming Qualitative Information: Thematic Analysis and Code Development*

- Aronson (1994): "A Pragmatic View of Thematic Analysis"

This process of "theming" the data can be especially useful in complex online studies that are conducted across various aspects of a networked field site—perhaps portals of an affinity space or a connected learning site. During such inquiry, researchers may create a data set from a variety of interactions, impressions, and interpretations that may not initially seem to fit particularly well together. As Boyatzis (1998) explained, "Because qualitative methods are often used in early stages of inquiry and to examine unusual or complex phenomena, the degree to which the information represents the phenomenon becomes an interpretive dilemma requiring theoretical as well as empirical support or justification of the sample studied" (p. 54).

Generating themes is one such way to build interpretive power, helping researchers to bring together theoretical frameworks and diverse data in early analyses and preliminary findings. It is important, however, for researchers to keep track of their theoretical assumptions. For example, is it a postpositivist account where reality is seen as stable, or a postmodern account where all "reality" is seen as constructed? Researchers also must be mindful of the saturation and prevalence of particular themes. For example, does the theme appear for all participants, or does it describe one or two participants' experiences? Do some participants have divergent stories that challenge the theme?

In addition, thematic analysis can be useful for researchers who are working to triangulate themes across data types. Spotlight Box 6.1, "Figment as a Multi-Sited Writing Space," examines this kind of work, showing how Magnifico (in press) coded postings from several loosely connected Internet sources to begin to map the affinity space of Figment.com. In other words, does looking solely at, say, participant interviews suggest one type of interpretation of a theme, while looking at discussion board posts suggest something different? Such comparisons can increase the trustworthiness of a researcher's interpretive coding processes. As mentioned in Chapter Five, researchers must note their sampling procedures and how these actions may affect the interpretations that they build during data analysis.

Questions to begin theming data include the following:

- What tools do participants use in this online space, and to what ends (e.g., spreadsheets, CSS code, hashtags)?

- What portals do participants use in this online space, and to what ends (e.g., Instagram, DeviantArt, a certain discussion board)?

- How, if at all, do participants take common actions (e.g., sharing particular kinds of problems, posting memes)?

- How, if at all, do participants use common markers of identity (e.g., similar avatars or genres)?

- What is happening in particular kinds of data (e.g., how does the group use Twitter)?

Grounded Theory Analysis

Constant comparison is one technique that is often employed in grounded theory studies. Grounded theory is an approach to qualitative research

Magnifico's (in press) thematic analysis of Figment.com examined the design of and public data associated with Figment, an online writing space aimed at young authors who write original fiction and fanfiction. Figment describes its own reach as "everywhere," allowing members to share their writing across a variety of popular social networks, including Facebook, Twitter, and Tumblr. She was primarily interested in the site as an intentional example of an affinity space; that is, an online space that stretches across portals by virtue of a design with a central site with links to social media where authors can socialize and share their stories more widely or for different audiences. Magnifico initially worked with two research questions.

1. How is the writing community of Figment structured or designed, and which structures seem especially salient to participants?

2. How are sites that are affiliated with Figment linked together in an affinity space?

To address these questions, she collected a variety of observations across several portals. She documented participation with screenshots, worked to determine connections among these artifacts, and wrote field notes and memos to capture events, interpretations, and various legitimate ways of participating in the Figment affinity space. The open-ended research questions helped her consider the practical, descriptive, and theoretical interests of the study.

To develop a better sense of participation across Figment's multiple sites for site-to-member and member-to-member contact, Magnifico conducted a thematic content analysis (Boyatzis, 1998; Saldaña, 2013) using observations from Figment users' most popular portals: Twitter, Tumblr, and The Daily Fig site blog. Beginning with descriptive coding of the official site account's communications, this analysis refined and triangulated meanings across the site content from different portals. The first codes were very specific (e.g., "Harry Potter fandom," "graphic mashup," "re-tweet of literary content"), and these were gradually refined into general themes that crossed portals (e.g., "books and literary" codes highlighted when users posted about reading various novels). These themes coalesced into patterns of typical actions that Figment participants were able to take.

While Figment presents itself as a unified writing space that encourages its writers to share their work across several social networks, this study documented that few of the writers actually did so. In fact,

(Continued)

(Continued)

while the Twitter, Tumblr, and main site portals— different parts of the broader Figment network—shared broad interests, few writers interacted across these portals or within multiple social networks. In this way, quantifying the contents of different posts by using a method like Chi's (1997) verbal analysis can allow researchers to understand the prevalence of various types of speech or action in which participants engage (see Figure 6.1).

These qualitative analyses presented a complex, conflicting picture of the context in which writing occurs in the Figment online community, and suggest that "affinity spaces," while they may host participation in many portals, may not look particularly unified around a "common endeavour" (Gee, 2004; Lammers, Curwood, & Magnifico, 2012). This multimodal observation, screenshot-gathering, coding, and theming were important for triangulating data from multiple portals (see Figure 6.2). When a coherent central story failed to emerge, these data helped to illustrate disconnects between the main site's apparent goals for participants—sharing writing *across* multiple networks—and the ways in which the participants in the different portals interacted with Figment users and representatives.

that initially was developed by sociologists Glaser and Strauss (1967) and has been extended by several others (e.g., Charmaz, 2000, 2006; Strauss & Corbin, 1990). Johnson and Christensen (2008) contended that the foundational question for a grounded theory analysis is: "What theory or explanation emerges from an analysis of the data collected about this phenomenon?" (p. 410). This direction is important for researchers to note, as it stresses the concept of **theory generation**, a central element of grounded theory studies. To generate theory directly from data, traditional grounded theory recommends that researchers avoid developing a priori codes or even conducting a literature review before beginning data analysis. Grounded theory analysis is meant to be as free as possible from presuppositions drawn from literature or existing theories. Researchers inductively study the collected data to better understand phenomena, events, or situations.

Many articles and books have discussed the utility of grounded theory. Understandings of this methodology have shifted considerably over time, however, largely because several scholars have pursued somewhat different formulas for what makes a successful grounded theory study. Researchers who are interested in the evolution of this conversation or wish to pursue

Figure 6.1   Data Spreadsheet of Themes

	A	B	C	D	E	F	G	H	I	J	K	L	M	N	O	P	Q	R
1	TWEET	RT?	Reply?	Fave-d?	RT-ed?	#RTs	interact w/-teens	authors sites	book blogs & sites	teachers	figs	contest players	include link	link to figment content	THEME / CATEGORY	SUBSEQUENT CONVO?	NATURE OF CONVO?	NOTES
39	@figment Imagines Your Dates with Fictional Men: http://ow.ly/hEkLU	1	0	3	1	4	4		1				1	1	figment content	0		this was RT-d by BookRiot, a book blog.
40	@figment: Find out what it would be like to date a fictional man! Heathcliff, Romeo, Edward Cullen, & Gatsby. http://bit.ly/Y9Yngi ahaha	1	0	0	1	2	2		1				1	1	figment content	0		
41	First dates with the greatest fictional men of all time: http://slate.me/12LY3KA via @figment	1	0	26	1	28	28		1				1	1	figment content	0		RT-d by slate
42	Is it weird that Heathcliff seems the most normal? @Slate 1st dates w/ greatest fictional men of all time: http://slate.me/12LY3KA @figment	1	0	1	1	2	2						1	1	figment content	0		
43	WHY ARE YOU EVEN A THING? Six possible reasons #ValentinesDay exists. http://bit.ly/Nqt2id	0	0	2	1	2	2						1	1	figment content	0		
44	In ONE HOUR, we will be tweeting angel facts! #Retweet for a chance to #Boundless by Cynthia Hand! http://bit.ly/14v8SxV	0	0	0	1	15	15					7	1	1	announcement	0	none	
45	Twenty minutes for your chance to retweet and win #BOUNDLESS, the latest in the Unearthly series. http://bit.ly/14v8SxV	0	0	0	1	14	14		7		2	1	1	1	contest announcement	1	2 sharing contest details	
46	Five minutes until your first chance to win #Boundless. You ready? http://bit.ly/14v8SxV	0	0	0	1	7	7		1	1	1	2	1	1	contest	1	3 answering question: yes ready for contest	
47	The word "angel" derives from the Greek "angelos" which means "messenger." RT to #win #Boundless. http://bit.ly/14v8SxV	0	0	2	1	66	66		6		1	10	1	1	contest RT	0		Strange: SAYS 66 RTs, but I can only document 24, all contest bitly links point to figment's boundless twitter contest
48	According to the Book of Revelations, there are 100 million #angels in existence. RT to win #Boundless! Rules: http://bit.ly/14v8SxV	0	0	1	1	59	59						1	1	contest RT	1	character / castiel in supernatural	
49	In the 13thC, angels were thought to control stars, planets, seasons, months, days, & hours. RT to #win #Boundless! http://bit.ly/14v8SxV	0	0	3	1	60	60						1	1	contest RT	1		
50	Dionysius described 9 angel ranks: seraphim, cherubim, thrones, dominions, virtues, powers, principalities, archangels, & angels. #Boundless	0	0	8	1	50	50						0	0	contest RT	0		
51	The first circle of angels—the seraphim, cherubim, and thrones—devote their time to contemplating God. http://bit.ly/14v8SxV RT #Boundless!	0	0	1	1	48	48						1	1	contest RT	1	contest player replies about angels (topic of contest); link to supernatural fandom?	
52	The second circle of angels—the dominions, virtues, and powers—govern the universe. http://bit.ly/14v8SxV RT to #win #Boundless!	0	0	1	1	50	50						1	1	contest RT	0		
53	The 3rd circle—principalities, archangels, angels—carry out the orders of the superior angels. http://bit.ly/14v8SxV RT for #Boundless!	0	0	1	1	48	48						1	1	contest RT	0		

Source: Alecia Magnifico.

Figure 6.2 Figment Twitter Screenshot (to Illustrate Coding)

this method further may find it useful to consult seminal texts, including the following:

- Johnson and Christensen (2008): *Educational research: Quantitative, qualitative, and mixed approaches.*

- Charmaz (2006). *Constructing Grounded Theory*

- Glaser (1998): *Doing Grounded Theory: Issues and Discussions*

- Strauss and Corbin (1990): *Basics of Qualitative Research: Grounded Theory Procedures and Techniques*

- Glaser and Strauss (1967): *The Discovery of Grounded Theory: Strategies for Qualitative Research*

As Strauss and Corbin (1990) pointed out, "One does not begin with a theory and then prove it. Rather one begins with an area of study and what is relevant to that area is allowed to emerge" (p. 23). Thus, grounded theory researchers begin to analyze data while collection is still occurring, comparing current theories about the field site with new insights and findings as their visits continue. Data collection may occur in several methods and stages, including participation in networked field sites (depending on the particular area of interest, such sites may involve online visits, face-to-face visits, or both), interviews in differing media, artifact collection, and the like. As data are collected in these various activities, researchers employ a "constant comparison" lens to test existing theories against new insights or data.

Traditional constant comparative analysis methods employ three cycles of coding: open coding, axial coding, and selective coding. The first stage, open coding, requires researchers to examine discrete data elements, generate a list of the major concepts that emerge, and compare these concepts across the data set. Open coding is quite similar to thematic analysis, and many researchers use similar techniques early in their data analytical procedures. In the second stage of constant comparative analysis, axial coding, researchers begin to transform the concepts from open coding into organized categories and look for potential relationships across categories. The final stage of constant comparison analysis is selective coding, where researchers begin to generate theories from the data set, return to the data set to test these ideas, and confirm the theory with the data, thus completing a process of validation.

Interviews and observations are the most common types of data in grounded theory studies, but as discussed throughout this book, online data sources are often multimodal in nature, and, therefore, may require different rounds or combinations of coding. For example, Gooden and Winefield (2007) labeled their analysis of gendered contributions to online forums for breast cancer and prostate cancer patients as both an example of "thematic qualitative method" and "grounded theory." The researchers, after having collected archives of forums for each of these cancers, described three stages of coding. Their open coding identified broad themes and behaviors in the discussions to capture the spread of writing that occurs on the boards (e.g., "quoting literature," "promoting choice"); then, axial coding helped to group these codes into larger categories of themes (e.g., "coping philosophy," "facts about the disease"). Finally, the researchers shaped two "central phenomena" that encompassed and described the smaller categories from the first rounds of coding: "information support" and "emotional support" (all quotations from p. 107).

Whereas the Gooden and Winefield (2007) study examined one data source, textual contributions to an online message board, some grounded theory studies employ several kinds of data. For example, Tyler Dodge and his colleagues (2008) drew on several multimodal data sources to conduct a modified ethnographic grounded theory study of Quest Atlantis, a virtual world developed for educational use. To better understand children's identity development and how it might be influenced by technological environments like Quest Atlantis, this research team collected data from a variety of sources. Their data were drawn from classroom observations (both face-to-face and within the virtual world Quest Atlantis), semi-structured interviews with participants, questionnaires, photographs taken by participants, and back-end data records of the students' virtual work and Quests.

Working across all of the data sources, Dodge and colleagues first "sort[ed] the data into the five focal components of identity work: agency (having voice or power); commitment (devoting to a course of action); meaning (constructing significance); learning (developing understandings); and participation (acting within a community)" (Dodge et al., 2008, p. 233). Then, they examined and constructed various levels of meaning and how aspects of the children's virtual experiences contributed to these meanings. Finally, they constructed broader themes and case studies of the participants and checked these interpretations with the participants themselves. Although this study did not detail how the team members made and revised their interpretations while still in the process of data collection, the researchers did describe several rounds of coding, analysis, and "grounded accounts of identity, agency, commitment, meaning, and learning" (Dodge et al., 2008, p. 233). Through this deliberate stepwise comparison, the authors showed how they created strongly systematic, empirical, and trustworthy data theories and structures about students' Quest Atlantis experiences. As such, the set-up and design of this study reflects the ethos of grounded theory methodologies.

Grounded theory has often been described in highly organized ways that encourage researchers to code and theorize first, track relationships and concepts across data sources second, and refine theories in the final phases of analysis; however, many researchers have modified these steps and rounds of coding to better suit their own studies. Many studies that purport to use a grounded theory methodology have reworked it to suit diverse needs or data types. For instance, Berente and Seidel (2014), noting that Glaser and Strauss's (1967) work did not specify that the method should be used only with qualitative data, adapted grounded theory to work with computationally generated "big data." Similarly, Wolfswinkel, Furmueller, and Wilderom (2013) developed a grounded theory method for reviewing and sorting literature.

Although grounded theory resists the idea of developing specific questions for a study in advance of data collection and analysis, researchers might begin by thinking broadly about how to approach the research:

- What patterns are emerging within particular data sources?
- What patterns are emerging across data sources?
- How do the data sources relate to each other?
- How is it possible to trace, document, and express those relationships?

Discourse Analysis

In this book, we focus on the important contributions that qualitative research makes to the understanding of online and blended spaces. Chapters One and Three, for example, consider several reasons why qualitative approaches and their alignment with sociocultural theories of learning have been valued by online researchers. Largely, when spaces for learning evolve as quickly as many online spaces do, it is important for those who study these spaces to reflect on how and why they arrive at the interpretations that they make. Further, Chapters Four and Five mention the importance of researchers' considerations of themselves and their participants for the same reason. Such methods support reflexive examinations of interpretive tools and discoveries of participant and researcher meaning making.

Bloome and his colleagues (2005) explained that no matter what an overall context for learning looks like, *all* macro-level events and environments are slowly constructed from micro-level events and contexts. People's relationships are constructed and maintained little by little: by the individuals involved, within particular environments (sometimes across several online portals), to particular ends, for different audiences, for particular reasons. These relationships are built through language and action, and **discourse analysis** is one way of making sense of such happenings.

Gee (2015) noted, "There are innumerable books on discourse analysis" (p. 5). For more information about discourse analysis, researchers may seek foundational discourse analysis texts that include the following:

- How-to manuals (e.g., Wood & Kroger, 2000)

- Specific applications to the social sciences (e.g., Potter & Wetherell, 1987)

- Critical discourse analysis (e.g., Fairclough, 1989, 1995; Rogers, 2011)

- "Big-D" discourse analysis (Gee, 1999, 2011)

- Microethnographic discourse analysis (Bloome et al., 2005)

- Mediated discourse analysis (Norris & Jones, 2005)

- Nexus analysis (Scollon & Scollon, 2004)

Discourse analysis is a theory about "the nature of language in use," and that "language in use is about saying-doing-being and gains its meaning from the 'game' or practice it is part of and enacts" (Gee, 2014, p. 11). In other words, language plays a central part of meaning creation in social situations, but it does so alongside many other contextual factors, helping to make sense of people's actions and activities. All of the relationships that learners develop have evolving meanings as a result of the accrual of long-term stories. This phenomenon is especially complicated by online settings in which people often develop relationships to and customs around technology tools themselves—reasons and stories about why they perform particular tasks using particular tools.

If researchers are interested in how learning happens in online spaces, then the primary task is to collect and interpret data around their participants' relationships with people and technologies, and how learners define their own learning in these particular settings. Such data might be gathered through face-to-face or online interviews, or they could be collected from online artifacts like discussion board postings or Wikipedia talk pages. In essence, researchers must uncover evidence of what the stories that people tell themselves mean, and construct data-driven stories about those meanings in a way that captures a narrative that rings true for the participants. These kinds of stories involve significant theoretical and interpretive work on the part of the researcher. For instance, researchers must come to understand the sociocultural, sociohistoric, and sociopolitical nature of the space as well as what learning and conversation mean there.

For example, Steinkuehler (2006) drew on concepts from Halliday's (1978) functional linguistics and Gee's "big-D" Discourse analysis (1999, 2011) to conduct a detailed analysis of one short utterance from her study of Lineage 2, a massively multiplayer online game. In this analysis, she examined how the speaker's use of abbreviations (e.g., "afk" for "away from keys"), truncated text (e.g., "regen" for "regenerate"), and specific references to in-game items and locations positioned him as an expert player in the "pledge hunt" in which he was collaboratively engaged. Even though the utterance in question was one where the player signaled his plans to leave the group to gain more necessary potions for the hunt, the culturally bound language that he used suggested his eventual return. (In her analysis, Steinkuehler noted that this supposition came to pass.) Not only did the player's direct, alphabetic text chat language express his intended actions, but also his words marked a certain kind of old-timer expertise.

Fairclough (1989, 1995, 2014) developed a specific **critical discourse analysis** (CDA) as a method to help researchers specifically analyze the ways in which social relationships and social power frame discourse (cf. Rogers, 2011). In a 2014 essay titled "What Is CDA? Language and Power Twenty-Five Years On," Fairclough positioned discourse analysis as "not just critique of discourse, but also explanation of how it relates to other elements of the existing reality" (p. 5). CDA can help inquirers to see critical elements of power in society and how they function through discourse, as well as potential ways to intervene in or disrupt that power for the purpose of positive societal change. Machin (2009) explained that one difficulty of the CDA methodology, however, is that the context of production (Philo, 2007) often has been overlooked. Citing work by Van Dijk (1993) and Fairclough (1995), Machin (2009) underscored the need for researchers to build contextual knowledge, something that "has not seriously been taken up by those working in this area and could be one major shortcoming of multimodal discourse analysis" (p. 189). Mediated discourse analysts, however, have begun to extend their work in the direction of working with multimodal interactions, which calls additional attention to the "emphasis on social actors and on the interaction between social actors and between social actors and their environments" (Norris, 2011, p. 81).

Perhaps as a result of this more recent entrance of CDA theorists into multimodal environments, there are relatively few studies of online communities and online learning that explicitly cite a CDA approach. In fact, Huckin, Andrus, and Clary-Lemon (2012) issued a call for researchers to continue thinking about how this method might be further developed in spaces where multimodal discourse has become the norm, including classrooms. Devane's (2009) study of a subforum of a hip hop message board devoted to financial matters, for example, examined how participants use African-American Vernacular English discourse markers both to share information about debt and finances and to signal their affiliation with hip hop culture. Employing discourse analysis (Gee, 1999, 2011; Fairclough, 1995) and narrative analysis (Labov, 1972; Linde, 1993), Devane's study showed how participants share information about banking and other privileged D/discourses while narrativizing their troubles and solutions online in a way that maintained connections to their home identities and struggles. While the participants were posing financial dilemmas and offering steps forward, they also used "hip hop vernacular" to present "values and sentiments" that "align with the values of the community" (p. 13).

Though researchers may claim that their work is primarily observational, they are themselves developing core theories as they develop methods for capturing and fixing their observations (Gee & Green, 1998). In later work, Gee (2014) reiterated this point even more strongly, writing that "method and theory cannot be separated, despite the fact that methods are often taught as if they could stand alone" (p. 11). Lemke (2012) further cautioned that all data analysis, particularly analysis involving observation, transcripts of dialogue, or field notes, is reductive. Even if archival studies of the Internet provide a relatively full view of online social events, researchers cannot reconstruct the full context. For instance, in the earlier discussion of Steinkuehler's (2006) work, did supporting materials, such as instant messages or voice calls, accompany the original in-game interactions, thereby solidifying the participant's expression of his expert status? Perhaps not in that case, but researchers do not always have access to all supporting materials. Further, as discussed in Chapters Four and Five, researchers will continue to use their own positionality and theoretical knowledge to make decisions about what is important and what must be collected. As such, even the fullest-available qualitative data set is necessarily a compromise.

To conduct qualitative examinations effectively and to mitigate some of the effects of researcher bias and positionality, many researchers use analytical methods that are grounded in discursive interactions and aid in such interpretations. Written and spoken discourse—what Gee (1999) noted as "discourse with a little 'd'" (p. 142)—are often primary drivers of meaning in the world, in both online and face-to-face interactions. Such communications become major components of how people choose particular actions as individuals and community members. This is one of the central insights of several lines of research on social linguistics, particularly Gee's (2012; 2014) insights about "big D" Discourses as "identity kits" or collections of broad practices (see Spotlight Box 6.2).

These are questions to begin analysis of discursive interactions:

- What kinds of language exist in this space (e.g., website comments, fanfiction stories)?

- Do participants communicate predominantly in alphabetic or textual language, or in something else (e.g., links, images, sound effects)?

- Are there particular meanings attached to those kinds of language (e.g., how do members of a role-play distinguish between in-character and out-of-character talk)?

- Do participants use fonts or layout tools to express meaning (e.g., using * characters to indicate action, like *laughs*)?

Spotlight Box 6.2
Black's Discourse Analysis Work on Fanfiction.net

Black's (2008, 2009) work on Fanfiction .net (FFN) was an exploratory case study that used discourse analysis techniques to capture the ways in which her participants used various written language features to write and otherwise communicate about the fanfictions that they shared on FFN.

This study set out to better understand the global group of writers who congregate on FFN, "with an underlying goal of understanding what aspects of FFN provided ELLs [English Language Learners] with access to and a means of affiliating with the literacy and social practices of the site" (Black, 2009, p. 402). More broadly, she described an interest in the identities of globalized youth, particularly youth who are raised within multiple cultures, and how young people interact and develop relationships with the media with which they develop affiliations. At the time Black conducted her research, the rise in online spaces where young people create and share their own stories and remixes was a new phenomenon, just beginning to be theorized, and she wanted to learn more about how such participation can support literacy skills and identity development. As such, her ethnographic work centered on these three research questions.

1. What languages and literacies did these youth engage with as they participated in online fanfiction writing sites?

2. What global and local resources did these youth draw on to support their fan-related activities?

3. As English Language Learners (ELLs), what online identities and relationships did these youth construct through their participation in fanfiction sites (Black, 2009, p. 399)?

To address these areas of interest, Black spent three years on FFN as a participant-observer, maintaining two accounts (one for writing and sharing her own fanfiction stories, and one for interacting with her informants). Her research design reflected her desire to better understand FFN from the position of two identities and contexts: that of a fanfiction writer and that of an education researcher.

Black's (2009) analysis of her participants' interviews, fanfiction stories, story header texts, and reviews followed Gee's (1999) discourse analytical techniques. She broke selected excerpts into lines and stanzas, both of which are discourse analysis terms of art that describe researchers' sectioning of participants' communications—in this study, interviews, narratives, or various kinds of correspondence. Black described these lines and stanzas "often" reflecting participants' own sections and line breaks. Finally, she noted that following this analysis, she worked to "[develop] a more detailed typology" of the ways in which these pieces of language established social meanings for the participants (p. 407).

In other words, Black's analysis of these texts stayed close to a wide variety of textual language that participants used to write stories and communicate about these narratives. Her focus on genre, discourse, and style helped her to document the ways in which her participants saw themselves as ELLs and fanfiction writers—their writerly and multicultural identities—as well as how the online space of FFN enabled social connections and shared representations of themselves and their work.

Using these techniques, Black concluded that an important aspect of FFN texts is, perhaps surprisingly, the story headers that begin each fanfiction. Black's (2009) discourse analysis of these headers, along with interviews with each participant, showed that her participants used this space to provide context for readers of the story. Primarily, the linguistic markers that they used in these headers functioned as "disclaimers" to reveal

(Continued)

(Continued)

the ELL status of the authors, the effect of which was to "implicitly [position] readers as experts who might notice errors in their texts and as responsive audience members who would provide feedback" (p. 413). In other words, while their fanfiction stories were, of course, central to these writers' English language learning, it was also important to them to get useful feedback on their pieces from reviewers. This availability to request feedback is a central affordance of writing on FFN, an Internet site with thousands of potential readers, all of whom had access to their stories. The header text disclaimers provided a central way for the authors to direct these audience interactions, and to more confidently assure progression in their learning.

Multimodal Analysis and Artifactual Analysis

Online and digital media have made it possible for a variety of users to employ the Internet to view and compose meanings that use such features as images, animations, sounds, videos, collages, text in multiple fonts, actions (especially in videogames), and coded page layouts. As such, few "texts" in online spaces may be comprehended by merely viewing the alphabetic text. Instead, textual features—from capital letters to colors to moving pictures—add layers of meaning to the compositions that participants consume and create. As Julie Coiro, Michele Knobel, Colin Lankshear, and Donald J. Leu argued (2008), textual representations are now often multiple, multimodal, and multifaceted. While print literacy relied primarily on a single mode, black-and-white words on the page (pictures did exist, of course, but were often limited to small numbers or certain genres, like picture books for children), multimodal literacy has opened up the possibilities. In response, researchers have developed theories and data analysis frameworks to aid in understanding how these complex texts are used and produced. For more information, readers may wish to consult these references.

- Multimodal analyses (Jewitt, 2009, 2013; Norris, 2004; Norris & Maier, 2014)

- Multimodality (Kress, 2010; Kress & van Leeuwen 1996, 2001; Rowsell, 2013)

- Multiliteracies (Cope & Kalantzis, 2000; Stein & Newfield, 2006)

- Media literacies (Burn, 2009)

- Artifactual literacies (Pahl & Rowsell, 2010)

- Nexus analysis (Scollon & Scollon, 2004)

There are a limited number of media and data that traditional, face-to-face, qualitative researchers might call artifacts. For instance, a classroom researcher who is doing research on how a particular project supports learning might interview students and teachers and collect student work samples over time. In the subsequent analysis, this researcher might transcribe the interviews and analyze the work samples as artifacts, perhaps looking at differences in the student work at the beginning and at the end of a project. In a project about literature, perhaps student drawings of characters include more details over time, or perhaps the paragraphs of student stories are longer and more unified at the end of the project.

As mentioned in Chapter Five, these artifacts may tell stories of individual learning that support the interviews or that diverge from them and complicate the analysis with new ideas. Although education research has often focused on how learners represent knowledge in the textual work that they do, an analysis that includes multimodal and artifactual elements may lead to more nuanced, thorough descriptions of learning. Technological and theoretical insights are continually making new analytical constructs possible.

Researchers who are interested in the role of artifacts like the ones described above often explicitly take on a theoretical framework that focuses on **multimodality** or one that focuses on **multiliteracies**. Multiliteracies, which was first described by the New London Group (1996; see also Cope & Kalantzis, 2000) is closely linked to the idea of "new literacies" and "literacies" as plural, rather than singular, terms. This broad theoretical position calls for researchers to recognize the validity of a variety of methods of communication and meaning making, as well as the frequent necessity of a variety of modes in that communication and meaning making.

Teaching students to recognize how meaning is made through a variety of modes and how to include such awareness in their own compositions are central facets of this work as well. In contrast, multimodality (e.g., Kress, 2010; Kress & van Leeuwen, 1996, 2001), which often refers to the more specific "multimodal social semiotics," examines the *ways in which* that variety of modes may work together to create meanings. Learning situations, whether online, in homes, or in classrooms, are often necessarily *both* multiliterate and multimodal, since they involve many communication modes (e.g., written text, oral text, links, videos, whiteboard drawings). These two schools of research, however, examine these situations using somewhat different theoretical frameworks and techniques. As Pippa Stein and Denise Newfield (2006) stressed: "Together, the linked concepts of multiliteracies and multimodality constitute a new way of conceptualising how teaching and learning occurs in contemporary classrooms" (p. 2).

Hull and Nelson (2005), for example, conducted digital artifact analysis using out-of-school participants' digital stories. Drawing on multiliteracies work from the New London Group (1996) that suggested educators must begin to recognize and teach diverse modes of communication, this piece pointed out that researchers, too, should consider the "individual and combinatory semiotic contributions made to the synesthetic whole by its material components" (Hull & Nelson, 2005, p. 234). In other words, compositions may be built from several modes that are combined in one piece, but their overall meanings are not merely the sum of the various components used. Multimodality allows for new, complex, different kinds of meanings. More recently, Halverson, Bass, and Woods (2012) developed a tool for creating transcripts of video data (or other complex learning settings) that sets various modes against each other (e.g., spoken audio, soundtrack, visual image, written text) and allows researchers to analyze the contributions of each, as well as the effect of the full film.

As Kate Pahl and Jennifer Rowsell (2010) stated, "Ideas can be represented visually as well as in writing" (p. 265), so if researchers are studying a space in which people are working with and learning from objects, an account of how and why they are using those objects may contribute significant understanding. This insight represents one of the major contributions of research on New Literacies, multiliteracies, and multimodality, all of which suggest that researchers (and teachers, too) must take students' use of artifacts seriously to understand learning and meaning making. A history of idea development is deeply enriched by a history of how the learners and developers interact with different kinds of objects. Pahl and Rowsell's (2010) work on artifactual literacies and Wohlwend's (2009) and Stein's (2008) work on children's interactions with toys described this necessary shift in understanding meaning, learning, and literacies, pointing out that because material objects help us to think and act, they are also integral parts of our literacies. Wohlwend and Buchholz's (2014) work particularly highlighted the possibilities of encouraging children to make digital videos of their play with physical objects, thus complicating distinctions between digital and physical artifacts. Rowsell and Burgess (2014) also addressed the complicated nature of artifacts and (im)materiality as they examined how community college students used Facebook and online artifacts to materialize instantiations of self. More specifically, they noted that "moving from the immaterial to the material is not moving from non-digital to digital—it is more about exerting self to an audience—it is about being heard and about knowing how to be heard through modal choice" (p. 107). In this way, the materiality of the artifact is not identified by prescriptions of online or offline spaces; rather, the focus shifts to learner agency and production.

At first, these insights may seem relatively straightforward. Researchers who are interested in learning may find evidence of progress or change in learners' work with objects as well as in their more traditional work with interviews and texts (also see Chapter Four for more about research that includes artifacts). One of the challenging things about doing research in online and blended spaces, however, is the number of "objects" that learners can interact with and use to represent their learning. Many methods of online communication are textual or imagistic in some way, which means that websites, virtual worlds, and games might be seen as artifacts that bring in a whole variety of modes that enable different kinds of thinking, reasoning, and learning. As Chapter Five points out, however, it is often important for researchers to find creative ways to capture *how* participants interact with various tools to think and learn (e.g., screen recording or video recording from behind the screen) so that these occasions for learning can be interpreted in trustworthy ways.

Gibbons (2010), as well as Halverson, Lowenhaupt, Gibbons, and Bass (2009), described the multimodal complexity of young people's learning about video production, for example. Not only were a variety of modes used to mark learners' progress and developing identity as filmmakers—for example, verbal discussions with mentors, textual pieces like pitches and scripts, and storyboards—but the videos themselves involved multiple modes of communication between the filmmaker and the viewer, including image, music, verbal and written language, and transitions between scenes.

Data sets like these are exciting and important since more and more people are learning to create and share images and videos as parts of their daily lives (witness the popularity of services like YouTube, Instagram, and Vine), but they are difficult to analyze in rigorous ways. Both Halverson and her team (2012) and Curwood and Gibbons (2009) have developed "multi-transcript" analytical methods for thinking through this kind of complexity. The table-based transcripts that they constructed were designed to help researchers understand the multiple modes that are co-present in what Gibbons (2010) calls "moving artifacts," as well as how these modes work together to create narrative meanings and portray filmmaker identities (see Spotlight Box 6.3).

The following are questions to begin **multimodal analysis** of artifacts:

- What kinds of digital artifacts exist in this space (e.g., YouTube videos, DeviantArt creative works)?
- What kinds of physical artifacts exist in this space (e.g., video cameras, markers, toys)?
- How do the participants use these different artifacts? Are they used together or separately?
- What (if any) kinds of meanings and rituals are attached to particular artifacts?
- What (if any) stories do participants tell about the artifacts?

In their piece on multimodal microanalysis, Jen Scott Curwood and Damiana Gibbons (2009) analyzed a digital poem produced in an English Language Arts class by a high school student. They described their analytical methods in detail and discussed how these methods helped them to understand the student's poem, which was written in response to Walt Whitman's "I Hear America Singing" and Langston Hughes's "I, Too, Sing America," and is a deliberate counternarrative to typical master narratives about American life. In this digital poem, Tommy used images, music, written language, and transitions to assert his gay, Asian, and second-generation immigrant identities. He tells his own story of being an American teenager in a majority-white high school where master narratives of Eurocentrism and homophobia were predominant (see the multimodal transcript of a digital poem below).

The researchers looked primarily to the digital poems themselves, although interviews were also conducted. First, they

I, too, am America

time	16	18	20	22
image				
action	text is fading (transition)	no action	image is being zoomed out	image is zooming out (will be zoomed out at 23 sec)
transition	dissolve	no transition	there was a fade to black screen at 17 sec	ken burns effect
music	Song is "Asian Beats"; continues throughout video	continued	continued	continued
language used	English	continued	continued	continued
written text	And live unnaturally	Don't make me do your homework	Because I'm a Sally and can't take a punch.	Because I'm a Sally and can't take a punch.
written text in use	Text in white, same font, placed at center vertically and at lower center horizontally	Text in same position as last image—lower half; text is white, same font as before; text is placed under girl in image and over the paper and pen	Text in same position as last image—lower half; same font and size; positioned "under the action" of bullying	Text position is exactly the same as the image is zooming out

Source: Curwood & Gibbons (2009).

used a multitranscription technique to understand what was happening with the text's images, action, transitions, music, and written text (sometimes animated or in multiple languages) at two-second intervals. Then, they narrativized this transcript to begin understanding Tommy's modal choices throughout the digital poem, and why he made the choices that he did at different times. Finally, once they had developed these descriptions of the modal choices and meanings over the space and time of the poem, Curwood and Gibbons began to look for patterns, repeated actions or series of modes that helped to develop his counternarrative. For instance, they noted that Tommy repeatedly combined transitions to blank screens of color with questions in his poem—questions that he also wanted the viewers in the audience to ask themselves.

The multimodal microanalysis ultimately focused on Tommy's use of remix and of multiple modes to communicate about his own America, and his own experiences in a school where many of his classmates and neighbors had rejected key elements of his identity. This detailed way of examining the various modes of a digital poem (or other kinds of multimodal texts), both alone and alongside each other, sheds light on the complexities of visual and textual meaning making.

Each of the prior sections that highlights a particular method (as well as the theoretical combination of methodology that surrounds this kind of sense-making) involves some kind of innovation, either in the methods themselves or in the interpretation of the associated data points. In the case of Magnifico's (2013) thematic analysis, she needed a method to capture participation and learning across portals within the same affinity space. She found that an initial sorting by topic and theme helped to support a case for participants in the various portals creating separate, distinct practices that did not hold true across the broader space. In Black's (2008, 2009) discourse analysis, looking closely at the text revealed the ways in which seemingly small bits of language in the story headers set the context for readers' feedback and participation. Finally, in Curwood and Gibbons's (2009) multimodal microanalysis, developing a technique for isolating the various modes so that they could be examined together and separately helped them to build a finely detailed case for how Tommy's digital poem created resistance to master narratives that were assumed by other members of his class. Many studies involve data analyses like these—instances where working with the data begins to call for a new approach or lens, or to show researchers something unexpected. Thinking about what artifacts are in play, how they are used by the participants, and what functions they serve can assist researchers in beginning to think about multimodal analyses.

Innovation With Methods

When beginning observations in a new space, the kinds of data analysis that are called for may be unclear, or the analytical plans may shift as observations or data points begin to suggest certain patterns. It is ideal for researchers to enter into a study with a mental model of how learning occurs, together with a well-developed logic of inquiry that maps how the collected data will model and describe the interactions; however, these tools do not always remain stable. Sometimes new or unexpected patterns become evident, and researchers must carefully reflect on the new situation and creatively meet this challenge, shifting or remixing traditional data collection or analysis protocols as necessary. They must make sure to think about ethics and consult their participants and ethics board if necessary. (For more on ethics see Chapter Seven.) Surprising and useful innovations may even result from unexpected shifts.

Halverson and Magnifico's (2013) work on bidirectional artifact analysis began in a similar way to many of the studies discussed earlier in this chapter (see Magnifico & Halverson, 2012; Magnifico, Halverson, Cutler, & Kalaitzidis, 2014). While examining students' work with creative writing and peer feedback, the researchers initially began with the insight that certain pairs of students were more productive when they were working together; these relationships were grounded in multiple observations and data points. They seemed to talk about their respective poems and stories more easily, to suggest changes more freely, to have more to say, and to revise their own work more eagerly after the conference had concluded. It was difficult, though, to pull an explanation of such differences that felt verifiable or reliable from the field notes on classroom observations, and the transcripts of the students' conferences did not include reflections on how the conversations had unfolded. In an attempt to see what was happening, Magnifico pasted one set of particularly "productive" peer conference discussions onto a huge sheet of butcher paper (see Figure 6.3).

As they viewed this larger timeline of the students' work together, they began to note that different students asked different kinds of questions of each other. The "productive" conferences seemed to refer more densely to the text at hand, and the readers shared their own responses to particular words or scenes, rather than to vague overall themes. This visual rendering of the drafts and conversations revealed how the young artists used their work to direct the conferences effectively (or not).

This insight led Magnifico and Halverson to begin examining the references that peers and mentors made to existing drafts of work artifacts during conference meetings, and to begin focusing on how these draft representations built on each other and helped young artists and writers think about what they wanted to say in a particular piece of work, or in its subsequent draft. An effort to chase down the roots of an interpretive claim—particular conferences seemed to have "better" results—led to a full rethinking of their approach to these kinds of data, and to an analysis that felt more dependable because it was well-grounded

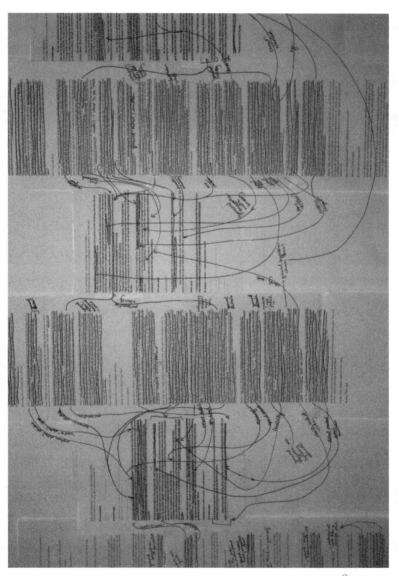

Alecia Magnifico

Figure 6.4 Bidirectional Artifact Analysis Showing Movement Among Drafts and Feedback in an Online Tool

Draft 1

Character
70s-80s
Husband died has dimensia
Very shy, quiet

Timeline of story
Friends pressure her into putting husband into a nursing home
Visits him every day
He starts forgetting her?

The doctor has only been telling me what I have known all along. He says that Stew should be watched more carefully because he may develop particular eating habits or neglect his hygiene. There's always something new to look for Dr. Frank Newhorn Newhorn has been a friend since my husband has been diagnosed with BVFTD. I don't expect you to know what that is. No one should have to know what that is. But it stands for Behavorial Behavioral Variant frontotemporal dementia, if you wanted to know; Which I doubt you did....

Stw Stewart was

Writers' Circle Feedback

Melanie: So I'm starting this story. Based on Sandra Day O'Connor... Her husband had dementia and she stayed home to take care of him, but she ended up putting him in a nursing home.... So I'm going to do a story about that. But... I don't know whether I should start, where he's already at the nursing home, or whether she has to take him to the nursing home, or if should start at the home life and how it gets worse...

Leanne: I think that you should probably start earlier on, so then we can get a sense of the wife, and then later on in the story... then probably it would be like more dramatic for the reader...[Sara: Yeah.] Cuz then we'll have developed a tie to the wife.

Kathy: I like that.

Sara: Like maybe you could start out when he does something weird, you could be like he's doing it again. Or some sort of random thing, that would like indicate dementia, I don't really know too much about it, so I couldn't say, but then you could do it from her wording and people would be able to guess.

Leanne: Or you could do it in flashbacks, like he could be in the home and then she could have flashbacks to whenever

Rica: I agree with Leanne, I think you should start as early as possible because it, just like the more you cover the more we're gonna understand the story. And like, if you're gonna have any of it from the wife's perspective, then it would make sense to work from there, do you know which perspective you're gonna put it in yet?

Melanie: I think it's the wife's, yeah. I could do his, I could do his, I was thinking about switching, back and forth, but... I wasn't sure I'd have time for that (camp transcript, 8/4/2009).

Draft 2

Marilyn
Stewart
Today I wake up and Stewart is still lying beside me, asleep. He normally is up and brushing around the kitchen, making breakfast. He looks like a fish
I wake up today and my

Dr. Frank Newhorn

"He only eats canned food. Can you work around that?" I can't believe I'm doing this. I feel like he is my child and I'm trying to find a daycare to take him to. Or an orphange [sic]. Except I know he can be nice if he tried. He wasn't always like this. We used to ... for dinner, we used to be able to go ... to go out to dinner when he wouldn't ... acrent [sic] or how the waiter's shoes ... ugh or how the couple next to us was ... to not be embarrased with him in ... the last time I felt comfortable with him. Although I do remember my birthday two years ago... had just turned 76

> Sara's comment influences Melie's revision: Draft 2 starts with "something weird" that Stewart does.

* * *

We went for Mexican at a little place down the road. I convinced him to order something other than chicken burritos. When his food came he yelled at the waiter. "Did this enchilada came from Mexico? I don't even taste the meat! You don't even know what I'm saying, do you? Can you speak English?" After that the waiter tuned him out and turned to look at me. He may not serve quality Mexican, he may not have understood English, or what Stewart was saying, even. That waiter looked at me, horrified by my husband, and felt sorry for me.

"Ma'am?" The receptionist at Sunny Hillside questions.

"All patients residing here at Sunny Hillside recieve the same meal plan. We don't do special orders.' "Okay," after going through all these phone calls I still find myself surprised by their inability to be flexible. She asks me if there is anything else she can help me with. I can still hear her voice coming

Source: Alecia Magnifico.

in both the draft texts and the transcripts of participants' activity. Despite the lack of full triangulation, the two data sources (participants' artifact "texts" and their conference conversations) supported each other and strengthened the interpretive power of the study (see Figure 6.4).

This short excerpt is included to suggest that researchers may need to try several approaches to data analysis, or to combine data points that might be initially seen as separate, to achieve an interpretation that feels worthwhile. While this chapter emphasizes the importance of establishing a study's logic of inquiry and a researcher's mental model for carrying out the analysis early on—such steps smooth the way for interpretive insight later on—it can also be significant to look at the data set in a new way if the planned methods do not lead to effective analytical progress.

Conclusion
....

This chapter addresses five commonly used frameworks for data analysis in qualitative studies: thematic analysis, grounded theory, discourse analysis, multimodal analysis, and artifactual analysis. In addition to explanations of the methods themselves, the chapter gives examples of studies that have employed these methods and discusses how the methods relate to the topics and research questions under investigation. Each of these topics comprises a wide range of practices, methods, opinions, and research studies; and an overview of each method provides a starting point for researchers who are looking ahead to develop protocols for data analysis.

CONNECTING TO YOUR WORK ───────────

As a qualitative researcher, it is important to consider not just your plans for data collection, but how you plan to use these data—perhaps data from several portals of a networked field site—in your analyses. As you begin to plan your study, consider how long you will be participating in the learning environment, what you will learn from each of the data sources that you plan to collect, and how these sources will create meaning as you examine them across different analyses.

- What opportunities might you have to strengthen your interpretations by examining, for instance, learners' online forum posts, their interviews, or their digital art?

- Is there a possibility that you might be able to ask participants to reflect on their own online videos, so that you can analyze both the multimodal texts themselves and participants' understandings of or intentions for these creations?

Guiding Questions for Chapter 7

- What is the principle of care, and how does it relate to researching learning in online spaces?
- What are some methods that support data anonymization and maintain confidentiality?
- How do the four degrees of concealment influence how a researcher might obscure a study's data?
- What are some of the steps toward achieving human subjects research approval for a study that occurs across multiple online spaces?

CHAPTER SEVEN

What Is Ethical Research?

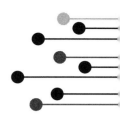

Introduction

The ethical issues that researchers must consider when conducting research in online spaces are diverse and complex. Examining the ethical considerations embraced by various researchers who study learning in online spaces brings to light the importance of adhering to ethical standards related to recruitment, consent, and confidentiality. Furthermore, layers of concealed identity underscore the complexities of online research. As researchers interrogate the ethical implications of studying online meaning making, they must respect various sites' terms of service, end-user licensing agreements, and Creative Commons licensing. Through examining the above concepts and principles, researchers will be better able to design studies that abide by ethical norms.

Research Ethics and Policies Across Multiple Contexts

Conducting ethical research is a crucial element in any research study. While research ethics provide a large arena for discussion, this chapter focuses predominantly on human subjects research ethics in online environments. **Human subjects review boards** oversee biomedical, behavioral, and social science research studies to ensure the thorough and consistent use of ethical research measures when research studies involve people. This often includes the anonymization of data and **beneficence** to the research participants and, subsequently, that methods are in place for participants to withdraw from the study without consequence (Boellstorff, Nardi, Pearce, & Taylor, 2012; Creswell, 2010; Kozinets, 2010).

Governed by law and policy, human subjects review boards protect the research participants and researchers (Creswell, 2015; Boellstorff et al., 2012). Many countries have their own national governing councils that ensure that independent, human subjects review boards follow national law and policy, such as Australia's Human Research Ethics Council governed by the National Health and Medical Research Council, or Institutional Review Boards as governed by the National Institutes of Health in the United States. Intergovernmental agencies, such as the United Nations Educational, Scientific, and Cultural Organization's Ethics of Science and Technology Research Council, also help to shape international policy related to human subjects research ethics. These organizations and agencies subject research to ethics review if it involves interaction with or involvement from human subjects. Studies that involve recording individual and collective behaviors, actions, or insights on various topics would fall under the purview of human subjects research—as would engaging with research participants in gaming cohorts, online discussions, online fanfiction, or online forums. Researchers in these studies might use surveys, interviews, or observation to collect data, as outlined in Chapter Five.

As noted in Chapter Two's discussion on multiple online spaces and Chapter Four's discussion on researcher positioning, the boundaries of online studies are porous and complex. Particularly when studying open social networks, researchers must attend to the presence of minors online, the acquisition of verifiable informed consent, and the identification of public or private data. As such, guidance from review boards can help researchers outline various methods for conducting ethical research within their chosen space (Markham & Buchanan, 2012).

To date, the national-level policies mentioned previously have not established standard all-encompassing guidelines that show researchers how to navigate ethical conduct of online research. In 2002, the Association of Internet Researchers (**AoIR**) created a working group to help researchers navigate the complexity of online research ethics, the outcome of which was a working document to help researchers make ethical decisions about their online studies. In 2012, the AoIR working group released a revised technical report, "Ethical Decision-Making and Internet Research: Recommendations from the AoIR Ethics Working Committee Version 2.0" (Markham & Buchanan, 2012). This document drew on theoretical, empirical, and field-based research to address the vast realm of online research ethics. The technical report provided overarching guidelines, and it posed specific questions for researchers to consider when designing studies within online spaces.

Rather than solidifying a specific set of principles or policies, the AoIR working group wrote guidelines in response to the dynamic and shifting nature of researching online spaces. The AoIR suggested that a national set of rules might, in fact, hinder the development of cutting-edge online research:

> We emphasize that no set of guidelines or rules is static; the fields of internet research are dynamic and heterogeneous. This dynamism is reflected in the fact that as of the time of this writing, no official guidance or "answers" regarding internet research ethics have been adopted at any national or international level. (Markham & Buchanan, 2012, p. 2)

As such, the guidelines developed by AoIR provide support to researchers, but they do not act as exact parameters or limitations for any particular study.

In addition to the guidelines set forth by the AoIR, a growing number of institutions and universities have established guidelines, many of which are freely available online, to help researchers understand the ethical elements concerning studies of online environments. Table 7.1 expands on the common elements of the guiding documents provided by the University of California at Berkeley, University of Georgia, Columbia University, and Pennsylvania State University. The table highlights key considerations and guiding questions for study design, such as:

- understanding scales of private and sensitive information

- obtaining permission, not just from the participants, but from the site's gatekeeper

- exercising caution when working with vulnerable populations, such as minors or those with disabilities

- ensuring that researchers gain ethical entry into online spaces

- ensuring that data are properly encrypted during the data transmission stage

Table 7.1	Common Elements in Institutional Policy for Online Research Ethics
Common Points	**Key Considerations**
Understanding public and private scales	• Are the data publicly available? • If identity were made public, could these data damage or stigmatize the participant?
Obtaining permission and gaining entry	• Who manages the site? • Are there site-use rules that govern becoming a member of the site? • Are opt-out procedures in place that do not force a participant to leave the community?
Exercising caution with vulnerable populations	• Are the participants minors or from other vulnerable populations? • Can consent be cross-validated to ensure that participants are, indeed, providing consent? In other words, can researchers use techniques that require participants to sign informed consent in two different methods and places that allow for cross-checking and validation of permission?
Using data encryption techniques	• Is the proper data encryption software being used during online data transmission? • Is the researcher using data encryption software that is approved by the site of study and the institution where the researcher is employed?

Because not all institutions have guidelines, it is important for researchers to consider the common elements listed in Table 7.1 and to think through the ways that these guidelines are related to their own study design and the unique aspects of their networked field sites. Researchers should then bring these guidelines forward to their own human subjects review boards as support for their ethical decisions.

Additionally, as researchers begin to design their own studies and write about their research protocols, it is important for them to think through the following questions:

- How much description of the online space needs to be in the research protocol?

- What are the various types of interactions that occur among participants in these spaces?

- What is (or are) the primary method(s) of interaction(s) that the researcher plans to use with participants?

- How does the researcher plan to gain entry when an online space is considered a public space?

- How does the researcher plan to gain entry when the online space includes minors or other vulnerable populations?

Because each online space and each study might be different, researchers must pay careful attention to provide the appropriate level of detail and supporting citations from the AoIR and other available guidelines to their respective review board. Missing or incomplete information can delay a review board's approval for a researcher to commence a study. Checking for completeness is especially important if the ethics board reviewing the research protocol is unfamiliar with the nuances of conducting qualitative research in online spaces.

The Public Versus the Private Web

How does one determine what is public and what is private within the spaces of the Internet? How do the boundaries of public and private spaces shape researchers' access to and perception of particular online environments and related data sources? How might researchers' understandings of public and private spaces influence their data analysis and subsequent findings?

Varying perceptions of research in online spaces can shape how researchers view the participants, the online space, and the various levels of public and private information. As McKee and Porter (2009) suggested, some researchers see the Internet as a vast repository of online texts that inform the world about society and culture, whereas others see the Internet as a cultural space filled with diverse humans enacting their lives. These differing views suggest that research involving networked field sites is specific to the space and topic being studied.

Additionally, the continuum of public and private can complicate a study. This means that content initially posted privately may become public through "sharing," "reblogging," and "liking" functions. Password-protected communities may have users who join communities just to lurk or troll, and some communities may move from private to public, such as Figment.com's recent move to publicly index reviews. As Breen (2015) indicated in her recent Huffington Post column, teens often post photos in a private social media account. Though initially highly restricted through privacy settings, these posts can, and often do, get screen-captured, shared, and re-Tweeted. Therefore, it behooves researchers to recognize that simply because they have been invited to join a particular community during a study, does not mean that the data that they are analyzing are necessarily viewable to the public. Neither the participant nor on-site friends or connections would necessarily want those data made public.

This example indicates that each research study comprises many ethical considerations and, as indicated by the AoIR, suggests that one approach cannot govern all studies. Some of these ethical considerations are related to gaining entry (see Chapter Four), data collection and generation methods (see Chapter Five), as well as data analysis and dissemination methods (see Chapter Six). By valuing ethical considerations during each of these stages, researchers can design a study that honors participants' privacy and rights.

Many researchers of online spaces (e.g., Boellstorff et al., 2012; Bruckman, 2002; Buchanan, 2004; Markham & Buchanan, 2012; McKee & Porter, 2009) believe that studies designed for the Internet are rich and dynamic and that views of public and private spaces cannot be governed by a one-size-fits-all approach. Thus, they contend that researchers must identify and abide by the rules that govern the space that they plan to study. For example, Wen, McTavish, Kreps, Wise, and Gustafson (2011) conducted case study research of a password-protected website dedicated to women diagnosed with breast cancer. The research team wanted to understand the coping strategies that women employed within discussion board forums related to cancer diagnoses. Though the data were from a password-protected site on which participants used their own pseudonyms, the sensitive nature of the online discussions required the team to use another pseudonym for participants. In other words, even participants in private spaces may need further protection.

Zimmer's (2010) research challenged the notion of public versus private data in his analysis of the ethical considerations of a large-scale data set collected by Kaufman, Christakas, Wimmer, Lewis, and Gonzalez in 2008. The data set included the Facebook profiles of approximately 1,700 college students. Zimmer posited that researchers should be especially careful in their discussion of social network data and that informed consent must be appropriately granted. There are special considerations if one is pulling data from social networks, like Facebook, or other sites that include various levels of privacy settings. Furthermore, Zimmer noted that many human subjects review boards are ill-equipped to review research protocols that outline studies taking place in online environments. As previously discussed, this means that researchers must take appropriate steps to provide additional support materials to inform their review boards of contemporary methods and policies. Spotlight Box 7.1 discusses Zimmer's analysis of the ethics of conducting research in online social networks with varying levels of privacy settings.

Spotlight Box 7.1

Analyzing the Ethics of Researching Online Social Networks: Public, Private, Continuum?

Michael Zimmer (2010) exposed the ethical issues related to the reported data set of a 2008 study of 1,700 college students' Facebook profiles. The researchers of this study (the T3 Team) paired Facebook profile data with identification data from the university where the data were drawn. Zimmer discussed the work of the "Tastes, Ties, and Time" (T3) research team. The T3 Team was made up of Harvard professors Jason Kaufman and George Christakas, University of California, Los Angeles, professor Andreas Wimmer, as well as Harvard sociology graduate students Kevin Lewis and Marco Gonzalez. Zimmer claimed that the team was negligent in grasping the importance of research ethics in online environments. Over four years, the T3 Team conducted a longitudinal study of a cohort of college students at a small, Northeastern, private university. The team wanted to understand relationships between online and offline social

networks and to establish a cultural fingerprint for the students from their interests, including favorite restaurants, movies, and books. Within days of the T3 Team releasing their data set online, several scholars were able to identify the university, individual identities of participants in the study, and other sensitive information including sexual preference and political affiliation.

As Zimmer (2010) discussed in his analysis, the data were culled by the Resident Assistants (RAs) of each dorm over the four-year period. However, because the RAs had personal network ties with the participants, the RAs were privy to information that might have been set as private by the individual. Those outside of each Facebook participant's network (namely those on the research team) would not have been able to see these private settings. Furthermore, as Zimmer explained, because the team believed the data to be public, informed consent was not given by any of the 1,700 participants. While the research team made efforts to clean the data and anonymize the data set by removing names, identification numbers, email addresses, physical addresses, and phone numbers, other data such as area of study/major, national identification, and race were included. As such, many students were identifiable.

While the T3 research team indicated that they had received appropriate permissions from the university, as well as from Facebook, to cull these data and create a widely usable data set for sociological research, Zimmer (2010) suggested that the lack of knowledge among ethics review boards on the impact of privacy settings of data collected from social networks is problematic. He argued that researchers who wish to study online spaces should bring together interdisciplinary teams to collaborate on study design to ensure that future ethical shortcomings in research design do not occur.

When researchers collect data in public arenas, it can be difficult to make judgments on age, race, and sex that often are not identifiable in online environments without extensive background information; even one's publicly viewable blog or discussion forum post may include deliberately false information. Comparing and contrasting online spaces with varying levels of privacy to public arenas, such as libraries, public squares, and supermarkets is inappropriate (Zimmer, 2010). Privacy settings and the public-private continuum must be fully considered when a researcher enters an online space for the purpose of conducting a study.

However, there is still valid work that can be done within online spaces, including studies of data that may be considered archival and public in nature. Ingram, Niemeyer, and Gerber (2015) examined the hashtag #psat on Tumblr to better understand high schoolers' dissidence with testing culture. Bounding the study by collecting only the hastag #psat from the three days that it was trending on Tumblr, the researchers found that youth expressed satirical dissidence against U.S. testing culture through the creation of memes, exaggerated stories using test information, and creative appropriation of test material. Because students signed a nondisclosure agreement before taking the test, the researchers concealed all identities and changed all of the direct quotes. Such caution in the anonymization of data is important. The next section addresses layers of data obfuscation by drawing on Bruckman's (2002) various levels of **concealment**.

Review Boards and Research Approval

If research involves interactions or interventions with participants, it first needs to undergo human subjects review and gain approval by the appropriate review board at an individual's institution (Bruckman, 2002; Buchanan, 2004). The researcher must also make sure that approval to conduct research has been procured from all parties involved, including site coordinators, school review boards, universities affiliated with coresearchers, and medical review boards. Research might involve analysis of texts that are publicly archived. Though according to some review boards, this data may qualify as exempt, it is the responsibility of the researcher to fully understand his or her review board's stance on this.

Governing boards are recognized by different names around the world. Institutional Review Boards (IRBs), Institutional Ethics Boards (IEBs), Human Research Ethics Committees (HRECs), and Research Ethics Committees (RECs) are just a few names that are used to describe the boards that have institutional-level ethical oversight of proposed research studies. For a research study to receive ethical approval, the researcher must first submit the research protocol to the appropriate review board. The board then determines whether the researcher has adequately described that a study will be conducted ethically or what changes need to be made to ensure that the study is conducted ethically. According to the historical cases that resulted from the Nuremberg trials, the Tuskegee experiments, and others, ethical research includes the following principles of care:

- Do no harm.

- Research participants give voluntary informed consent.

- Confidentiality is maintained throughout the study.

- Beneficence is regarded.

Do No Harm

The principle of care, or do no harm, governs *all* research, and implies that the researchers in the study do not cause undue harm or stress to the research participants or the population that surrounds the participants (Kraut, Olson, Banaji, Bruckman, Cohen, & Cooper, 2010). As evidenced throughout this book, the spaces a researcher chooses to enter are often connected to participants' daily lives (Boellstorff et al., 2012; Roberts, Smith, & Pollock, 2002; Whitty, 2002). For example, online spaces such as massive open online courses (MOOCs) have physical connections to groups of people who inhabit those spaces. Carelessly entering sites and engaging in unethical interactions—intended or unintended—may have a negative impact on a participant's daily income and way of life. Whenever researchers enter into online spaces, they should enter with the guiding principle that they will do no harm.

This principle of care refers to the way in which participants trust the researcher to treat them with tact and sensitivity (Kozinets, 2010). The "do no harm" principle of care recognizes and attempts to mitigate the power dynamics that are at play between the researched and the researcher. When research participants open up their worlds and let researchers in, they may become vulnerable. A participant's online representation (e.g., an avatar) does not signal human detachment; the participant is not devoid of feelings about an online persona. Furthermore, sometimes, online personas are attached to a participant's reputation or livelihood. For an example of the do no harm principle, see Spotlight Box 7.2.

Spotlight Box 7.2
Do No Harm and World of Warcraft: Chat Log Analysis to Protect Nonparticipants

Yun Joon "Jason" Lee (2014) conducted ethnographic case study research to understand incidental second-language acquisition within the game spaces of one of the largest massively multiplayer online role-playing games in history, World of Warcraft. Lee's one-year study involved extensive interaction with one Korean, second-language, World of Warcraft player who opted to play on an English, not Korean, language server.

During the study, Lee conducted online and face-to-face interviews with the participant and collected chat logs between the research participant and players during in-game raids and other sessions. Lee had access to all of the guild's chat logs because he was a member of the guild. However, Lee had informed consent from only one person in the guild—the participant in his study. To ensure that he practiced the principle of do no harm, Lee analyzed only chat sequences he had with the participant. In so doing, he upheld the ethical integrity of the study because he was able to examine the way that the participant navigated learning the English language while keeping the other players from becoming unwilling or uninformed research participants.

Informed Consent

Contemporary research studies must deal with **informed consent**, which means that the research participants have foreknowledge that they will be studied, and they have given permission for the research to occur (Sveningsson, 2002). When a researcher plans to work with minors or other vulnerable populations, there are additional steps involved in consent procedures, such as securing parental (or guardian) consent and participant assent.

Many governments and intergovernmental agencies have guidelines and legal parameters that outline the protection of child populations in online environments, including what information can be collected on children and how this information can be used. For example, the Child Online Protection Initiative (COP) provides an online collaborative network focused on the legalities of protecting youth and children online within an international and transcultural arena. The Child Online Protection Initiative was developed by the information communication and technology sector of the United Nations in response to the Global Cybersecurity Agenda Framework. It was endorsed by various heads of state and international organizations in 2008.

In the United States, the Children's Online Privacy Protection Act (COPPA) is a federal law that outlines the procedures that websites and companies must abide by when they create child-friendly online products. In the United Kingdom, the National Crime Agency has created the Child Exploitation and Online Protection Centre (CEOP) to ensure that online environments are safe for children by exploring threats to children's online safety. The CEOP works closely with various agencies and companies to ensure that guidelines are developed and followed to ensure the safety of present and future technology development. Table 7.2 provides practical examples of the child protection principles. The principles used by COP, COPPA, and CEOP can guide researchers in ethical and responsible methods of obtaining informed consent from minors. These include:

- providing language that is accessible to children;
- gaining parental notice, verification, and permission; and
- using birth date validation and verification protocols and procedures created specifically for online environments.

Table 7.2 Internationally Recognized Child Protection Principles and Case Examples

Principle for Child Protection	Example

Providing accessible language	• Have three to four consent forms available for varying levels of children's readability and comprehension levels.
	
	  o Ages 5–7
	  o Ages 8–11
	  o Ages 12–14
	  o Ages 15–18

Gaining parental notice	• Have secondary email verification for parental consent. • Conduct phone and videoconference verification with parents and guardians.
Birth date validation	• Ask youth to verify their birth date at several different points in the informed consent process through electronic date verification methods.

As a result of the Nuremberg Code, it is expected that all research studies allow research participants the opportunity to give voluntary informed consent. However, how do researchers gain informed consent from participants that they might never encounter physically in a face-to-face environment? How do they verify that the person giving consent is indeed the study participant? If the participants are minors, how can researchers verify that the participants have parental consent? As many scholars have indicated, these are the same questions that have concerned researchers who have conducted studies through methods such as phone interviews, where the identity of the participant is not as easily verifiable as that of a face-to-face participant (Boellstorff et al., 2012). What can be done as a researcher to mitigate this concern?

Niemeyer and Gerber (2015) studied the walkthroughs and YouTube channels of several youth Minecraft players. Using a snowball sampling scheme, they conducted collective case study research of five youth. The data that Niemeyer and Gerber collected included analyses of artifacts posted on YouTube channels, discussion board posts within the user's YouTube channel, and interviews. To verify the informed consent of the participants in the study, the researchers required a phone interview with the parent. Because of the use of snowball sampling, Niemeyer and Gerber were able to gain access to participants who were known to the researchers at initial point of entry into the Minecraft community. This facilitated access to conduct interviews with parents. However, what should researchers do if they do not use a sampling scheme that gives them this type of access? What if the participants live in other countries, or places where time zone differences make phone interviews with parents and guardians a more difficult task? Some of the suggestions in Table 7.2, such as birth date verification and secondary email contact with parents, might be most useful in those cases.

Anonymity

Anonymity is an important component of all research studies, particularly those dealing with research in online spaces, where a simple search on any public search engine might highlight identifying information about research participants. Internet research has many components to it that risk revealing participants' identities if they are not properly protected from the outset. Though not all information divulged to researchers during a research study might be available through public search engines, all data must be kept confidential and anonymized so that research participants' identities are protected at all times.

Anonymity becomes an interesting facet to explore, as many research participants in online environments often already go by pseudonyms. For many participants, their online pseudonyms carry a level of expertise or respect, and often research participants want to be credited for the work and creative productions that they have completed in their respective online environments. In the book *Ethnography* and *Virtual Worlds: A Handbook of Method,* coauthored by Boellstorff, Nardi, Pearce, and Taylor (2012), Pearce described an instance when one of the research participants felt slighted because during the prepublication, member checking stage, she believed that the researcher had misattributed her work to someone else. However, the research participant had failed to read the fine print of the consent form that stated that all work would be credited to pseudonyms.

Researchers may ask participants to help create their own pseudonyms; doing so works to mitigate confusion and helps participants to feel that they are working *with* the researchers. On the other hand, as illustrated in the previous example of Pearce's work, participants may want to use the real names of their online personas. This option should be explored with the ethics review board, and if it is an option, then related risks should be clearly noted in the consent forms.

Other researchers have created methods to create leveled "cloaking," or concealing, of the data (Kozinets, 2010, p. 154). This means the level of anonymity is related to the sensitivity level of the data. Researchers have noted that there are instances in which keeping participants anonymous may not be realistic, or desired, such as when dealing with writing about public figures, famous individuals, or individuals who have gained notoriety within their respective online environments (Boellstorff et al., 2012; Kozinets, 2010). This method of concealment requires the researcher to take a somewhat subjective stance, but at the same time, to exercise good judgment as to the sensitivity of the data.

Bruckman (2002) suggested four levels of **data concealment**: from no concealment to heavy concealment, depending on the sensitivity levels of the data. One end of the spectrum, unconcealed, allows for researchers to write openly about their research using the participant's real name, the online persona's real pseudonym or community name, and direct or verbatim quotes. In this case, of course, the participant must give the researcher permission to do so. This is particularly helpful when copyrights of creative productions are involved. If using this method of concealment, care should be exercised in using data that could be potentially damaging or embarrassing to the research participant.

Researchers using minimum concealment include the name of the community being researched but use pseudonyms to protect the anonymity of the individuals in the community. Direct, verbatim quotes are used. This is a method to use when the context to the research is so important that concealing it would be detrimental to understanding the research. Again, it is important to make sure researchers do not reveal any damaging information that could potentially harm research participants.

In medium concealment cases, researchers would most likely alter the participants' pseudonyms but might keep the group or community name, and they would practice care and good judgment in using verbatim quotes. The final level, maximum concealment, obscures all identifying information so that it would be nearly impossible to identify a research participant. Pseudonyms are used for all participants, group and community names are altered, and all quotes are reworded and rephrased so that even a simple online search would not reveal the identity of the participant or the group.

Bruckman (2002) provided an example of concealment levels related to the case of journalist Julian Dibbell's (1993) work titled "A Rape in Cyberspace." In addition to the sensitive nature of the data presented in the article, which examined the antisocial behaviors that occurred within the LambdaMoo virtual environment, the article received a lot of attention from mainstream media, which led Dibbell to later publish a book-length account of his work. When he published the book, he used pseudonyms to obscure every name and key identifying information. However, to give ownership to those who were a part of the LambdaMoo study, he created a detective game that allowed those within the LamdaMoo community to identify the key characters and participants discussed within the book. The levels of concealment that Dibbell engaged in were directly tied to the level of protection dictated by the reach of his work. Table 7.3 provides a quick reference of Bruckman's suggested levels of concealment for anonymity.

It is important to realize that the level to which researchers conceal a participant's identity is directly related to the sensitivity of the information and the online arena that they are researching. As McKee and Porter (2009) suggested, there are varying degrees of sensitive information that need to be considered when determining the extent to which anonymity

Table 7.3 Bruckman's Levels of Concealment	
Level	**Key Elements**
Unconcealed	Participants' names and community are revealed and verbatim quotes are used.
Minimum Concealed	Participants' names are changed; however, community names may remain the same.
Medium Concealed	There is a blend of changing participants' names, community name, and rephrasing of direct quotes.
Maximum Concealed	All identifying information is changed; fictive language is used for pseudonyms and the rephrasing of direct quotes.

is needed. Drawing from Sveningsson's (2002) work on the public-private dichotomy that still exists in Internet research, McKee and Porter proposed mapping the levels to which informed consent and identity concealment are necessary depending on whether the information is deemed private-sensitive or public-nonsensitive. As such, researchers must make judgment calls as to what level of concealment they will employ. For example, an SAT study skills discussion forum may have less sensitive data than a forum on "coming out" for individuals in countries where homosexuality can lead to the penalty of death.

Benefits and Risk

All research has certain risks and benefits. Without appropriately obscuring the data to protect participants, researchers risk creating potentially hazardous situations for the participants. This might include a participant's loss of status, loss of an employment, loss of a romantic relationship, or in other cases, lawsuits or death threats.

Researchers should try to give back to the participants and involved communities, and such beneficence is an important component of research ethics. The research should be conducted to benefit both the research community and the participants. These efforts can be as informal as offering editing services to participants or as formal as pro bono professional development for the community studied. Spotlight Box 7.3 discusses beneficence by providing professional development to a group of teachers interested in developing games-based learning environments.

Spotlight Box 7.3
Pro Bono Professional Development and Game-Based Learning

Gerber and Price (2013) engaged in community beneficence by designing and conducting pro bono professional development related to research that involved discussion boards on the topic of games-based learning. Their study looked at thirteen in-service teachers' perceptions of games-based learning. The findings of their study indicated that teachers often feel overwhelmed when presented with new pedagogies, that teachers are concerned with their teacherly identity when implementing new technologies such as gaming, and that teachers fear that a lack of professional support will exist when trying out new pedagogies.

After the completion of the study, Gerber and Price (2013) offered their participants a district-wide professional development model. There, teachers could receive guidance in developing their own games-based curricula as well as engage in face-to-face dialogue and discussion about gaming and literacy, with a peer support network. For six months, Gerber and Price hosted monthly workshops on a variety of games-based learning topics, such as working with multiple game titles versus a single game title; supporting videogames with young adult literature; and expanding students' writing opportunities through games-based topics. Additionally, they provided a forum where teachers enrolled in the professional development could voice their concerns about using games-based learning in resource-poor environments, and working with nongamer students in a games-based classroom. Finally, Gerber and Price mentored several first- and second-year teachers in conducting action research on their games-based curricular materials so that the teachers would be able to provide evidence-based support to parents and administrators on these curricular changes.

Some researchers offer financial compensation to underpaid participants, such as teachers, police officers, and public service workers, who they feel deserve monetary compensation. When researchers offer financial compensation to research participants, it must be approved by the appropriate review board, and specific information about the financial compensation must be included on the informed consent form. Other scholars believe that this type of monetary compensation might taint the data, and that participants might be more apt to tell researchers what they believe the researchers want to hear instead of their true opinions (Miles, Huberman, & Saldaña, 2014). Regardless of financial compensation, when it comes to risks and benefits, the community where one is conducting research should not be left worse off when the researcher leaves. Following the principles of care will help researchers ensure that they are adequately and accurately representing their participants, that they are actively minimizing any risk, and—when possible—that they are providing proper benefits to their research participants.

Copyright, Terms of Service, End-User License Agreements, Creative Commons, and Fair Use

When researchers conduct qualitative studies in online spaces, there also can be issues related to data ownership. Often, in the fine print of the end-user license agreement, researchers will find that the online service provider owns the information hosted on a website, including materials created by users. From Disney's Club Penguin to Google's YouTube, most spaces are owned by large corporations that use terms of service and end-user licensing policies to protect their best interests. In *Connected Play: Tweens in a Virtual World*, Kafai and Fields (2013) discussed the importance of digital content creation within online spaces and the resulting issues of ownership and copyright on youth participation in these spaces. Kafai and Fields explained that these creations are generally recorded, replicable, and searchable by invisible entities, namely the corporation that owns the site.

However, Creative Commons licensing agreements, otherwise known as public copyright licenses, give individuals the right to share, use, build on, and redistribute works to which they have contributed. Though Creative Commons licensing provides researchers and participants more flexibility in the use and distribution of materials, the researcher must still uphold principles of care. Additionally, fair use policies often provide researchers a level of flexibility in how they approach data collection, generation, and analysis because research is viewed as supporting the social good (Lessig, 2002; 2005).

Ethically, researchers must consider the unique aspects of terms of service, end-user licensing agreements, and Creative Commons licensing when they set out to conduct research in online spaces. From the way that the data are represented in publications, to the legality of analyzing and publishing data that might, in fact, not be owned by the participants, researchers must exercise care and caution. Furthermore, without a universal copyright law, researchers must be familiar with the laws that govern where they are conducting research, as different countries follow different laws and different codes regarding copyright (Hawkins, 2011; World Intellectual Property Organization, n.d.; Xalabarder, 2002). As noted in the Berne Convention, Article 5.2, "Choice of Law," the country claiming copyright on the work(s) being used would also use its laws to govern that document's use. For example, a researcher from Thailand who is living in Cyprus, but is conducting research dealing with documents under copyright in the United States, would need to abide by U.S. copyright laws. However, the Choice of Law Article in the Berne Convention was written many years before the Internet was conceived and developed. Therefore, the World Intellectual Property Organization Copyright Treaty was established and ratified in 1996 to help individuals stay abreast of changes in copyright and intellectual property brought about by the Internet. However, given that laws evolve, researchers should remain up-to-date on current copyright laws and, when in doubt, access legal counsel.

Conclusion

This chapter traces the historical underpinnings of research ethics and presents contemporary guidelines and issues related to researching learning in online environments. The chapter closes with a discussion about the principles of care and vulnerable populations, as well as an exploration of international guidelines that provide insight into the complexity of research ethics.

CONNECTING TO YOUR WORK

Research ethics is a complicated topic but one that must be carefully considered before beginning a study. The following questions will help you to think through some of the ethics issues that surround the study of online spaces:

- What are your main concerns related to ethical research? What are some ideas that were presented in this chapter that might help you to mitigate these concerns?

- What are some ways that you might conceal the identities of the participants in your research study?

- Determine if your institution has a policy in place for conducting online research. If so, examine this policy and see what areas of the policy you would like to have clarified by the ethics review board.

- If your institution does not have a policy in place specifically for conducting online research, examine one of the institutional policies introduced in the chapter. What aspects of the policy need additional clarification? Why?

Guiding Questions for Chapter 8

- What are some characteristics of the changing nature of research?
- How might the participatory culture of learning influence research design?
- How does the research of learning in online spaces remain an evolving process?

CHAPTER EIGHT

How Might Research Change in New Times?

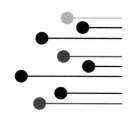

Introduction

In this final chapter, we draw on discussions from across the previous seven chapters as we look ahead and address implications and applications of conducting qualitative research of learning in online spaces. We also present additional contemporary frameworks regarding online participation and pedagogy for researchers to contemplate as they design their study.

The Complicated Nature of Studying Learning in Online Spaces

In 1998, *Journal of Adolescent & Adult Literacy* editors Allan Luke and John Elkins looked to the turn of the century and contemplated what literacy would look like in what they called "New Times." Though their focus was specific to literacy when they questioned, "What will it mean to be a reader and writer in the 21st century" (p. 4), contemplating the impact of "New Times" extends into multiple fields in the humanities and social sciences. Now, after eighteen years of rapid technological changes, researchers continuously attempt to identify and (re)evaluate learning practices. Given that what is new inherently becomes old (Cope & Kalantzis, 2015), the focus is on contemporary and changeable forms of meaning making.

As these examinations have increasingly included activities in online spaces, researchers have had to rethink research design and aspects of participation, such as inhabitation, learning artifacts, and ways of being. In addition to expanding or reconceptualizing terms, researchers have had to contemplate what it means to investigate learning in online spaces, as well as to collect and analyze data of learning in those spaces. At times, this has included the perforation of methodological boundaries and a combination of tools and theoretical constructs to achieve the collection of in-depth, rich data. In this book, we extend Luke and Elkins's question to include methodologies and tools. Knowing well that we cannot predict the future, we look to contemporary practices, distinguish how we conceptualize learning in online spaces, and call on extant investigations to address methodological approaches and data analyses, keeping in mind that these discussions will help to inform what research will look like in current and future "New Times."

Across this book, there is careful attention to the description and discussion of learning, online spaces, and methodological tools. Chapter One points to the ubiquity of learning, especially when researchers account for networked field sites. In a similar vein, throughout the book, it is clear that not all sites can be treated in the same ways. As noted in Chapters Two and Seven, there are various levels of public access, consumption, and contribution. Some sites, like Wikipedia, support public viewing, but collaborative authorship requires registration for a free account. This approach—keeping material open to the public to view, but requiring a login to add or comment on content—is common among sites that provide information. For instance, the site gamefaqs .com hosts a message board, as well as archives of walkthroughs, cheats, and answers to frequently asked questions. Like Wikipedia, the content is open to the public to read; but, if users want to contribute to the site, they must register with a valid email address. Additionally, there are programs created or overseen by academics, such as Scholar (Cope & Kalantzis, 2013) and Barnsborough (Merchant, 2010), which were designed for academic purposes and specifically feature co-constructed meaning-making opportunities (for more about these programs, see Chapters Three and Four, respectively). These online spaces build on contemporary participatory practices to engage students in metacognitive and critical thinking and help to keep the interaction and feedback student-driven and relevant. Finally, other sites, including, but not limited to, social networking forums (noted in Chapter Two), hinge on user registration and feature a spectrum of participation and privacy options. For example, Facebook users have the ability to create a semiclosed circle of "friends," making only selected individuals privy to posted information. However, as with most online content, there is a lack of control of the update and distribution of information. Facebook users may be able to select the initial people with whom they want to share their posts, but the caveat is that users cannot control if and how their "friends" modify or share the content.

Important to consider, however, is not only the space and its affordances and limitations, but also the inhabitants of the space, movement within and beyond the space, and the generation of artifacts. Addressed throughout this book is the concept of tracing an individual's interactions and movements across spaces by examining networking residues (Grimes & Fields, 2012). As explained in Chapter Two, researchers must consider the aspect of multi-sited research, and the investigation of movement and specific practices within and across sites. For instance, Fields and Kafai (2009) examined the teleporting that took place in the online gaming space Whyville as a means to understand how knowledge sharing not only existed among peers but also extended across and beyond the Whyville site. Additionally, as Fields and Kafai noted, there were methodological affordances to their approach:

Our strategic choice of focusing on a practice rather than individuals . . . allowed us to leverage the record-keeping facility of log files to focus our multimodal analysis on particular time points. In further analyses, we are using the log files to reconstruct participation portraits of individual Whyville players revealing their trajectories of participation and often hidden activities—hidden because they were neither captured in our field notes or video recordings, nor reported in interviews. (p. 65)

In other words, participation in online spaces can be complicated to trace and to analyze, and the examination of movement can offer new insights into participation and meaning making.

Equally important is how the researcher bounds the study, considers his or her positioning within the site, and designs the data collection and analyses (for more see Chapters Four and Six). Returning to the example of Fields and Kafai's (2009) Whyville study, one may see how, despite rigorous data collection including videos, log files, field notes, and interviews, they still encountered difficulty reassembling conversations "because accounts logged in chronological sequence do not capture concurrent interactions in multiple spaces" (p. 65). The multidimensional nature of online spaces and participatory practices, therefore, presents a challenge to researchers not only to collect, but also to analyze in ways that aptly capture the dynamism in meaning making across multiple sites.

(Re)Imagining Research Techniques

Given that contemporary learners continuously layer their online and offline experiences in unanticipated ways (Abrams, 2015), researchers are challenged to think beyond convention and consider a combination of methods to capture dynamic interaction and creation. In his research of five college students' use of Facebook as an educational tool, Barden (2014) did not ascribe to any one particular qualitative approach (e.g., ethnography, phenomenology). Rather, he argued that calling on a variety of methods, including, but not limited to, participant observation, protocol analysis, video recordings, and screen capture–facilitated, "multidimensional" data collection. Barden explained that "using multiple methods enables researchers to move beyond triangulation or corroboration, and enhances our ability to develop an in-depth understanding of complex phenomena (Denzin & Lincoln, 2003): what Mason (2006, p. 12) called the 'heart and soul' of lived experience" (p. 556). In a similar vein, researchers, such as Kafai and Fields (2012) and Maxwell (2015), have asserted the need to break down methodological silos to aptly and appropriately capture and analyze complex contemporary meaning making. These researchers called attention to the affordances of multiple data sources and approaches to data collection:

Some researchers have begun to acknowledge that the dividing lines between the quantitative and qualitative methodologies create a false dichotomy because each of the perspective[s] contributes to our understanding of what, when and why players engage in these worlds. Furthermore, the complexity of virtual worlds indicates that not any one data source alone but the triangulation of many may do better justice in understanding player practices, purposes, and psychology. (Kafai & Fields, 2012, p. 265)

What these researchers bring to the fore is the importance of moving beyond methodological traditions to find the appropriate combination of techniques to identify, record, and analyze data. Such an approach to research affords one the ability not only to take a pragmatic stance and tailor the design to the needs of his or her study, but also to address learning within and across multifarious practices and sites. In other words, researchers need not be limited to the approaches from any one single tradition; however, mixing multiple approaches should be adopted with care. There must be a rationale for the approaches used, as haphazard intermixing of traditions can lead to the misalignment of concepts and, potentially, unfounded or disorganized interpretations. Further, by acknowledging their experiences and expectations, researchers can build on their mental model to select appropriate paradigmatic and methodological frameworks that align with their logic of inquiry, or to modify these choices as their understanding of the research questions evolves. With care, methodological combinations can be creatively advantageous, especially given the increasingly participatory nature of contemporary research.

Calling attention to issues of power in research, as discussed in Chapter One, Onwuebguzie and Frels (2013) suggested that the equal inclusion of the participant as researcher will help to support and sustain egalitarian, democratized, and progressive research. A recent study of adolescent gaming in a high school classroom assumed a critical dialectical pluralistic approach that included the students as coresearchers and co-presenters (Gerber, Abrams, Onwuebguzie, & Benge, 2014). Critical dialectical pluralism draws from dialectical pluralism (Johnson, 2012), a philosophy that allows researchers to engage with multiple competing paradigms, disciplines, and values, and to purposefully work toward creating meaning in their research studies. The "critical" aspect of dialectical pluralism acknowledges that power dynamics exist in all studies between researcher and participant. To upend these power dynamics, researchers must begin to engage in participatory approaches in their studies, calling on participants to help shape the research. In so doing, the students in the aforementioned study were instrumental in the analysis and reanalysis of the data, as well as co-presentation of the findings. The research involved an iterative process for collecting, interpreting, and reinterpreting the data, with the students providing immediate and retrospective insight into their learning practices. This feedback occurred through ongoing dialogue and regular conferencing with the student-participants in this study. Through this talk, the students helped to shape the revision of artifacts, assignments, and subsequent curricular decisions. The use of critical dialectical pluralism enabled students to take a creative and agentic stance toward their own meaning making within the class, and their involvement in the process became central to the analysis and dissemination of the findings as co-presenters in conference presentations. Though not specifically pragmatic, such a critical dialectical pluralistic approach seems to support a mixing of traditions and methodologies.

Similarly, mixing multiple approaches when studying learning in online spaces honors "scaffolded co-construction" of meaning (Lankshear & Knobel, 2003). With a related egalitarian ethos of critical dialectical pluralism, scaffolded co-construction includes the researcher working with groups of various participants and "ideally, the groups would contain a mix of mindsets, offering scope for negotiation and for developing mutual understandings within a relaxed environment" (p. 180). Scaffolded co-constructed learning, therefore, involves the participants as active collaborators in the investigation of their own learning.

Shifting Cultures, Shifting Boundaries

Combining multiple approaches to designing and implementing research also supports investigations of an evolving learning landscape. After all, researching learning in online spaces also includes the examination of shifting cultures and participatory networks. In *Confronting the Challenges of Participatory Culture*, Jenkins, Purushotma, Weigel, Clinton, and Robison (2009) called attention to contemporary norms that hinge on active participation, social connection, and, often, artistic reinvention. A contemporary participatory culture includes prompts to share experiences and rely on mobile technologies and digital tools to support impulsive and deliberate social networking. Commercial vendors have built on and exploited these norms to support product promotion, using hashtags, QR codes, or prompts to encourage further consumption and mass participation. One need not look beyond a preprinted Dunkin' Donuts cup, which encourages consumers to "Share your Dunkin' story," to contribute to a public, social narrative about Dunkin' Donuts experiences. Though such marketing seems to superficially reveal how users traverse and contribute to online spaces, it calls attention to a variety of ways that commercialism thrives on and extends new norms and ways of being.

To more clearly understand how there can be a "convergence" (Jenkins, 2006) of behavioral and cultural shifts, one could consider how the Harry Potter Alliance (HPA) builds on fandom and the multifaceted relationship between media and consumers. More specifically, with a vision to embrace "a creative and collaborative culture that solves the world's problems" (Harry Potter Alliance, 2015) the site has spurred social activism from a range of online contributions. From collective discussions of lessons gleaned from the popular J. K. Rowling series to fundraising efforts, book drives, and awareness campaigns, the HPA has drawn attention to social issues and has ignited social awareness and fan-based activism. As such, online participatory cultures build on mass media (and vice versa), and they can support the sharing, resharing, and reshaping of experiences and practices that can promote not only new forms of meaning making, but also new ways of addressing social issues.

What also comes to the fore is the shifting nature of learning ecologies. Kalantzis and Cope (2010) explained that many social changes are related to the "knowledge society" that supports independent thinking and emphasizes creativity and innovation. They asserted that in contrast to previous generations of learners who passively accepted information they read in textbooks, a new generation of learners, "Generation P," for "participatory," is actively and collaboratively involved in learning, creating, and assessing their work:

> The new learners will take greater responsibility for their learning in part because they are given greater autonomy and scope for self-control. They will be a knowledge producer, drawing together a range of available knowledge resources— instead of a knowledge consumer, fed just one source, the old textbook. They will work effectively in pairs or groups on collaborative knowledge projects, creating knowledge to be shared with peers. They will continue to learn beyond the classroom, using the social media to learn anywhere and anytime—a phenomenon called "ubiquitous learning." They will critically self-assess and reflect upon their learning. They will give feedback to their peers in 'social-networking' interactions. They will be comfortable players in environments where intelligence is collective—not just the sum of things that can be retained in the individual's head, but with a capacity to source knowledge online or from other students or from experts, parents and community members. (p. 204)

Conceptual and participatory shifts, therefore, translate into complex and multisourced meaning making (see Chapter Three for a comprehensive discussion of conceptualizing learning in online spaces and the role of participatory culture).

When contemplating qualitative research in light of shifting and evolving practices, it is important to account for principles of contemporary learning, as they call attention to the modes and practices that are seminal to meaning making. This book opened with a discussion of established qualitative approaches in Chapter One, and the concept of combining these methodologies has been

Table 8.1 Select Perspectives of Contemporary Learning

Perspective	Scholarship	Description
Learning by Design	Cope & Kalantzis (2015); Kalantzis & Cope (2012)	Learning is interest-driven, social, and networked. Learners are involved in self-assessment, and knowledge is collective.
Connected Learning	Ito et al. (2010)	Learning is interest-driven, social, and networked, which supports collaborative knowledge generation. There is an interconnection among production, peer culture, and mentorship.
Participatory Learning	Jenkins (2010); Reilly, Vartabedian, Felt, & Jenkins (2012)	Learning involves multiple forms of media, tools, and practices. Stemming from understandings of participatory culture, there is an emphasis on collaborative learning that is relevant, engaging, and draws on out-of-school practices.

threaded throughout the chapters. What also has come to the fore, however, is how research methods can promote agentive, creative, and collaborative perspectives on learning in online spaces. Extending the conversation, Table 8.1 showcases three select perspectives of contemporary learning and how collaborative, interest-driven, and agentive practices exist across these different discussions of learning. Though all three include the examination of artifacts and interaction, there is a nuanced focus for each perspective.

• Learning by Design addresses the knowledge processes and how learners experience, conceptualize, analyze, and apply information (Cope & Kalantzis, 2015; Kalantzis & Cope, 2012). The Learning by Design approach also attends to pedagogy and how shifts in learning must be accompanied by shifts in pedagogy and school culture and the creation of new learning ecologies. In terms of qualitative research, the Learning by Design perspective helps to draw attention to socioculturally situated understandings and re-created or transformed meaning evidenced in artifacts and peer interaction. The program Scholar, addressed in Chapter Three, builds on a Learning by Design approach. Agentive and networked meaning making are core components that have guided the design and implementation of the program.

• Connected Learning underscores the various trajectories of meaning making. As illustrated in the infographic in Figure 8.1 and addressed in Chapter Three, the Connected Learning framework honors meaning making with multiple entry points and "genres of participation" (Ito et al., 2013, p. 36). Further, the framework highlights connections to in-school pursuits and out-of-school interests, and how the presence of others—from peers to caring adults— is seminal to the advancement of knowledge and practice. For qualitative researchers, the connected learning perspective supports a nuanced view of participant interactions and media use, as well as the examination of distributed knowledge and networks online and offline.

- Participatory Learning, which also is discussed in Chapter Three, focuses on the knowledge and skills necessary for making meaning in a new multimedia, multimodal learning landscape. The five principles of participatory learning, which are inspired by Ito and colleagues' (2010) examination of participatory practices and Jenkins and colleagues' (2006, 2009) discussion of participatory culture, place an emphasis on the learning experience. The five principles include (1) creating with various media and modes; (2) coproduction; (3) intrinsic and extrinsic motivation and engagement; (4) meaningful activities with personal resonance; and (5) the connection across online and offline, traditional and progressive spaces (Reilly, Vartabedian, Felt, & Jenkins, 2012). Foci of related studies have included students' or educators' new media literacies and digital tool use, as well as pedagogical applications (Vartabedian & Felt, 2012). For qualitative researchers, the principles of Participatory Learning emphasize the actions and knowledge of the learning within a particular cultural milieu.

These three perspectives focus not only on representing learning as a networked ecology, but also on effecting a pedagogical change that recognizes contemporary teaching and learning as a collection of meaning-making practices that are multimodal, digital, and interconnected. Additionally, each perspective honors the porosity of online spaces and the importance of the offline component when conceptualizing and studying learning in and across online spaces.

The juxtaposition of the principles also calls attention to the networked and social nature of learning, and it highlights a level of agency in meaning making. Agentive learning suggests that the meaning maker has a sense of control and power within the space. For instance, Jackie Marsh's (2013) examination of children's interaction in Club Penguin revealed how the participants would determine and seek friendships:

> One of the first activities children undertook when they encountered an avatar who either interested them or who had approached them with a request for friendship was to click on their avatar profile to read them. If this reading of the data led them to feel comfortable about the avatar, the next step would be to send a postcard inviting friendship. (p. 81)

Depending on the framework or perspective, a researcher could consider this interaction by examining the design and normative structures of the online space that support such interaction and agency. One also could investigate the ways literacies and networked practices develop and evolve through such agentive

Figure 8.1   A Visual Representation of the Connected Learning Framework

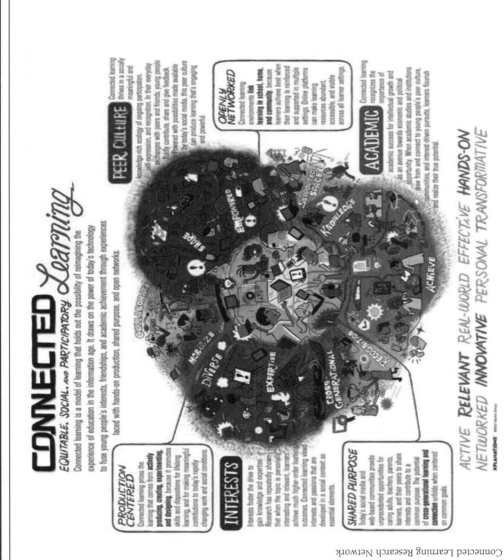

Connected Learning Research Network

interaction. Additionally, one could consider how friendships in the space contribute to online (and perhaps offline) identities and practices.

As with traditional inquiry, the direction and design of the study depend on the focus of the investigation. What complicates research of learning in online spaces, however, are the various directionalities of and entry points to learning, as well as the aspect of opportunity and choice. Further, whereas issues of access to traditional offline field sites, such as face-to-face classrooms, may constrain research, many online sites offer immediate—and sometimes public—access to data. Such immediacy not only simplifies time line considerations that may delay or stymie data collection but also gives researchers the ability to continuously document meaning making over an extended period of time.

Traditional qualitative research of offline environments has some presupposed constants. For instance, researchers know that barring any major ecological or weather-related disaster, the space that they have visited (e.g., a home, a classroom, a museum, a park) will be there the following day. The people who inhabit the space may have different experiences within that space, but the physical setting acts as a relative constant. In the virtual space, though, that is not the case. The introduction of new user content continuously shifts the interior design of many sites. For instance, Facebook may archive posts, but the influx of new posts creates a new landscape for one to view, modify, and traverse. Furthermore, given that the Internet is continuously on—as opposed to most institutions that have hours of operation—the rate of growth and change can be exponential in a short period of time. Additionally, there are situations when sites (or components of sites) are removed by webmasters or when participants cease to inhabit a space.

Though the concern of maintaining participant involvement can be a tenuous factor in any research study, the online element creates a fragility and instability that is both challenging and exciting. The rapid change and interaction present a host of opportunities for investigating learning and extending research studies. However, these aspects of online meaning making also highlight common questions related to the role of the researcher, the tools necessary for data collection, and the approaches for data analysis. These and similar concerns have been addressed earlier in this text (see Chapters Four through Six), but they continue to remain important points to consider when studying (and confronted with) new technologies, spaces, and practices.

Additionally, researching learning in online spaces has a number of ethical considerations, many of which have been addressed in Chapter Seven. In terms of research design and approaches to collecting data, Knobel (2003) specifically expressed concern with viewing the Internet as a repository of information that can be easily tapped, analyzed, and generalized. She addressed the lure of "hit-and-run research, where the researcher spends a few days or even a few hours observing the interactions of online participants in a given community, then writes about them as though everything to be known about the community and its make-up has been observed and understood in that short period of time" (p. 192). The various studies featured throughout our book do not include such "snatch-and-grab" techniques (p. 192); rather, all have included longitudinal examinations of inhabitation, participation, and related meaning making. Despite the limitations of researching online spaces, longitudinal examinations provide insight into evolving practices, environments, and cultures.

Knobel (2003) also advocated for researchers to be careful in their identification and analysis of interactions online. She called attention to the nuances of behavior, noting how a "rant" and a "flame" are different forms of expression that run the risk of conflation and subsequent inaccurate discussions of interaction:

> For example, if a rant—an extended, always passionate monologue about a usually-narrow topic that is of almost obsessive interest to the author—is equated with a flame, which in turn is equated with an ongoing feudal exchange between two participants, and then with direct contributions to the discussion, and all are treated as equivalent within analysis and reporting, interpretations cannot provide a fair or even accurate account of what took place within the studied space. (p. 193)

Accuracy in reporting is always important in any research. With qualitative inquiry, researchers must take extra caution in the ways they represent a practice or a space. Likewise, researchers must be mindful of how they label or identify a space. Affinity space research (Gee, 2004, Gee & Hayes, 2010; Hayes & Duncan, 2012) has created a language for addressing participation that is guided by shared interests and activities. The concept of affinity spaces also acknowledges that digital language and behavior can be bounded by context and practice, but it also recognizes the various trajectories for participation (Lammers, Curwood, & Magnifico, 2012). However, it is important not to simply describe an online environment as an affinity space; not all online practices take place in an affinity space. Echoing Knobel's point (2003), we contend that the research design must be concrete and logical. It should be "framed by a well-formed and manageable research question and a workable theory or set of theories, [and it] has carefully selected data collection and analysis tools and techniques that will produce the kinds of data and outcomes needed for addressing the research questions" (Knobel, 2003, p. 201).

Conclusion

It is clear that the research of learning in online spaces is not without its challenges. As with the creation of any study's design, researchers must carefully bound their investigation. Across this book, we advocate for contemporary research to embrace pragmatic, appropriate, and ethical approaches to data collection and analysis. When contemplating future inquiry, readers can draw on the discussions in Chapters Four through Seven and use the prompts below to contemplate a study's design—from ways to conceptualize learning, to researcher positioning, to data collection and analysis, to ethical considerations.

With the purpose of the inquiry in mind, researchers must consider the following:

- how to conceptualize the examination of participatory practices that exist online and extend offline;

- how online spaces may complicate or support data collection and analysis;

- how the inquiry's design positions the researcher and the participants; and

- how the researcher will have to negotiate access to the site, participants, and texts.

When examining learning in online spaces, researchers should bear in mind the porosity of online spaces and the importance of examining offline activities. As discussed throughout this text and highlighted in Chapter Four, learning in online spaces may not be relegated solely to on-screen practices. Researchers have been grappling with ways to design and conduct research that includes learning in online spaces (see Chapters Four and Five). In this way, challenges can become opportunities to investigate rich, interconnected meaning making.

Across this text, the positioning of the researcher has remained in the foreground. Whether the discussion has centered on ethics, data collection, data analysis, or the role of the researcher, the responsibility for quality and thoroughness remains on the researcher. However, this focus is not to deny the changing, participatory nature of inquiry and the new possibilities of co-construction and coproduction of meaning *with* participants. This approach underscores and supports the multidimensional nature of investigating learning in online spaces, and it calls for greater sensitivity and accuracy in research. Such an approach will be warranted as technologies continue to permeate public and private spaces and as movement among digital and nondigital text continues to become routine.

Finally, qualitative inquiry has been a primary component across discussions in this text. However, it is important to acknowledge that the combination of multiple methodologies, including those extending into the quantitative realm, supports an approach to inquiry that honors online and offline perspectives and privileges participant voices. Such an approach accounts for multi-sited, hyperlinked, and hypermobile practices that are otherwise difficult to trace, document, and analyze with traditional or singular methodologies. Increased flexibility and reflexivity are essential when researching learning in online spaces.

CONNECTING TO YOUR WORK

Before you begin your research, consider how participatory practices exist within and across spaces:

- How do you plan to trace these practices?

- What combination(s) of approaches will support the rich examination and discussion of the data?

- How will your study include the voices of the participants?

- How, if at all, will your research resemble a learning process?

GLOSSARY

Affinity spaces: Sites of informal, interest-driven learning where a variety of novice and experienced participants interact around a common goal, topic, or project. These physical, virtual or blended spaces are often spread across many sites including online message boards, blogs, web pages, and face-to-face meetings.

Anthropological orientation to studying learning: Learning research in the anthropological tradition often takes the form of close description. Researchers spend long periods of time documenting the particularities of learning spaces and practices, focusing on how the learning of a certain group works, and how it is useful and distinct.

AoIR: The Association of Internet Researchers is a multidisciplinary, international academic association dedicated to the study of online spaces. The AoIR hosts an annual academic conference that is held in different locations around the globe, and it strives to provide researchers with up-to-date and cutting-edge methods for Internet-based research. For more information on AoIR, visit its website: http://aoir.org/

Behaviorism: A theory that human and animal behavior—not thoughts, emotions, or learning—can explain action because all behavior is an observable response to the environment. This theory assumes that psychological disorders or upsets are best treated through conditioning by which the behavior patterns are altered.

Beneficence: A concept that is related to the positive impact that all research studies should strive to maintain within their local and broader research communities. Ethically research studies should leave their communities as good as, or better than, when they entered.

Blended spaces: Learning spaces that contain both face-to-face and online elements. For example, friends in a World of Warcraft guild may meet both online and at a guild member's house to strategize.

Cognitivism: An information-processing theory that deals with how people perceive, learn, remember, and think about information. It sees learning as taking place within the learner as a result of mental processing (not just observable behavior).

Collective case study: This is also known as multicase design. Collective case studies allow researchers to compare similarities and differences among and between single cases in order to gain a more comprehensive understanding about a theory or issue.

Concealment: Related to research ethics and indicates the amount of anonymity that is applied to a research participant's identity.

Confirmability: The degree to which researchers acknowledge the subjective nature of qualitative inquiry and disclose their predispositions, which may include sharing the beliefs that underpin their methodological decisions.

Connected learning: A theory of learning and social change whereby learners are encouraged to develop links and connections among their in-school, out-of-school, civic, and family-oriented activities and interests—and to use these links to create opportunities for greater access or positive change.

Connective ethnography: A qualitative method where researchers act as participant observers to trace participants' lifeworlds within online and offline practices and environments.

Constructivism: A social theory of knowledge and learning. Because new knowledge must be built from preexisting knowledge, what humans know is based on what we learn from others in various social settings.

Co-presence: When researchers simultaneously inhabit the same online or offline space as participants.

Credibility: Focuses on ensuring that the research findings are congruent with reality; can be enhanced through member checking and peer examination.

Critical discourse analysis: A type of discourse analysis that focuses on how social or political power and equity are gained, lost, or maintained through discursive interactions.

Critical theorist: A paradigm that seeks to understand various situations and multiple realities. The researcher must take into account social, political, cultural, economic, ethnic, and gender factors.

Data concealment: Considering elements of confidentiality, as well as anonymity of participants within a study, data concealment is related to the various degrees that a participant's information is concealed and kept confidential. The sensitivity of a study's data suggests the level of concealment that a researcher should consider: minimum, medium, and maximum. These levels of concealment provide researchers with a guiding framework for the amount of identifying information that they should allow to be disseminated in publications.

Dependability: Research findings are more dependable when the researchers have taken care to explicate the research design and implementation, to detail the process of recruiting participants and collecting data, and to engage in member checking.

Discourse analysis: A qualitative analytical technique that focuses on how human meanings are constructed and maintained through language and action by the individuals involved, within particular environments, to particular ends, for different audiences, and for particular reasons.

Emic research: An emic approach is inductive, and understandings emerge from participants' voices. For more on emic versus etic, please see http://isites.harvard.edu/icb/icb .do?keyword=qualitative&pageid=icb.page340911

Fanfiction: A narrative or poetic text created by enthusiasts of a popular media in which they extend characters, ideas, and information from a particular book, movie, videogame, or other fandom community.

Generalizability: Findings from research that hold true for the population sampled and, over time and through repeated study, can be statistically extended (or generalized) to the population at large or to a broader theory.

Grounded theory: A qualitative data collection and analysis technique in which the researcher generates theory directly from data and observations, moving between collecting new data and comparing it to emerging themes and patterns.

Human subjects review boards: Responsible for approving or denying research protocols submitted by researchers by determining if the research design is ethical. In different parts of the world, this board is known by various names, such as Institutional Review Board, Ethics Review Committee, and Human Subjects Review Boards.

Informed consent: A state in which research participants have foreknowledge that they will be studied and have given permission for the research to occur.

Instrumental case studies: A research approach that allows researchers to gain insight into a variety of issues that inform other situations and sites. Instrumental case studies provide a broader examination of a larger picture in a research study.

Intrinsic case studies: A research approach that allows researchers to gain insight into a particular person or concept to better understand that particular situation.

Learning scientist: People who identify themselves as part of the learning sciences discipline take a pragmatic, cross-paradigm, and interdisciplinary approach to studying learning. They often draw on multiple theories to describe and explain learning, design new learning environments, and study its processes and outcomes.

Legitimate peripheral participation:
Describes trajectories by which novices become experts in a community of practice (Lave & Wenger, 1991). Newcomers in such communities learn vital skills and procedures by first contributing to activities and tasks that are low risk or secondary ("peripheral"), but still important to the overall action ("legitimate"). As they gain expertise, their participation becomes increasingly central.

Machinima: A portmanteau of machine and cinema, machinima is the creation of video through manipulation of videogame graphics. Machinima provides creators a platform to create video that can act as parody, satire, or irony, and allows creators to develop expository, persuasive, and narrative structures.

Mash-ups: These creations are made up of remixed musical tracks that blend two or more songs together to create a hybrid song. Mash-ups often combine instrumental music with vocals from another song.

Massively descriptive: Studies that may be descriptive in nature, but in a way that distinguishes their questions from ethnographies that focus on a small number of individuals.

Memes: Cultural transmissions, often graphics or short animations with textual captions, which are passed from one person to the next, with slight variations occurring between each passing.

Metacognition: The consideration and evaluation of one's own thinking, knowledge, or skills.

Microblogging: A type of blogging that is typically smaller in actual and aggregated file size; examples include Twitter and Tumblr.

Multiliteracies: First described by the New London Group (1996) and closely linked to the idea of "new literacies" and "literacies" as plural, rather than singular, terms. This theoretical position calls for researchers to recognize the validity of a variety of methods and modes of communication and meaning making.

Multimethod approach: An approach to the design of research studies that draws on multiple qualitative methods, or quantitative methods in a single study in order to access or generate the most relevant data for a given research study. This is different from mixed method approach, which relies on both qualitative and quantitative data within a single study.

Multimodal analysis: An analytical technique that expands the qualitative analysis of human language to multiple meaning-making modes, including alphabetic text, sounds, images, photographs, graphical layout, and the like.

Multimodality: The ways in which a variety of modes may work together in a text or composition to create meanings.

Networked field sites: Dynamic sites of study that are user-driven, social, and collaborative, which allow researchers to actively trace meaning-making activities in, around, and through tools, spaces, and participants.

Networking residues: Include traces of an individual's social connection to others within and across specific online spaces; include participating in groups, taking part in collaborative projects, creating friend lists, and "favoriting" posts and comments.

Online ethnography: A qualitative approach concerned with data collection methods used to understand interactions within online spaces. Online data collection methods build on traditional ethnographic principles, such as a bricolage of methods and tools that are continually refashioned and reworked to address the needs of the researcher.

Participatory learning: Related to understandings of participatory culture, such collaborative learning draws on out-of-school practices and involves multiple forms of media, tools, and practices.

Participatory research: The focus on including participants in data collection and interpretation, which also supports participant reflexivity.

Portals: Entry points to affinity spaces, such as social media tools and websites.

Positivist: A paradigm that assumes realities can be hypothesized and tested through research methods.

Postpositivist: A paradigm that assumes that reality exists, but that researchers can know only part of the reality.

Pragmatism: A research paradigm concerned with the practical and what works. Adopting a pragmatic frame allows researchers to purposefully select methods and approaches that work for their particular study.

Prior knowledge: Concepts, facts, and procedures that students believe to be true or useful. Learning becomes more complicated when previously learned concepts are, in fact, misconceptions.

Psychological orientation to studying learning: Learning research in the psychological tradition often takes the form of controlled studies with large populations. In such studies, learning is measured mathematically, using statistics to note whether or not the learning phenomenon in question is generalizable to a larger group.

Reinforcement: Often used in conjunction with behavioral conditioning. Behaviors are changed by repeatedly associating specific stimuli and responses. For example, students may be trained to raise their hands before speaking if teachers reinforce this behavior with praise.

Remix: A lens that allows for user engagement to creatively appropriate materials and artifacts. When used as a framework in research design, remix provides researchers creativity, flexibility, and agency in the design of their study.

Researcher as research tool: A researcher's methodological and theoretical knowledge, as well as his or her familiarity with the study's context, impact the design and implementation of a study. The concept of the researcher as research tool acknowledges one's role in data collection (e.g., interviewing, observing) and data analysis.

Researcher positioning: How the researcher approaches and situates himself or herself in the space and in relation to participants.

Researcher reflexivity: The researcher's continuous reflection of self, research, and the relationship between the two; this includes reflecting on perspective and bias that could impact a study's design, implementation, and analysis.

Research paradigms: Inform the methodological approaches a researcher takes in a given study. Major research paradigms are positivism, postpositivism, critical theories, constructivism, and pragmatism.

Research questions: Questions that guide a study. They are shaped by researchers' experiences and expectations and typically show the alignment of paradigmatic and methodological frameworks with the logic of inquiry.

Sampling: Directly relates to research questions and occurs before or during data collection. Probability sampling allows researchers to generalize findings from the sample to the population from which it was drawn; nonprobabilistic sampling (such as purposeful sampling) is specific to the research context.

Schema: A cognitive understanding of how knowledge is organized in the mind. Knowledge is stored in durable conceptual structures that we compare to new situations at hand. For instance, "going to a restaurant" is a script-like procedure that many people in the Western world invoke regularly.

Situated learning: A theory of learning that is anthropological in orientation. This theory suggests that all learning is drawn from and specific to a person's particular cultural situation, and it is based in naturalistic studies of participants' own actions and interpretations.

Social accounts of learning: Philosophical positions on learning that focus on learning as a cultural experience that occurs in situ and in practice with other participants in a social situation.

Social network: A technology-enabled platform that is allows users to build and trace social links among friends, family members, and acquaintances. Facebook is one of the largest social networks in the English-speaking world, but many other examples exist, including Orkut, Renren, Bebo, and Ello. Additionally, other sites include social networking features in addition to other features. Twitter allows for news posting and social networking, whereas Instagram allows for image sharing and social networking.

Social networking forums: Encompass a broad and inclusive range of online social activities, practices, and platforms; participation can be both interest-driven and socialization-based.

Stimulated recall: A method for studying cognitive processes wherein a learner is video-recorded as he or she completes a task or solves a problem. Immediately thereafter, the learner watches the recording and discusses his or her thoughts and procedures related to completing various steps of the task or problem.

Stimulus: Often used in conjunction with behavioral conditioning. A thing or event that causes a specific behavioral reaction or response.

Thematic analysis: An open-ended analytical technique wherein qualitative data are flexibly sorted and grouped into initial themes; used to organize early findings into larger patterns and interpretations.

Theory generation: An element of grounded theory methods, wherein the larger analytical concepts and insights of the study are drawn directly from its data by engaging in an iterative approach to analyzing data through constant comparison analysis.

Think-aloud protocol: A method for studying learning or expertise wherein a learner completes a task while verbalizing her or his processes as a researcher (or an audio recorder) listens. Her or his words reveal at least some of the complexities of the knowledge or cultural context that she or he is employing in order to complete the task.

Transfer: The idea that when a concept or procedure is learned sufficiently, it can be applied by analogy to similar situations. For example, if students learn how to add and subtract at school, they will be able to transfer this knowledge to balancing their bank accounts.

Transferability: The extent to which the findings of one study can be applied to others.

Transformative works: The kinds of writing and designing practices that take an original work and turn it into something with a new purpose, function, or mode of expression. This includes, but is not limited to, fanfiction, art, videos, and games, which involve a variety of modes, semiotic resources, and literacy practices.

Triangulation: Includes the use of multiple data sources and different methods to check on one another; may also involve multiple investigators or multiple theories to confirm emergent findings. Triangulation reduces the risk that the conclusions reflect the biases of a single method and contributes to the trustworthiness of the study.

Trustworthiness: Often involves interdisciplinary, reflexivity, and transparency, which includes the public disclosure of decisions made during the research process. Trustworthiness generally demands that researchers have familiarity with the research context, a strong theoretical knowledge, an ability to take a multidisciplinary approach, and methodological expertise.

REFERENCES

Abrams, S. S. (2009a). A gaming frame of mind: Digital contexts and academic implications. *Educational Media International, 46,* 335–347.

Abrams, S. S. (2009b). *Real benefits from virtual experiences: How four avid video gamers used gaming as a resource in their literate activity* (Doctoral dissertation, Rutgers University, New Brunswick, NJ). Available from https://rucore.libraries.rutgers.edu/rutgers-lib/25703/

Abrams, S. S. (2010, February). *Digital communication and ethnography: New pathways for qualitative research.* Paper presented at the 31st Annual Ethnography in Education Research Forum, University of Pennsylvania, Philadelphia.

Abrams, S. S. (2011). Association through action: Identity development in real and virtual videogame environments. *Teachers College Record/Yearbook of the National Society for the Study of Education, 110*(1), 220–243.

Abrams, S. S. (2013, April–May). *A wealth of modal shifts: Reconsidering directionality and cross-modal understandings of virtual and place-based practices.* Paper presented at the American Educational Researchers Association Annual Meeting, San Francisco, CA.

Abrams, S. S. (2015). *Integrating virtual and traditional learning in 6–12 classrooms: A layered literacies approach to multimodal meaning making.* New York, NY: Routledge.

Abrams, S. S., & Gerber, H. R. (2014). Cross-literate digital connections: Contemporary frames for meaning making. *English Journal, 103*(4), 18–24.

Abrams, S. S., & Rowsell, J. (2011). Dynamic learning in virtual spaces: Producers and consumers of meaning. *Journal on School Educational Technology, 7*(1), 7–13.

Abrams, S. S., & Walsh, S. (2014). Gamified vocabulary. *Journal of Adolescent & Adult Literacy, 58,* 49–58.

Adler, P. A., & Adler, A. (1994). Observational techniques. In N. K. Denzin & Y. S. Lincoln (Eds.), *Handbook of qualitative research* (pp. 377–392). Thousand Oaks, CA: Sage.

Altheide, D. L., & Johnson, J. M. (1994). Criteria for assessing interpretive validity in qualitative research. In N. K. Denzin & Y. S. Lincoln (Eds.), *Handbook of qualitative research* (pp. 485–499). Thousand Oaks, CA: Sage.

Alvesson, M. (2011). *Interpreting interviews.* Thousand Oaks, CA: Sage.

Ames, C. (1992). Classrooms: Goals, structures, and student motivation. *Journal of Educational Psychology, 84,* 261–271.

Androutsopoulos, J. (2008). Potentials and limitations of discourse-centered online ethnography. *Language@ Internet, 5*(9), 1–20.

Anfara, V. A., Brown, K. M., & Mangione, T. L. (2002). Qualitative analysis on stage: Making the research process more public. *Educational Researcher, 31*(7), 28–38.

Angrosino, M. (2007). *Doing ethnographic and observational research.* Thousand Oaks, CA: Sage.

Annand, D. (2011). Social presence within the community of inquiry framework. *The International Review of Research in Open and Distance Education, 12*(5), n.p.

Appadurai, A. (1996). *Modernity at large: Cultural dimensions of globalization.* Minneapolis: University of Minnesota Press.

Aronson, J. (1994). A pragmatic view of thematic analysis. *The Qualitative Report, 2*(1), 1–3.

Barab, S., Thomas, M., Dodge, T., Carteaux, R., & Tuzun, H. (2005). Making learning fun: Quest Atlantis, a game without guns. *Educational Technology Research & Development, 53,* 86–107.

Barden, O. (2014). Winking at Facebook: Capturing digitally mediated classroom learning. *E-Learning and Digital Media, 11,* 554–568.

Bartlett, F. C. (1932/1995). *Remembering: A study in experimental and social psychology.* Cambridge, England: Cambridge University Press.

Barton. D. (2012). Participation, deliberate learning and discourses of learning online. *Language and Education: An International Journal, 26,* 139–150.

Baym, N. K. (2000). *Tune in, log on: Soaps, fandom, and online community.* Thousand Oaks, CA: Sage.

Berente, N., & Seidel, S. (2014, August). *Big data & inductive theory development: Towards computational grounded theory?* Paper presented at the Americas Conference on Information Systems. Savannah, GA.

Bergold, J., & Thomas, S. (2012). Participatory research methods: A methodological approach in action. *Forum: Qualitative Social Research, 13*(1). Retrieved from http://www.qualitative-research.net/index.php/fqs/article/view/1801

Best, S. J., & Krueger, B. S. (2008). Internet survey design. In N. Fielding, R. M. Lee, & G. Blank (Eds.), *The SAGE handbook of online research methods* (pp. 217–235). Thousand Oaks, CA: Sage.

Biddolph, C., & Curwood, J. S. (in press). #PD: Exploring the intersection of English education, Twitter, and professional learning. In M. Knobel & J. Kalman (Eds.), *Literacies, digital technologies, and teachers' professional development.* New York, NY: Peter Lang.

Black, R. W. (2008). *Adolescents and online fiction.* New York, NY: Peter Lang.

Black, R. W. (2009). Online fan fiction, global identities, and imagination. *Research in the Teaching of English, 43,* 397–425.

Black, R. W., & Reich, S. M. (2011). Affordances and constraints of scaffolded learning in a virtual world for young children. *International Journal of Game-Based Learning, 1*(2), 52–64.

Bloome, D. (2012). Classroom ethnography. In M. Grenfell, D. Bloome, C. Hardy, K. Pahl, J. Rowsell, & B. Street (Eds.), *Language, ethnography, and education: Bridging New Literacy Studies and Bourdieu* (pp. 7–26). New York, NY: Taylor & Francis.

Bloome, D., Power-Carter, S., Christian, B. M., Otto, S., & Shuart-Faris, N. (2005). *Discourse analysis and the study of classroom language and literacy events.* Mahwah, NJ: Lawrence Erlbaum.

Boellstorff, T., Nardi, B., Pearce, C., & Taylor, T. L. (2012). *Ethnography and virtual worlds: A handbook of method.* Princeton, NJ: Princeton University Press.

Bogost, I. (2011, May 3). *Persuasive games: Exploitationware* [Column]. Retrieved from http://www.gamasutra.com/view/feature/6366/persuasive_games_exploitationware.php

Bombardieri, M. (2014, May 18). Harvard goes all in for online courses. *The Boston Globe.* Retrieved from http://www.bostonglobe.com/metro/2014/05/17/behind-harvard-explosion-online-classes-flurry-lights-camera-action/BybPhkyfX59D9a7icmHz5M/story.html

Borman, K. M., LeCompte, M. D., & Goetz, J. P. (1986). Ethnographic and qualitative research design and why it doesn't work. *American Behavioral Scientist, 30,* 42–57.

Bowker, N., & Tuffin, K. (2004). Using the online medium for discursive research about people with disabilities. *Social Science Computer Review, 22,* 228–241.

Boyatzis, R. E. (1998). *Transforming qualitative information: Thematic analysis and code development.* Thousand Oaks, CA: Sage.

boyd, d. (2006). Friends, friendsters, and myspace top 8: Writing community into being on social network sites. *First Monday, 11*(12). Retrieved from http://firstmonday.org/ojs/index.php/fm/article/view/1418

boyd, d. (2008a). A response to Christine Hine. In A. N. Markham & N. K. Baym (Eds.), *Internet inquiry: Conversations about method* (pp. 26–32). Thousand Oaks, CA: Sage.

boyd, d. (2008b). Why youth (heart) social network sites: The role of networked publics in teenage social life. In D. Buckingham (Ed.), *Youth, identity, and digital media* (pp. 119–142). The John D. and Catherine T. MacArthur Foundation Series on Digital Media and Learning. Cambridge, MA: MIT Press.

boyd, d. (2014). *It's complicated: The social lives of networked teens.* New Haven, CT: Yale University Press.

boyd, d., & Ellison, N. B. (2007). Social network sites: Definition, history, and scholarship. *Journal of Computer-Mediated Communication, 13,* 210–230.

Bransford, J. D., & Schwartz, D. (1999). Rethinking transfer: A simple proposal with multiple implications. In A. Iran-Nejad & P. D. Pearson (Eds.), *Review of research in education* (Vol. 24, pp. 61–100). Washington, DC: American Educational Research Association.

Braun, V., & Clarke, V. (2006). Using thematic analysis in psychology. *Qualitative Research in Psychology, 3,* 77–101.

Breen, G. (2015, March 18). Your tween's private photo could go viral. Retrieved from http://www.huffingtonpost.com/galit-breen/your-tweens-private-photo-could-go-viral-heres-how_b_6892708.html

Brennan, K., Monroy-Hernandez, A., & Resnick, M. (2010). Making projects, making friends: Online community as catalyst for interactive media creation. *New Directions for Youth Development, 128*(Winter), 75–83.

Brooker, W., & Jermyn, D. (Eds.). (2003). *The audience studies reader.* London, England: Routledge.

Broudy, H. S. (1977). Types of knowledge and purposes of education. In R. C. Anderson, R. J. Spiro, & W. E. Montague (Eds.), *Schooling and the acquisition of knowledge* (pp. 1–17). Hillsdale, NJ: Lawrence Erlbaum.

Brown, J. S., Collins, A., & Duguid, P. (1989). Situated cognition and the culture of learning. *Educational Researcher, 18*(1), 32–42.

Bruckman, A. (2002). Studying the amateur artist: A perspective on disguising data collected in human subjects research on the Internet. *Ethics and Information Technology, 4,* 217–231.

Buchanan, E. (Ed.). (2004). *Readings in virtual research ethics: Issues and controversies.* Hershey, PA: Information Science.

Burn, A. (2009). *Making new media: Creative production and digital literacies.* New York, NY: Peter Lang.

Burnett, C. (2011). Shifting and multiple spaces in classrooms: An argument for investigating learners' boundary-making around digital networked texts. *Journal of Literacy and Technology, 12*(3), 2–23.

Burnett, C., & Bailey, C. (2014). Conceptualising collaboration in hybrid sites: Playing *Minecraft* together and apart in a primary classroom. In C. Burnett, J. Davies, G. Merchant, & J. Rowsell. (Eds.) *New literacies around the globe: Policy and pedagogy* (pp. 50–71). Abingdon, Oxon, England: Routledge.

Burnett, C., Davies, J., Merchant, G., & Rowsell, J. (2014). *New literacies around the globe.* London, England: Routledge.

Burnett, C., & Merchant, G. (2014). Points of view: Reconceptualising literacies through an exploration of adult and child interactions in a virtual world. *Journal of Research in Reading, 37,* 36–50.

Burrell, J. (2009). The field site as a network: A strategy for locating ethnographic research. *Field Methods, 21,* 181–199.

Cappello, M., & Hollingsworth, S. (2008). Literacy inquiry and pedagogy through a photographic lens. *Language Arts, 85,* 442–449.

Charmaz, K. (2000). Grounded theory: Objectivist and constructivist methods. In N. K. Denzin & Y. S. Lincoln (Eds.), *Handbook of qualitative research* (2nd ed., pp. 509–536). Thousand Oaks, CA: Sage.

Charmaz, K. (2003). Qualitative interviewing and grounded theory analysis. In J. Holstein & J. Gubrium (Eds.), *Inside interviewing* (pp. 311–330). Thousand Oaks, CA: Sage.

Charmaz, K. (2006). *Constructing grounded theory.* Thousand Oaks, CA: Sage.

Checkoway, B. N., & Gutierrez, L. M. (2006). Youth participation and community change. *Journal of Community Practice, 14*(1–2), 1–9.

Chen, M. (2012). *Leet noobs: The life and death of an expert player group in World of Warcraft.* New York, NY: Peter Lang.

Chi, M. T. H. (1997). Quantifying qualitative analyses of verbal data: A practical guide. *Journal of the Learning Sciences, 6,* 271–315.

Chi, M. T. H., Feltovich, P., & Glaser, R. (1981). Categorization and representation of physics problems by experts and novices. *Cognitive Science, 5,* 121–152.

Chiseri-Strater, E. (1996). Turning in upon ourselves: Positionality, subjectivity, and reflexivity in case study and ethnographic research. In P. Mortensen & G. E. Kirsch (Eds.), *Ethics and responsibility in qualitative studies of literacy* (pp. 115–133). Urbana, IL: National Council of Teachers of English.

Clifford, J., & Marcus, G. E. (1986). *Writing culture: The poetics and politics of ethnography*. A School of American Research Advanced Seminar. Berkeley: University of California Press.

Cody, R. (2010). Learning and collaborating in Final Fantasy XI. In M. Ito, S. Baumer, M. Bittanti, d. boyd, R. Cody, B. Herr-Stephenson, . . . L. Tripp. (2010). *Hanging out, messing around, and geeking out: Kids living and learning with new media* (pp. 216–219). The John D. and Catherine T. MacArthur Foundation Series on Digital Media and Learning. Cambridge, MA: MIT Press.

Coiro, J., Knobel, M., Lankshear, C., & Leu, D. J. (Eds.). (2008). *Handbook of research on new literacies*. Mahwah, NJ: Lawrence Erlbaum.

Cole, M., Gay, J., Glick, J., & Sharp, D. (1971). *The cultural context of learning and thinking: An exploration in experimental anthropology*. New York, NY: Basic Books.

Constas, M. (1992). Qualitative analysis as a public event: The documentation of category development procedures. *American Educational Research Journal, 29*, 253–266.

Coopman, S. J. (2009, June). A critical examination of Blackboard's e–learning environment. *First Monday, 14*(6). Retrieved from http://firstmonday.org/ojs/index.php/fm/article/view/2434/2202

Cope, B., & Kalantzis, M. (Eds.). (2000). *Multiliteracies: Literacy learning and the design of social futures*. New York, NY: Routledge.

Cope, B., & Kalantzis, M. (2013). Towards a new learning: The *Scholar* social knowledge workspace, in theory and practice. *E-Learning and Digital Media, 10*, 332–356.

Cope, B., & Kalantzis, M. (2015). The things you do to know: An introduction to the pedagogy of multiliteracies. In B. Cope & M. Kalantzis (Eds.), *A Pedagogy of Multiliteracies* (pp. 1-36). Hampshire, England: Palgrave.

Corbin, J. M., & Strauss, A. C. (2007). *Basics of qualitative research: Techniques and procedures for developing grounded theory* (3rd ed.). Thousand Oaks, CA: Sage.

Creswell, J. W. (1998). *Qualitative inquiry and research design: Choosing among five approaches*. Thousand Oaks, CA: Sage.

Creswell, J. W. (2007). *Qualitative inquiry and research design: Choosing among five approaches* (2nd ed.). Thousand Oaks, CA: Sage.

Creswell, J. W. (2010). Mapping the developing landscape of mixed methods research. In A. Tashakkori & C. Teddlie (Eds.), *SAGE handbook of mixed methods in social & behavioral research* (2nd ed., pp. 45–68). Thousand Oaks, CA: Sage.

Creswell, J. W. (2012). *Educational research: Planning, conducting, and evaluating quantitative and qualitative research* (4th ed.). Boston, MA: Pearson

Creswell, J. W. (2013). *Qualitative inquiry and research design: Choosing among five approaches* (3rd ed.). Thousand Oaks, CA: Sage.

Creswell, J. W. (2015). *A concise introduction to mixed methods research*. Thousand Oaks, CA: Sage.

Creswell, J. W., & Miller, D. L. (2000). Determining validity in qualitative inquiry. *Theory Into Practice, 39*, 124–130.

Crittenden, E. (2006). Grounded theory: A research methodology for e-learning. *Malaysian Journal of Distance Education, 8*(1), 1–13.

Curwood, J. S. (2013a). Fan fiction, remix culture, and The Potter Games. In V. E. Frankel (Ed.), *Teaching with Harry Potter* (pp. 81–92). Jefferson, NC: McFarland.

Curwood, J. S. (2013b). *The Hunger Games*: Literature, literacy, and online affinity spaces. *Language Arts, 90*, 417–427.

Curwood, J. S. (2014a). English teachers' cultural models about technology: A microethnographic perspective on professional development. *Journal of Literacy Research, 46*, 9–38.

Curwood, J. S. (2014b). Reader, writer, gamer: Online role-playing games as literary response. In H. R. Gerber & S. S. Abrams (Eds.), *Bridging literacies with videogames* (pp. 53–66). Rotterdam, Netherlands: Sense.

Curwood, J. S. & Gibbons, D. (2009). "Just like I have felt": Multimodal counternarratives in youth-produced digital media. *International Journal of Learning and Media, 1*(4), 59-77.

Curwood, J. S., Magnifico, A. M., & Lammers, J. C. (2013). Writing in the wild: Writers' motivation in fan-based affinity spaces. *Journal of Adolescent & Adult Literacy, 56*, 677–685.

Dabbagh, N. (2007). The online learner: Characteristics and pedagogical implications. *Contemporary Issues in Technology and Teacher Education, 7*, 217–226.

Dawkins, R. (1976). *The selfish gene*. Oxford, England: Oxford University Press.

de Certeau, M. (1984). Reading as poaching. In S. Rendall (Ed.), *The practice of everyday life* (pp. 165–176). Berkeley: University of California Press.

De Gagne, J. C., & Walters, K. J. (2010). The lived experience of online educators: Hermeneutic phenomenology. *Journal of Online Learning and Teaching, 6*, 357–366.

deMarrais, K. (2004). Qualitative interview studies: Learning through experience. In K. de Marrais & S. D. Lapan (Eds.), *Foundations for research: Methods of inquiry in education and the social sciences* (pp. 51–68). Mahwah, NJ: Lawrence Erlbaum.

Denzin, N. K. (1978). *Sociological methods: A sourcebook*. New York, NY: McGraw Hill.

Denzin, N. K., & Lincoln, Y. S. (2000). Introduction: The discipline and practice of qualitative research. In N. K. Denzin & Y. S. Lincoln (Eds.), *Handbook of qualitative research* (pp. 1–28). Thousand Oaks, CA: Sage.

Denzin, N. K., & Lincoln, Y. S (Eds.). (2003). *9/11 in American culture: Crossroads in qualitative inquiry*. Walnut Creek, CA: AltaMira Press.

Denzin, N. K., & Lincoln, Y. S. (2005). *The SAGE handbook of qualitative research*. Thousand Oaks: Sage.

Denzin, N. K., & Lincoln, Y. S., Eds. (2013). *The SAGE handbook of qualitative research* (3rd ed.). Thousand Oaks, CA: Sage.

DeSantis, L., & Ugarriza, D. N. (2000). The concept of theme as used in qualitative nursing research. *Western Journal of Nursing Research, 22*, 351–372.

Deterding, S., Dixon, D., Khaled, R., & Nacke, L. E. (2011). From game design elements to gamefulness: Defining "gamification". In *MindTrek 2011 Proceedings* (pp. 9–15). Tampere, Finland: ACM Press.

Devane, B. (2009). "Get some secured credit cards homey": Hip hop discourse, financial literacy and the design of digital media learning environments. *E-Learning and Digital Media, 6*, 4–22.

Dibbell, J. (1993, December 23). A rape in cyberspace: How an evil clown, a Haitian trickster spirit, two wizards, and a cast of dozens turned a database into a society. *The Village Voice*. Retrieved from http://www.juliandibbell.com/texts/bungle_vv.html

Dodge, T., Barab, S., Stuckey, B., Warren, S., Heiselt, C., & Stein, R. (2008). Children's sense of self: Learning and meaning in the digital age. *Journal of Interactive Learning Research, 19*, 225–249.

Domokos, M. (2007). Folklore and mobile communication. *Fabula, 48*(1/2), 50–59.

Drake, M. (2014, February 9). Old School rules! Wisdom of massive open online courses now in doubt. *The Washington Times*. Retrieved from http://www.washingtontimes.com/news/2014/feb/9/big-plan-on-campus-is-dropping-out/print/

Dreyfus, H. L., & Dreyfus, S. E. (1986). *Mind over machine: The power of human intuition and expertise in the era of the computer*. Oxford, England: Blackwell.

Duncan, S. C., & Hayes, E. R. (2012). Expanding the affinity space: An introduction. In E. R. Hayes & S. C. Duncan (Eds.), *Learning in videogame affinity spaces* (pp. 1–23). New York, NY: Peter Lang.

Dweck, C. S., & Leggett, E. L. (1988). A social-cognitive approach to motivation and personality. *Psychological Review, 95*, 256–273.

Einarsdottir, J. (2005). Playschool in pictures: Children's photographs as a research method. *Early Child Development and Care, 175*, 523–541.

Ellis, C. (2009). *Revision: Autoethnographic reflections on life and work*. Walnut Creek, CA: Left Coast Press.

Erickson, F. (1973). What makes school ethnography 'ethnographic?' *Council on Anthropology and Education Newsletter, 4*(2), 10–19.

Ericsson, K. A., & Simon, H. A. (1980). Verbal reports as data. *Psychological Review, 87*, 215–251.

Fairclough, N. (1989). *Language and power*. London, England: Longman.

Fairclough, N. (1995). *Critical discourse analysis*. London, England: Longman.

Fairclough, N. (2014). *Language and power* (3rd ed.). London, England: Longman.

Fairclough, N. (2014). What is CDA? Language and power twenty-five years on. Academia.edu. Retrieved from https://www.academia.edu/8429277/What_is_CDA_Language_and_Power_twenty-five_years_on

Feeler, W. G. (2012). *Being there: A grounded theory study of student perceptions of instructor presence in an online class* (Doctoral dissertation). Retrieved from DigitalCommons@University of Nebraska–Lincoln http://digitalcommons.unl.edu/cehsedaddiss/122/

Fields, D. A., & Kafai, Y. B. (2009). A connective ethnography of peer knowledge sharing and diffusion in a tween virtual world. *International Journal of Computer Supported Learning, 4,* 47–68.

Fields, D. A., Magnifico, A. M., Lammers, J. C., & Curwood, J. S. (2014). DIY media creation. *Journal of Adolescent & Adult Literacy, 58,* 19–24.

Fine, M., Bloom, J., Burns, A., Chajet, L., Guishard, M., Payne, Y., . . . Torre, M. E. (2005). Dear Zora: A letter to Zora Neale Hurston fifty years after *Brown. Teachers College Record, 107*(3), 496–528.

Flewitt, R. (2011). Bringing ethnography to a multimodal investigation of early literacy in a digital age. *Qualitative Research, 11,* 293–310.

Flick, U. (2009). *An introduction to qualitative research.* Thousand Oaks, CA: Sage.

Gaiser, T. J. (1997). Conducting on-line focus groups: A methodological discussion. *Social Science Computer Review, 15,* 135–144.

Garrison, D. R., Anderson, T., & Archer, W. (1999). Critical inquiry in a text-based environment: Computer conferencing in higher education. *The Internet and Higher Education, 2,* 87–105.

Gauntlett, D. (2007). *Creative explorations: New approaches to identities and audiences.* London, England: Routledge.

Gee, J. P. (1999). *An introduction to discourse analysis.* New York, NY: Routledge.

Gee, J. P. (2003). *What video games have to teach us about learning and literacy.* New York, NY: Palgrave-Macmillan.

Gee, J. P. (2004). *Situated language and learning: A critique of traditional schooling.* New York, NY: Routledge.

Gee, J. P. (2005). *Why video games are good for your soul.* Sydney, Australia: Common Ground.

Gee, J. P. (2007). *What video games have to teach us about learning and literacy* (2nd ed.). New York, NY: Palgrave-Macmillan.

Gee, J. P. (2008). *Social linguistics and literacies* (3rd ed.). Bristol, PA: Taylor & Francis.

Gee, J. P. (2011). *How to do discourse analysis: A toolkit.* New York, NY: Routledge.

Gee, J. P. (2012). The old and the new in the new digital literacies. *The Educational Forum, 76,* 418–420.

Gee, J. P. (2014). *An introduction to discourse analysis: Theory and method.* New York, NY: Routledge.

Gee, J. P. (2015). *Social linguistics and literacies: Ideology in discourses* (3rd ed.). New York, NY: Routledge.

Gee, J. P., & Green, J. L. (1998). Discourse analysis, learning, and social practice: A methodological study. *Review of Research in Education, 23,* 119–169.

Gee, J. P., & Hayes, E. R. (2010). *Women and gaming: The Sims and 21st century learning.* New York, NY: Palgrave Macmillan.

Geertz, C. (1973). *The interpretation of cultures.* New York, NY: Basic Books.

Gerber, H. R. (2008). *New literacies studies: Intersections and disjunctures between in-school and out-of-school literacies among adolescent males* (Unpublished doctoral dissertation). University of Alabama, Tuscaloosa.

Gerber, H. R. (2014). Problems and possibilities in gamifying learning: A conceptual review. *Internet Learning Journal, 3*(2), n.p. doi:10.18278/il.3.2.4

Gerber, H. R., Abrams, S. S., Onwuegbuzie, A. J., & Benge, C. (2014). From Mario to FIFA: What qualitative case study research suggests about games-based learning in a U.S. classroom. *Educational Media International, 51*, 16–34.

Gerber, H. R., & Price, D. P. (2013). Fighting baddies and collecting bananas: Teachers' perceptions of games-based literacy learning. *Educational Media International. 50*, 51–62.

Gibbons, D. (2010). Tracing the paths of moving artifacts in youth media production. *English Teaching: Practice and Critique, 9*(1), 8–21.

Gibbs, G. (2007). *Analyzing qualitative data.* Thousand Oaks, CA: Sage.

Glaser, B. G. (1998). *Doing grounded theory: Issues and discussions.* Mill Valley, CA: Sociology Press.

Glaser, B. G. (1999). The future of grounded theory. *Qualitative health research, 9*, 836–845.

Glaser, B. G., & Strauss, A. L. (1967). *The discovery of grounded theory: Strategies for qualitative research.* New York, NY: Aldine.

Glazer, K., & Hergenrader, T. (2014). A world filled with darkness, dungeons, and dragons: Using analog role playing game creation to enhance literature and writing instruction in high school English classes. In A. Ochsner, J. Dietmeier, C. C. Williams, & C. Steinkuehler (Eds.), *Proceedings of the 10th Annual Games, Learning, and Society Conference, Madison, WI* (pp. 102–108). Retrieved from http://press.etc.cmu.edu/files/GLS10-Proceedings-2014-web.pdf

Gooden, R. J., & Winefield, H. R. (2007). Breast and prostate cancer online discussion boards: A thematic analysis of gender differences and similarities. *Journal of Health Psychology, 12*, 103–114.

Graffigna, G., & Bosio, A. C. (2006). The influence of setting on findings produced in qualitative health research: A comparison between face-to-face and online discussion groups about HIV/AIDS. *International Journal of Qualitative Methods, 5*(3), 55–76.

Greene, J. C. (2007). *Mixed methods in social inquiry.* San Francisco, CA: Jossey-Bass.

Greeno, J. G., Collins, A. M., & Resnick, L. B. (1996). Cognition and learning. In D. Berliner & R. Calfee (Eds.), *Handbook of educational psychology* (pp. 15–41). New York, NY: MacMillian.

Grimes, J. M., Fleischmann, K. R., & Jaeger, P. T. (2010). Research ethics and virtual worlds. In C. Wankel & S. K. Malleck (Eds.), *Emerging ethical issues of life in virtual worlds* (pp. 72–99). Charlotte, NC: Information Age.

Grimes, S. M., & Fields, D. A. (2012). *Kids online: A new research agenda for understanding social networking forums*. New York, NY: The Joan Ganz Cooney Center. Retrieved from http://www.joanganzcooneycenter.org/publication/kids-online-a-new-research-agenda-for-understanding-social-networking-forums/

Groves, R. M. (1989). *Survey errors and survey costs*. New York, NY: John Wiley.

Guba, E. G., & Lincoln, Y. S. (1981). *Effective evaluation: Improving the usefulness of evaluation results through responsive and naturalistic approaches*. San Francisco, CA: Jossey-Bass.

Guba, E. G., & Lincoln, Y. S. (1982). The epistemological and methodological bases of naturalistic inquiry. *Educational Communications and Technology Journal, 30*, 233–252.

Guba, E. G., & Lincoln, Y. S. (1989). *Fourth generation evaluation*. Newbury Park, CA: Sage.

Guba, E. G., & Lincoln, Y. S. (1994). Competing paradigms in qualitative research. In N. K. Denzin & Y. S. Lincoln (Eds.), *The handbook of qualitative research* (pp. 105–117). Thousand Oaks, CA: Sage.

Guest, G. S., MacQueen, K. M., & Namey, E. E. (2012). *Applied thematic analysis*. Thousand Oaks, CA: Sage.

Gutierrez, K. D. (2008). Developing a sociocritical literacy in the third space. *Reading Research Quarterly, 43*, 148–164.

Halliday, M. A. K. (1978). *Language as social semiotic*. London, England: Edward Arnold.

Halverson, E. R. (2013). Participatory media spaces: A design perspective on learning with media and technology in the twenty-first century. In C. Steinkuehler, K. Squire, & S. Barab (Eds.), *Games, learning, and society: Learning and meaning in the digital age* (pp. 244–268). New York, NY: Cambridge University Press.

Halverson, E. R., Bass, M., & Woods, D. (2012). The process of creation: A novel methodology for analyzing multimodal data. *The Qualitative Report, 17*, 1–27.

Halverson, E. R., Lowenhaupt, R., Gibbons, D., & Bass, M. (2009). Conceptualizing identity in youth media arts organizations: A comparative case study. *E-Learning and Digital Media, 6*, 23–42.

Halverson, E. R., & Magnifico, A. M. (2013). Bidirectional artifact analysis: A method for analyzing digitally mediated creative processes. In R. Luckin, S. Puntambekar, P. Goodyear, B. Grabowski, J. Underwood, & N. Winters (Eds.), *Handbook of design in educational technology* (pp. 406–416). New York, NY: Routledge.

Halverson, E. R., & Sheridan, K. M. (2014). The maker movement in education. *Harvard Educational Review, 84*, 495–504.

Hammersley, M., & Atkinson, P. (1995). *Ethnography: Principles in practice* (2nd ed.). London, England: Routledge.

Hargittai, E. (2010). Digital na(t)ives? Variation in Internet skills and uses among members of the "Net Generation." *Sociological Inquiry, 80*(1), 92-113.

Hanna, P. (2012). Using Internet technologies (such as Skype) as a research medium: A research note. *Qualitative Research, 12*, 239–242.

Harry Potter Alliance. (2015). What we do. Retrieved from http://thehpalliance.org/what-we-do/

Hawkins, S. (2011, November 23). Copyright fair use and how it works for online images. Retrieved from http://www.socialmediaexaminer.com/copyright-fair-use-and-how-it-works-for-online-images/

Hayes, E. R., & Duncan, S. C. (Eds.). (2012). *Learning in video game affinity spaces*. New York, NY: Peter Lang.

Herrera, L. (2012). Youth and citizenship in the digital age: A view from Egypt. *Harvard Educational Review*, *82*, 333–352.

Hewson, C. (2014). Qualitative approaches in Internet-mediated research: Opportunities, issues, possibilities. In P. Leavy (Ed.),*The Oxford Handbook of Qualitative Research* (pp. 423–449). Oxford University Press.

Hewson, C., & Laurent, D. (2008). Research design and tools for Internet research. In N. Fielding, R. M. Lee, & G. Blank (Eds.), *The SAGE handbook of online research methods* (pp. 58–78). Thousand Oaks, CA: Sage.

Hidi, S., & Renninger, K. A. (2006). The four-phase model of interest development. *Educational Psychologist*, *41*, 111–127.

Hine. C. (2000). *Virtual ethnography*. Thousand Oaks, CA: Sage.

Hine, C. (2008). How can qualitative Internet researchers define the boundaries of their projects? In A. N. Markham & N. K. Baym (Eds.), *Internet inquiry: Conversations about method* (pp. 1–20). Thousand Oaks, CA: Sage.

Hine, C. (2013). *The Internet: Understanding qualitative research*. New York, NY: Oxford University Press.

Hookway, N. (2008). 'Entering the blogosphere': Some strategies for using blogs in social research. *Qualitative Research*, *8*, 91–113.

Howe, K. R. (1988). Against the quantitative-qualitative incompatibility thesis or dogmas die hard. *Educational Researcher*, *17*(8), 10–16.

Hsu, W. (2012, October 27). On digital ethnography. What do computers have to do with ethnography? (Part1 of 4). [Web log post]. Retrieved from http://ethnographymatters.net/blog/2012/10/27/on-digital-ethnography-part-one-what-do-computers-have-to-do-with-ethnography/

Huckin, T., Andrus, J., & Clary-Lemon, J. (2012). Critical discourse analysis and rhetoric and composition. *College Composition and Communication*, *64*, 107–129.

Hull, G. A., & Nelson, M. E. (2005). Locating the semiotic power of multimodality. *Written Communication*, *22*, 224–261.

Hull, G. A., Stornaiuolo, A., & Sahni, U. (2010). Cultural citizenship and cosmopolitan practice: Global youth communicate online. *English Education, 42*, 331–367.

Hutchins, E. (1995). *Cognition in the wild*. Cambridge, MA: MIT Press.

Ingram, J., Niemeyer, D., & Gerber, H. R. (2015). *Satire, fandom, and the U.S. testing culture*. Paper presented at the nineteenth European Conference on Literacy, Klagenfurt, Austria.

Ito, M., Baumer, S., Bittanti, M., boyd, d., Cody, R., Herr-Stephenson, B., . . . Tripp, L. (2010). *Hanging out, messing around, and geeking out: Kids living and learning with new media*. Cambridge, MA: MIT Press.

Ito, M., & Bittani, M. (2010). Gaming. In M. Ito, S. Baumer, M. Bittani, D. boyd, R. Cody, B. Herr-Stephenson, . . . L. Tripp (Eds.). *Hanging out, messing around, and geeking out: Kids living and learning with new media* (pp. 195–242). Cambridge, MA: MIT Press.

Ito, M., Gutierrez, K., Livingstone, S., Penuel, B., Rhodes, J., Salen, K., . . . Watkins, S. C. (2013). *Connected learning: An agenda for research and design.* The John D. and Catherine T. MacArthur Foundation Series on Digital Media and Learning. Irvine, CA: Digital Media and Learning Research Hub.

Jacobs, G. E. (2004). Complicating contexts: Issues of methodology in researching the language and literacies of instant messaging. *Reading Research Quarterly, 39,* 394–406.

Jackson, L. (2013). Learning from *Adventure Rock.* In G. Merchant, J. Gillen, J. Marsh, & J. Davies (Eds.), *Virtual literacies: Interactive spaces for children and young people* (pp. 208–225). Oxon, England: Routledge.

Jamison, A. (2013). *Fic: Why fanfiction is taking over the world.* Dallas, TX: Smart Pop Books.

Jenkins, H. (1992). *Textual poachers: Television fans & participatory culture.* New York, NY: Routledge.

Jenkins, H. (2006). *Convergence culture: Where old and new media collide.* New York, NY: NYU Press.

Jenkins, H. (2010). Multiculturalism, appropriation, and the new media literacies: Remixing *Moby Dick.* In S. Sonvilla-Weiss (Ed.), *Mashup cultures* (pp. 98–119). New York, NY: Springer.

Jenkins, H. (2012). "Cultural acupuncture": Fan activism and the Harry Potter Alliance. *Transformative Works and Culture, 10.* Retrieved from http://journal.transformativeworks.org/index.php/twc/article/view/305

Jenkins, H., Clinton, K., Purushotma, R., Robison, A. J., & Weigel, M. (2006). *Confronting the challenges of participatory culture: Media education for the 21st century.* The John D. and Catherine T. MacArthur Foundation Series on Digital Media and Learning. Cambridge, MA: MIT Press.

Jenkins, H., Purushotma, R., Clinton, K., Weigel, M., & Robison, A. J. (2007). *Confronting the challenges of participatory culture: Media education for the 21st century.* The John D. and Catherine T. MacArthur Foundation Series on Digital Media and Learning. Cambridge, MA: MIT Press. Retrieved from http://mitpress.mit.edu/sites/default/files/titles/free_download/9780262513623_Confronting_the_Challenges.pdf

Jenkins, H., Purushotma, R., Weigel, M., Clinton, K., & Robinson, A. J. (2009). *Contronting the challenges of participatory culture: Media education for the 21st century.* The John D. and Catherine T. MacArthur Foundation Series on Digital Media and Learning. Cambridge, MA: MIT Press.

Jewitt, C. (2009, 2013). *The Routledge handbook of multimodal analysis.* New York, NY: Routledge.

Johnson, E. (2008). Simulating medical patients and practices: Bodies and the construction of valid medical simulators. *Body & Society, 14,* 105–128.

Johnson, R. B. (2012). Dialectical pluralism and mixed research. *American Behavioral Scientist 56,* 751–754.

Johnson, R. B., & Christensen, L. B. (2008). *Educational research: Quantitative, qualitative, and mixed approaches* (3rd ed.). Thousand Oaks, CA: Sage.

Johnson, R. B., & Christensen, L. B. (2014). *Educational research: Quantitative, qualitative, and mixed approaches* (5th ed.). Thousand Oaks, CA: Sage.

Johnson, R. B., & Onwuegbuzie, A. J. (2004). Mixed methods research: A research paradigm whose time has come. *Educational Researcher, 33*(7), 14–26.

Jordan, B. (1989). Cosmopolitical obstetrics: Some insights from the training of traditional midwives. *Social Science and Medicine, 28*, 925–944.

Kafai, Y. B., & Fields, D. (2012, October). Connecting play: Understanding multimodal participation in virtual worlds. In *Proceedings of the 14th ACM International Conference on Multimodal Interaction* (pp. 265–272). New York, NY: ACM.

Kafai, Y. B., & Fields, D. A. (2013). *Connected play: Tweens in a virtual world.* Cambridge, MA: MIT Press.

Kafai, Y. B., Fields, D. A., Roque, R., Burke, W. Q., & Monroy-Hernandez, A. (2012). Collaborative agency in youth online and offline creative production in Scratch. *Research and Practice in Technology Enhanced Learning, 7*, 63–87.

Kafai, Y., & Peppler, K. (2011). Beyond small groups: New opportunities for research in computer-supported collective learning. In H. Spada, G. Stahl, N. Miyake, & N. Law (Eds.), *Proceedings of the Computer-Supported Collaborative Learning Conference* (pp. 17–24). Hong Kong, China: International Society of the Learning Sciences.

Kafai, Y. B., & Peppler, K. A. (2011). Youth, technology, and DIY: Developing participatory competencies in creative media production. *Review of Research in Education, 35*, 89–119.

Kalantzis, M., & Cope, B. (2010). The teacher as designer: Pedagogy in the new media age. *E-learning and Digital Media, 7*, 200–222.

Kalantzis, M., & Cope, W. (2012). *Literacies.* New York, NY: Cambridge University Press.

Kaufmann, J., Christakas, N., Wimmer, A., Lewis, K., & Gonzalez, M. (2008). Tastes, ties, and time: Facebook data release. Cambridge, MA: Berkman Center for Internet & Society, Harvard University. Retrieved from http://cyber.law.harvard.edu/node/4682

Kazmer, M. M., & Xie, B. (2008). Qualitative interviewing in Internet studies: Playing with the media, playing with the method. *Communication & Society, 11*, 257–278.

Kendall, A., & McDougall, J. M. (2013). Telling stories out of school: Young male gamers talk about literacies. In G. Merchant, J. Gillen, J. Marsh, & J. Davies (Eds.), *Virtual literacies: Interactive spaces for children and young people* (pp. 89–102). Oxon, England: Routledge.

Kincheloe, J. L. (2001). Describing the bricolage: Conceptualizing a new rigor in qualitative research. *Qualitative Inquiry, 7*, 679–692.

Kincheloe, J. L. (2005). On to the next level: Continuing the conceptualization of the bricolage. *Qualitative Inquiry, 11*, 323–350.

Kirk, J., & Miller, M. L. (1986). *Reliability and validity in qualitative research.* Beverly Hills, CA: Sage.

Knobel, M. (2003). Rants, ratings, and representation: Ethical issues in researching online social practices. *Education, Communication & Information, 3*, 187–210.

Knobel, M., & Lankshear, C. (2007). Online memes, affinities, and cultural production. In M. Knobel & C. Lankshear (Eds.), *A new literacies sampler* (199–227). New York, NY: Peter Lang.

Knobel, M., & Lankshear, C. (2008). Remix: The art and craft of endless hybridization. *Journal of Adolescent & Adult Literacy, 52,* 22–33.

Kozinets, R. V. (2009). *Netnography: Doing ethnographic research online.* Thousand Oaks, CA: Sage.

Kraut, R., Olson, J., Banaji, M., Bruckman, A., Cohen, J., & Couper, M. (2010). Ethics Working Paper.

Kress, G. (2010). *Multimodality: A social-semiotic approach to contemporary communication.* London, England: Routledge.

Kress, G., & van Leeuwen, T. (1996). *Reading images: The grammar of visual design.* New York, NY: Routledge.

Kress, G., & van Leeuwen, T. (2001). *Multimodal discourse: The modes and media of contemporary communication.* Oxford, England: Oxford University Press.

Kuhn, T. (1962) *The structure of scientific revolutions.* Chicago, IL: University of Chicago Press.

Kuzel, A. J. (1992). Sampling in qualitative inquiry. In B. F. Crabtree & W. L. Miller (Eds.), *Doing qualitative research* (pp. 31–44). Newbury Park, CA: Sage.

Labov, W. (1972). *Sociolinguistic patterns.* Philadelphia: University of Pennsylvania Press.

Lam, W. S. E. (2000). Literacy and the design of the self: A case study of a teenage writing on the Internet. *TESOL Quarterly, 34,* 457–482.

Lammers, J. C. (2012). Is the hangout . . . the hangout? Exploring tensions in an online gaming-related fan site. In E. R. Hayes & S. C. Duncan (Eds.), *Learning in video game affinity spaces* (pp. 23–50). New York, NY: Peter Lang.

Lammers, J. C. (2013). Fangirls as teachers: Examining pedagogic discourse in an online fan site. *Learning, Media and Technology, 38,* 368–386.

Lammers, J. C. (2014, April). *Sims Fanfiction as innovative literacy learning: Stories from three young women.* Paper presented at the American Educational Research Association annual meeting, Philadelphia, PA.

Lammers, J. C., Curwood, J. S., & Magnifico, A. M. (2012). Toward an affinity space methodology: Considerations for literacy research. *English Teaching: Practice and Critique, 11*(2), 44–58.

Lammers, J. C., Magnifico, A. M., & Curwood, J. S. (2014). Exploring tools, places, and ways of being: Audience matters for developing writers. In K. E. Pytash & R. E. Ferdig (Eds.), *Exploring technology for writing and writing instruction* (pp. 186–201). Hershey, PA: IGI Global.

Lange, P. G. (2010). All in the Family. In M. Ito, S. Baumer, M. Bittanti, d. boyd, R. Cody, B. Herr-Stephenson, . . . L. Tripp. (2010). *Hanging out, messing around, and geeking out: Kids living and learning with new media* (pp. 263–269). The John D. and Catherine T. MacArthur Foundation Series on Digital Media and Learning. Cambridge, MA: MIT Press.

Lankshear, C., & Knobel, M. (2003). *New literacies. Changing knowledge and classroom learning.* Buckingham, England: Open University Press.

Lave, J., Murtaugh, M., & de la Rocha, O. (1984). The dialectic of arithmetic in grocery shopping. In B. Rogoff & J. Lave (Eds.), *Everyday cognition: Its development in social context* (pp. 67–94). New York, NY: Cambridge University Press.

Lave, J., & Wenger, E. (1991). *Situated learning: Legitimate peripheral participation*. Cambridge, England: Cambridge University Press.

Leander, K. (2008). Toward a connective ethnography of online/offline literacy networks. In J. Coiro, M. Knobel, C. Lankshear, & D. Leu (Eds.). *Handbook of research on new literacies* (pp. 33–66). New York, NY: Lawrence Erlbaum.

Leander, K., & Boldt, G. (2013). Rereading "A pedagogy of multiliteracies": Bodies, texts, and emergence. *Journal of Literacy Research*, 45, 22–46.

Leander, K. M., & Lovvorn, J. F. (2006). Literacy networks: Following the circulation of texts, bodies, and objects in the schooling and online gaming of one youth. *Cognition and Instruction*, 24, 291–340.

Leander, K. M., & McKim, K. K. (2003). Tracing the everyday 'sitings' of adolescents on the Internet: A strategic adaptation of ethnography across online and offline spaces. *Education, Communication, Information*, 3, 211–240.

Leavy, P. (2014). Introduction. In P. Leavy (Ed.), *The Oxford handbook of qualitative research* (pp. 1–13). Oxford, England: Oxford University Press.

Lee, J. (2014). *Working hypothesis in second language development in natural settings: Twenty-one-year-old adult's second language development in the game play of World of Warcraft* (Unpublished doctoral dissertation). The Pennsylvania State University, University Park.

Lemke, J. L. (2012). Analyzing verbal data: Principles, methods, and problems. In B. J. Fraser, K. G. Tobin, & C. J. MacRobbie (Eds.), *Second international handbook of science education* (Vol. 2, pp. 1471–1484). New York, NY: Springer Science + Business Media.

Lenhart, A., Madden, M., Smith, A., & Magill, A. (2007). *Teens and social media*. A Pew Internet & American Life Project. Retrieved from http://www.pewinternet.org/files/old-media/Files/Reports/2007/PIP_Teens_Social_Media_Final.pdf.pdf

Lenhart, A., Purcell, K., Smith, A., & Zickhur, K. (2010). *Social media and young adults*. A Pew Internet & American Life Project. Retrieved from http://pewinternet.org/Reports/ 2010/Social-Media-and-Young-Adults.aspx.

Lessig, L. (2002). *The future of ideas: The fate of the commons in a connected world*. New York, NY: Random House.

Lessig, L. (2005). *Free culture: The nature and future of creativity*. New York, NY: Penguin Books.

Lévi-Strauss, C. (1962). *Structural anthropology*. New York, NY: Basic Books.

Li, J., & Greenhow, C. (2015). Scholars and social media: Tweeting in the conference backchannel for professional learning. *Educational Media International*, 52, 1–14.

Lincoln, Y. S. (2001). Varieties of validity: Quality in qualitative research. In J. Smart & W. Tierney (Eds.), *Higher education: Handbook of theory and research* (pp. 25–72). New York, NY: Agathon.

Lincoln, Y. S., & Guba, E. G. (1985). *Naturalistic inquiry*. Beverly Hills, CA: Sage.

Lincoln, Y. S., & Guba, E. G. (2000). Paradigmatic controversies, contradictions, and emerging confluences. In N. K. Denzin & Y. S. Lincoln (Eds.), *Handbook of qualitative research* (pp. 163–188). Thousand Oaks, CA: Sage.

Lincoln, Y. S., & Guba, E. G. (2002). The only generalization is: There is no generalization. In R. Gomm, M. Hammersley, & P. Foster (Eds.), *Case study method* (pp. 27–44). London, England: Sage.

Linde, C. (1993). *Life stories: The creation of coherence*. New York, NY: Oxford University Press.

Livingstone, S. (2003). The changing nature of audiences: From the mass audience to the interactive media user. In A. Valdivia (Ed.), *The Blackwell companion to media research* (pp. 337–359). Oxford, England: Blackwell.

Luke, A., & Elkins, J. (1998). Reinventing literacy in 'New Times.' *Journal of Adolescent & Adult Literacy, 42*, 4–7.

Lyle, J. (2003). Stimulated recall: A report on its use in naturalistic research. *British Educational Research Journal, 29*, 861–878.

Lynch, H. (2014, November). Being and becoming: A theoretical model of learning and identity through video games. Paper presented at the National Council of Teachers of English Convention, Washington, D.C.

Lynch, M. (2011). After Egypt: The limits and the promises of online challenges to the authoritarian Arab state. *Perspectives on Politics, 9*, 301–310.

Machin, D. (2009). Multimodality and theories of the visual. In C. Jewitt (Ed.), *The handbook of multimodal analysis* (pp. 181–190). London, England: Routledge.

Magnifico, A. M. (2012). The game of Neopian writing. In E. R. Hayes & S. C. Duncan (Eds.), *Learning in videogame affinity spaces* (pp. 212–234). New York, NY: Peter Lang.

Magnifico, A. M. (2013). "Well, I have to write that": A cross-case qualitative analysis of young writers' motivations to write. *International Journal of Educational Psychology, 2*, 19–55.

Magnifico, A. M. (in press). Theorizing context: A design-based analysis of an online affinity space. In M. Knobel & J. Kalman (Eds.), *Researching new literacies: Design, theory and data in sociocultural investigation*. New York: Peter Lang.

Magnifico, A. M., & Curwood, J. S. (2012, July). *Affinity space ethnography: Qualitative research in online spaces.* Invited poster session presented at the Early Career Workshop at the International Conference of the Learning Sciences. Sydney, NSW, Australia.

Magnifico, A. M., Curwood, J. S., & Lammers, J. C. (2015). Words on the screen: Broadening analyses of interactions among fanfiction writers and reviewers. *Literacy, 49*, 158–166.

Magnifico, A.M. & Halverson, E.R. (2012). Bidirectional artifact analysis: A method for analyzing creative processes. In J. van Aalst, K. Thompson, M. J. Jacobson & P. Reimann (Eds.), *The Future of Learning: Proceedings of the 10th International Conference of the Learning Sciences* (Vol. 2, pp. 276–280). Sydney, NSW, Australia: International Society of the Learning Sciences.

Magnifico, A. M., Halverson, E. R., Cutler, C. T., & Kalaitzidis, T. J. (2014). Bidirectional analysis of creative processes: A tool for researchers. In J. Polman, E. Kyza, I. Tabak, & K. O'Neill (Eds.), *Proceedings of the 11th International Conference of the Learning Sciences* (pp. 839–846). Boulder, CO: International Society of the Learning Sciences.

Magnifico, A. M., Lammers, J. C., & Curwood, J. S. (2013). Collaborative learning across time and space: Ethnographic research in online affinity spaces. In N. Rummel, M. Kapur, M. Nathan, & S. Puntembekar (Eds.), *Proceedings of the 10th International Conference on Computer Supported Collaborative Learning* (Vol. 2, pp. 81–84). Madison, WI: International Society of the Learning Sciences.

Marcus, G. E. (1995). Ethnography in/of the world system: The emergence of multi-sited ethnography. *Annual Review of Anthropology, 24,* 95–117.

Marcus, G. E. (Ed.). (1998). *Ethnography through thick and thin.* Princeton, NJ: Princeton University Press.

Markham, A., & Buchanan, E. (2012). *Ethical decision-making and Internet research (version 2.0): Recommendations from the AoIR Ethics Working Committee.*

Markham, A. N. (1998). *Life online: Researching real experience in virtual space.* Lanham, MD: AltaMira Press.

Markham, A. N. (2003, October). *Images of Internet: Tool, place, way of being.* Paper presented at the Fourth Annual Conference of the Association of Internet Researchers. Toronto, Canada.

Marsh, J. (2010). Young children's play in online virtual worlds. *Journal of Early Childhood Research, 8,* 23–39.

Marsh, J. (2012). Purposes for literacy in children's use of the online virtual world *Club Penguin. Journal of Research in Reading, 37*(2), 179–195.

Marsh, J. (2013). Countering chaos in *Club Penguin*: Young children's literacy practices in a virtual world. In G. Merchant, J. Gillen, J. Marsh, & J. Davies (Eds.), *Virtual Literacies* (pp. 75–88). London: Routledge.

Marshall, C., & Rossman, G. B. (2006). *Designing qualitative research.* Thousand Oaks, CA: Sage.

Martin, C. (2012). Video games, identity, and the constellation of information. *Bulletin of Science, Technology & Society, 32,* 384–392.

Martin, C., Williams, C. C., Ochsner, A., Harris, S., King, E., Anton, G., . . . Steinkuehler, C. (2013). Playing together separately: Mapping out literacy and social synchronicity. In G. Merchant, J. Gillen, J. Marsh, & J. Davies (Eds.), *Virtual literacies* (pp. 226–243). London, England: Routledge.

Martinez, R., Martin, C., Harris, S., Squire, K. D., Lawley, E., & Phelps, A. (2012, June). Just press play: Implications for gamifying the undergraduate experience. In C. Martin, A. Ochsner, & K. Squire (Eds.), *Proceedings of the GLS 8.0 Games + Learning + Society Conference, Madison, WI* (pp. 9–13). Pittsburgh, PA: ETC Press.

Mason, J. (2006). Mixing methods in a qualitatively driven way. *Qualitative Research, 6,* 9–25.

Maxwell, J. A. (2013). *Qualitative research design: An interactive approach.* Thousand Oaks, CA: Sage.

Maxwell, J. A. (2015). Evidence: A critical realist perspective for qualitative research. In N. K. Denzin & M. D. Giardina (Eds.), *Qualitative Inquiry—Past, Present, and Future: A Critical Reader* (pp. 88–102). Walnut Creek, CA: Left Coast Press.

McKee, H. A., & Porter, J. E. (2009). *The ethics of Internet research: A rhetorical case-based approach.* New York, NY: Peter Lang.

Merchant, G. (2010). 3D virtual worlds as environments for literacy learning. *Educational Research, 52,* 135–150.

Merriam, S. B. (1998). *Qualitative research and case study applications in education.* San Francisco, CA: Jossey-Bass.

Merriam, S. B. (Ed.). (2002). *Qualitative research in practice: Examples for discussion and analysis.* San Francisco, CA: Jossey-Bass.

Merriam, S. B. (2009). *Qualitative research: A guide to design and implementation.* San Francisco, CA: Jossey-Bass.

Mertens, D. M. (2005). *Research methods in education and psychology: Integrating diversity with quantitative and qualitative approaches.* Thousand Oaks, CA: Sage.

Miles, M. B., & Huberman, A. M. (1984). *Qualitative data analysis: A sourcebook of new methods.* Beverly Hills, CA: Sage.

Miles, M. B., & Huberman, A. M. (1994). *Qualitative data analysis: An expanded sourcebook.* Thousand Oaks, CA: Sage.

Miles, M. B., Huberman, A. M., & Saldana, J. (2014). *Qualitative data analysis: A methods sourcebook* (3rd ed.). Thousand Oaks, CA: Sage.

Mitchell, W. J. (1996). *City of bits: Space, place, and the infobahn.* Cambridge, MA: MIT Press.

Morford, Z. H., Witts, B. N., Killingsworth, K. J., & Alavosius, M. P. (2014). Gamification: The intersection between behavior analysis and game design technologies. *The Behavior Analyist, 37,* 25–40.

Morgan, D.L. (2007). Paradigms lost and pragmatism regained : Methodological implications of combining qualitative and quantitative methods. *Journal of Mixed Methods Research, 1*(1), 48–76.

Morrell, E. (2006). Critical participatory action research and the literacy achievement of ethnic minority youth. In C. M. Fairbanks, J. Worthy, B. Maloch, J. Hoffman, & D. Schallert (Eds.), *55th Yearbook of the National Reading Conference* (pp. 60–78). National Reading Conference: Oak Creek, WI.

Moustakas, C. (1994). *Phenomenological research methods.* Thousand Oaks, CA: Sage.

Nardi, B. (2010). *My life as a night elf priest: An anthropological account of world of warcraft.* Ann Arbor: University of Michigan Press.

Nardi, B., Ly, S., & Harris, J. (2007). Learning conversations in world of warcraft. Retrieved from http://www .artifex.org/~bonnie/pdf/Nardi-HICSS.pdf

New London Group. (1996). A pedagogy of multiliteracies: Designing social futures. *Harvard Educational Review, 66,* 60–92.

Niemeyer, D. J., & Gerber, H. R. (2015). Maker culture and Minecraft: implications for the future of learning. *Educational Media International, 52*(3), 1–11.

Norris, S. (2004). *Analyzing multimodal interaction: A methodological framework.* New York: Routledge.

Norris, S. (2011). Modal density and modal configurations: Multimodal actions. In C. Jewitt (Ed.), *The Routledge handbook of multimodal analysis* (pp. 78–90). London, England: Routledge.

Norris, S. & Jones, R.H. (2005). *Discourse in action: Introducing mediated discourse analysis.* New York: Taylor & Francis.

Norris, S., & Maier, C. D. (Eds.). (2014). *Interactions, images and texts: A reader in multimodality.* Berlin, Germany: De Gruyter Mouton.

Onwuegbuzie, A. J., & Frels, R. K. (2013). Introduction: Towards a new research philosophy for addressing social justice issues: Critical dialectical pluralism 1.0. *International Journal of Multiple Research Approaches, 7,* 9–26.

Orgad, S. (2009). How can researchers make sense of the issues involved in collecting and interpreting online and offline data? In A. N. Markham & N. K. Baym (Eds.), *Internet inquiry: Conversations about method* (pp. 33–53). Thousand Oaks, CA: Sage.

Pahl, K., & Rowsell, J. (2010). Artifactual literacies. In J. Larson & J. Marsh. (Eds.) *The SAGE handbook of early childhood literacy* (2nd ed., pp. 263–279). Thousand Oaks, CA: Sage.

Pahl, K., & Rowsell, J. (2011). The material and the situated: What multimodality and new literacy studies do for literacy research. In D. Lapp & D. Fisher (Eds.). *Handbook of research on teaching the English language arts* (pp. 175–181). Oxon, England: Routledge.

Pascoe, C. J. (2010). Intimacy. In M. Ito, S. Baumer, M. Bittani, D. Boyd, R. Cody, B. Herr-Stephenson, . . . L. Tripp (Eds.). *Hanging out, messing around, and geeking out* (pp. 117–148). Cambridge, MA: MIT Press.

Pascoe, C. J. (2012). Studying young people's new media use: Methodological shifts and educational innovations. *Theory Into Practice, 51,* 76–82.

Pahl, K., & Rowsell, J. (2011a). Artifactual critical literacy: A new perspective for literacy education. *Berkeley Review of Education, 2,* 129–151.

Pahl, K., & Rowsell, J. (2011b). The material and the situated: What multimodality and new literacy studies do for literacy research. In D. Lapp & D. Fisher (Eds.), *Handbook of research on teaching the English language arts* (pp. 175–181). Oxon, England: Routledge.

Patton, M. (1990). *Qualitative evaluation and research methods* (2nd ed.). Beverly Hills, CA: Sage.

Patton, M. Q. (2002). *Qualitative research and evaluation methods* (3rd ed.). Thousand Oaks, CA: Sage.

Phillips, D.C. (1996). Philosophical perspectives. In D. C. Berliner & R. C. Calfee (Eds.), Handbook of educational psychology. Old Tappan, NJ: Macmillan.

Philo, G. (2007). Can discourse analysis successfully explain the content of media and journalistic practice? *Journalism Studies 8*(2), 175–196.

Piaget, J., & Inhelder, B. (1969). *The psychology of the child.* New York, NY: Basic Books.

Pillow, W. (2003). Confession, catharsis, cure? Rethinking the uses of reflexivity as methodological power in qualitative research. *International Journal of Qualitative Studies in Education, 16,* 175–196.

Polit, D. F., & Beck, C. T. (2004). *Nursing research principles and methods.* Philadelphia, PA: Lippincott Williams & Wilkins.

Potter, J., & Wetherell, M. (1987, 2005). *Discourse and social psychology: Beyond attitudes and behaviour.* London, England: Sage.

Prensky, M. (2006). *Don't bother me Mom—I'm learning! How computer and video games are preparing your kids for 21st century success and how you can help!* New York, NY: Paragon House.

Reid, E. M. (1994). *Cultural formations in text-based virtual realities* (Master's thesis, University of Melbourne, Australia). Retrieved from www.lastplace.com/page210.htm

Reilly, E., Vartabedian, V., Felt, L. J., & Jenkins, H. (2012). *PLAY!* Los Angeles: Annenberg Innovation Lab at the University of Southern California. http://www.annenberglab.org

Resnick, M., Maloney, J., Monroy-Hernandez, A., Rusk, N., Eastmond, E., Brennan, K., . . . Kafai, Y. (2009). Scratch: Programming for all. *Communications of the ACM, 52*(11), 60–67.

Rish, R. M. (2014). Students' transmedia storytelling: Building fantasy fiction storyworlds in videogame design. In H. R. Gerber & S. S. Abrams (Eds.), *Bridging literacies through videogames* (pp. 29–52). Rotterdam, The Netherlands: Sense.

Roberts, L. D., Smith, L. M., & Pollock, C. M. (2002). MOOing till the cows come home: The sense of community in virtual environments. In C. C. Sonn (Ed.), *Psychological sense of community: Research, applications, implications* (pp. 223–245). New York, NY: Kluwer Academic/Plenum.

Rogers, R. (Ed.) (2011). *An introduction to critical discourse analysis in education.* New York, NY: Routledge.

Rowsell, J. (2013). *Working with multimodality: Rethinking literacy in a digital age.* London, England: Routledge.

Rowsell, J. & Burgess, J. (2014). A tale of two selves: Im/materializing identities on Facebook. In C. Burnett, J. Davies, G. Merchant, & J. Rowsell (Eds.). *New Literacies Around the Globe: Policy and Pedagogy* (pp. 103–120). New York, NY: Routledge.

Saldaña, J. (2013). *The coding manual for qualitative researchers* (2nd ed.). Thousand Oaks, CA: Sage.

Salen, K. (2008). Toward an ecology of gaming. In K. Salen (Ed.), *The ecology of games: Connecting youth, games, and learning* (pp. 1–20). The John D. and Catherine T. MacArthur Foundation Series on Digital Media and Learning. Cambridge, MA: MIT Press.

Salen, K., & Zimmerman, E. (2004). *Rules of play: Game design fundamentals.* Cambridge, MA: MIT Press.

Sandoval, W. A., & Bell, P. (2004). Design-based research methods for studying learning in context: Introduction. *Educational Psychologist, 39,* 199–201.

Schön, D. A. (1995). *The reflective practitioner: How professionals think in action.* Surrey, England: Ashgate.

Scollon, R., & Scollon, S. W. (2004). *Nexus analysis*. New York, NY: Routledge.

Scribner, S., & Cole, M. (1981). *The psychology of literacy*. Cambridge, MA: Harvard University Press.

Seale, C. (1999). *The quality of qualitative research*. London, England: Sage.

Shaffer, D. W. (2006) *How computer games help children learn*. New York, NY: Palgrave Macmillan.

Shaffer, D. W., Squire, K. D., Halverson, R., & Gee, J. P. (2005). Video games and the future of learning. *Phi Delta Kappan, 87*, 104–111.

Shenton, A. K. (2004). Strategies for ensuring trustworthiness in qualitative research projects. *Education for Information, 22*, 63–75.

Skinner, B. F. (1976). *About behaviorism*. New York, NY: Vintage Books.

Slator, B. M., Borchert, O., Brandt, L., Chaput, H., Erickson, K., Groesbeck, G., . . . Vender, B. (2007). From dungeons to classrooms: The evolution of MUDs as learning environments. *Studies in Computational Intelligence, 62*, 119–159.

Smith, M. L. (1997). Mixing and matching: Methods and models. In J. C. Greene & V. J. Caracelli (Eds.), *Advances in mixed-method evaluation: The challenges and benefits of integrating diverse paradigms* (New Directions for Evaluation No. 74, pp.73–85). San Francisco, CA: Jossey-Bass.

Squire, K. (2011). *Video games and learning: Teaching and participatory culture in the digital age*. New York, NY: Teachers College Press.

Squire, K. D. (2002). Cultural framing of computer/video games. *Game studies, 2*(1). Retrieved from http://gamestudies.org/0102/squire/?ref=HadiZayifla

Squire, K. D. (2006). From content to context: Videogames as designed experience. *Educational Researcher, 35*(8), 19–29.

Stake, R. E. (1995). *The art of case study research*. Thousand Oaks, CA: Sage.

Stein, P. (2008). *Multimodal pedagogies in diverse classrooms: Representation, rights and resources*. New York, NY: Taylor & Francis.

Stein, P., & Newfield, D. (2006). Multiliteracies and multimodality in English in education in Africa: Mapping the terrain. *English Studies in Africa, 49*(1), 1–21.

Steinkuehler, C. (2006). Massively multiplayer online video gaming as participation in a discourse. *Mind, Culture, and Activity, 13*, 38–52.

Steinkuehler, C. (2007). Massively multiplayer online gaming as a constellation of literacy practices. In B. E. Shelton & D. Wiley (Eds.), *The design and use of simulation computer games in education* (pp. 187–212). Rotterdam, Netherlands: Sense.

Steinkuehler, C., Black, R., & Clinton, K. (2005). Researching literacy as tool, place, and way of being. *Reading Research Quarterly, 40*, 95–100.

Steinkuehler, C. A., & Duncan, S. C. (2008). Scientific habits of mind in virtual worlds. *Journal of Science Education and Technology, 17*, 530–543.

Steinkuehler, C. A., & Williams, D. (2006). Where everybody knows your (screen) name: Online games as "third places." *Journal of Computer-Mediated Communication, 11*, 885–909.

Stevens, R., Satwicz, T., & McCarthy, L. (2008). In-game, in-room, in-world: Reconnecting video game play to the rest of kids' lives. In K. Salen (Ed.), *The ecology of games: Connecting youth, games, and learning* (pp. 41–66). Cambridge, MA: MIT Press.

Strauss, A. L., & Corbin, J. (1990). *Basics of qualitative research: Grounded theory procedures and techniques.* Newbury Park, CA: Sage.

Sveningsson, M. (2002). Cyberlove: Creating romantic relationships on the net. In J. Fornas, K. Klein, M. Ladendorf, J. Sunden & M. Svenigsson (Eds.), *Digital borderlands: Cultural studies of identity and interactivity on the Internet* (pp. 48–78). New York, NY: Peter Lang.

Swan, K., Garrison, D. R., & Richardson, J. C. (2009). A constructivist approach to online learning: The Community of Inquiry framework. In C. R. Payne (Ed.), *Information technology and constructivism in higher education: Progressive learning frameworks* (pp. 43–57). Hershey, PA: IGI Global.

Swan, K., Shea, P., Richardson, J., Ice, P., Garrison, D. R., Cleveland-Innes, M., & Arbaugh, J. B. (2008). Validating a measurement tool of presence in online communities of inquiry. *E-mentor, 2*(24), 1–12.

Szabo, M. & Flesher, K. (2002). CMI theory and practice: Historical roots of learning management systems. In M. Driscoll & T. Reeves (Eds.). *Proceedings of World Conference on E-Learning in Corporate, Government, Health Care, and Higher Education 2002.* Montreal, Canada.

Tashakkori, A., & Creswell, J. W. (2007). Editorial: The new era of mixed methods. *Journal of Mixed Methods Research, 1*, 3–7.

Tashakkori, A., & Teddlie, C. (1998). *Mixed methodology: Combining qualitative and quantitative approaches.* Thousand Oaks, CA: Sage.

Taylor, A. S., & Harper, R. (2003). The gift of *gab*? A design-oriented sociology of young people's use of mobiles. *Computer Supported Cooperative Work, 12,* 267–296.

Taylor, S. J., & Bogdan, R. (1989). On accepting relationships between people with mental retardation and non-disabled people: Towards an understanding of acceptance. *Disability, Handicap & Society, 4*, 21–36.

Tesch, R. (1990). *Qualitative research: Analysis types and software.* New York, NY: Routledge.

Trainor, A. A., & Graue, E. (2014). Evaluating rigor in qualitative methodology and research dissemination. *Remedial and Special Education, 35*, 267–274.

Turkle, S. (1995). *Life on the screen. Identity in the age of the age of Internet.* New York, NY: Simon & Schuster.

Turner, K. H., Abrams, S. S., Katic, E., & Donavan, M. J. (2014). Demystifying digitalk: The what and why of the language teens use in digital writing. *Journal of Literacy Research, 46*, 157–193.

Van Dijk, T. A. (1993). Principles of critical discourse analysis. *Discourse & Society, 4*, 249–283.

van Manen, M. (1990). *Researching lived experience*: New York, NY: State University Press.

Vartabedian, V., & Felt, L. J. (2012). PLAY! (Participatory Learning and You!) Pilot: Professional Development with Los Angeles Unified School District Educators (LAUSD), Grades 6–12. In E. Reilly & I. Literat (Eds.), *Designing with teachers: Participatory approaches to professional development in education* (pp. 50–66). Los Angeles, CA: Annenberg School for Communication & Journalism.

Vehovar, V., & Manfreda, K. L. (2008). Overview: Online surveys. In N. Fielding, R. M. Lee, & G. Blank (Eds.), *The SAGE handbook of online research methods* (pp. 177–194). Thousand Oaks, CA: Sage.

Verba, J. M. (2003). *Boldly writing: A Trek fan and Fanfiction history, 1967–1987* (2nd ed.). Minnetonka, MN: FTL.

Viegas, F., Wattenberg, M., & McKeon, M. (2007, July). The hidden order of Wikipedia. In D. Schuler (Ed.), *Online Communities and Social Computing: Second International Conference, Beijing, China,* (pp. 445–454). Berlin, Germany: Springer-Verlag.

Vygotsky, L. S. (1978). *Mind in society*. Cambridge, MA: Harvard University Press.

Walsh, J., & Simpson, A. (2013). Touching, tapping . . . thinking? Examining the dynamic materiality of touch pad devices for literacy learning. *Australian Journal of Language and Literacy, 36,* 148–157.

Wargo, J. M. (2015). Spatial stories with nomadic narrators: Affect, *Snapchat*, and 'feeling' embodiment in youth mobile composing. *Journal of Language & Literacy Education, 11*(1), 47–64.

Watson, W. R. (2007). An argument for clarity: What are learning management systems and what are they not, and what should they become? *Tech Trends, 51*(2), 28–34.

Wen, K. Y., McTavish, F., Kreps, G., Wise, M., & Gustafson, D. (2011). From diagnosis to death: A case study of coping with breast cancer as seen through online discussion group messages. *Journal of Computer-Mediated Communication, 16,* 331–361.

Wenger, E. (1998). *Communities of practice: Learning, meaning, and identity*. Cambridge, England: Cambridge University Press.

Wertsch, J. V. (1991). *Voices of the mind: A sociocultural approach to mediated action*. Cambridge, MA: Harvard University Press.

Whitty, G. (2002) *Making sense of education policy: Studies in the sociology and politics of education*. London, England: Sage.

Williams, D. (2005). Bridging the methodological divide in game research. *Simulation & Gaming, 36*(4), 1–17.

Williams, J. B., & Jacobs, J. (2004). Exploring the use of blogs as learning spaces in the higher education sector. *Australasian Journal of Educational Technology, 20,* 232–247.

Williams, M. (2007). Avatar watching: Participant observation in graphical online environments. *Qualitative Research, 7,* 5–24.

Wohlwend, K. E. (2009). Damsels in discourse: Girls consuming and producing identity texts through Disney princess play. *Reading Research Quarterly, 44,* 57–83.

Wohlwend, K. E., & Buchholz, B. A. (2014). Making paper pterodactyls and Popsicle sticks: Expanding school literacy through filmmaking and toymaking. In C. Burnett, J. Davies, G. Merchant, & J. Rowsell. (Eds.) *New literacies around the globe: Policy and pedagogy* (pp. 33–50). New York, NY: Routledge.

Wolcott, H. (1975). Criteria for an ethnographic approach to research in schools. *Human Organization, 34,* 111–127.

Wolcott, H. F. (2011). *Ethnography: A way of seeing* (2nd ed.). Lanham, MD: AltaMira Press.

Wolfswinkel, J. F., Furtmueller, E., & Wilderom, C. P. M. (2013). Using grounded theory as a method for rigorously reviewing literature. *European Journal of Information Systems, 22,* 45–55.

Wood, L. A., & Kroger, R. O. (2000). *Doing discourse analysis: Methods for studying action in talk and text.* Thousand Oaks, CA: Sage.

World Intellectual Property Organization (n.d.). Understanding copyright and related rights. WIPO Publication No. 909(E). Retrieved from http://www.wipo.int/edocs/pubdocs/en/intproperty/909/wipo_pub_909.pdf

Xalabarder, R. (2002). Copyright: Choice of law and jurisdiction in the digital age. *Annual Survey of International & Comparative Law, 8*(1), art. 5.

Yalof, B. (2014). Marshaling resources: A classic grounded theory study of online learners. *Grounded Theory Review, 13*(1). Retrieved from http://groundedtheoryreview.com/2014/06/22/marshaling-resources-a-classic-grounded-theory-study-of-online-learners/

Yin, R. K. (1994). *Case study research: Design and methods* (2nd ed.). Thousand Oaks, CA: Sage.

Yin, R. K. (2009). *Case study research: Design and methods* (4th ed.). Thousand Oaks, CA: Sage.

Yin, R. K. (2014). *Case study research: Design and methods* (5th ed.). Thousand Oaks, CA: Sage.

Yin, R. K. (2011). *Qualitative research from start to finish.* New York, NY: Guilford Press.

Zimmer, M. (2010). "But the data is already public": On the ethics of research in Facebook. *Ethics and Information Technology, 12,* 313–325.

INDEX